Kind comments regarding *Elegant Small Hotels* (North America)

Thank you, Pamela, for unerring good taste, for quality and for your talent in telling us about it.
—Peter Balas, President
International Hotel Association

. . . devoted to pleasing the most discriminating . . . . the text and side notes offer explicit answers.
—Los Angeles Times

It is indeed very good and full of fascinating addresses for people who travel as much as we do.
—Duchess of Bedford

They were chosen, both for their elegant decor and because they possess an ambience like that of a fine residence.
—Washington Post

Let me tell you that we are proud to collaborate with you. . . .
—Pierre Cardin

*The entries for each hotel include rates, service and facilities available, as well as a short description of the **style** and **mood** of the establishment.*
—San Francisco Chronicle

My schedule is so hectic that when I can steal a few days for myself, they are very precious to me. I always choose small, out-of-the-way places, which give me and my family privacy, while providing excellent service and luxury accommodations.
—Donna Karan

Elegant Small Hotels *makes a seductive volume for window shopping. . . . Handsomely illustrated . . . Hotels that provide the atmosphere of a fine residence: beauty in design, color and furnishings, fresh flowers, luxurious toiletries and linens. Other considerations are select business and physical fitness facilities, excellence of cuisine and concierge services.*

—Chicago Sun Times

All the best for a sure success.

—Valentino

Services, facilities and amenities nationwide. . . . Available in retail outlets.

—Travel Age West

What I love about managing a fine hotel is the same that makes me choose these houses for staying: Elegance, efficiency, and smoothness, accuracy and actuality and that personal touch I like so much to feel.

—Count Johannes Walderdorff

Every great hotel in this guide is unique . . . handsome photographs.

—Hideaways International

The elegant ones make staying in hotels a little more bearable. The elegant ones don't seem like hotels at all.

—Phillip Glass

If you've enjoyed the charming personalized hotels of Europe, you will love Pamela Lanier's selection of. . . .outstanding hotels here at home. The information and photographs will allow the discerning traveller to choose from among the best.

—Traveller's Bookstore

Dignified and classy.

—Publish

ELEGANT

HOTELS OF THE
PACIFIC RIM

A CONNOISSEUR'S GUIDE

PAMELA LANIER

A *Lanier* Guide

▲

This book is dedicated to international travellers as our best ambassadors for understanding and world peace.

Other books from Lanier Guides

Elegant Small Hotels—A Connoisseur's Guide
Condo Vacations—The Complete Guide
All-Suite Hotel Guide—The Definitive Directory
Complete Guide to Bed & Breakfast Inns & Guesthouses in the United States & Canada
Golf Courses—The Complete Guide
Golf Resorts—The Complete Guide
Golf Resorts International
22 Days in Alaska
Cinnamon Mornings
The Back Almanac

Copyright © 1994 Lanier Publishing International, Ltd.
Cover Copyright @ 1994 Lanier Publishing International, Ltd.

Cover photograph: The Terrace, Adelaide, Australia
Design & Production: J.C. Wright, Futura Graphics
Editorial Assistants: Leslie Chan, Ann Chandler, Marianne Barth, Judy Berman, Eleanor Rush, Sarah Morse, Lisa Ruffin

Library of Congress Catalogue-in-Publication Data
Lanier, Pamela
    Elegant hotels of the pacific rim: a connoisseur's guide/Pamela Lanier.
        Includes index.
    ISBN 0-89815-583-5
    1. Hotels, taverns, etc.—United States—Pacific—Guidebooks.

First Edition February 1994
Published by Lanier Publishing International, Ltd.
P.O.Box 20429
Oakland, CA 94620

Distributed to the trade by Ten Speed Press
P.O.Box 7123
Berkeley, CA 94707
Printed in the United States of America on recycled paper

All information in this book is subject to change without notice. We strongly recommend that you call ahead and always verify the information in this book before making final plans or reservations. The author and publisher of this directory make no representation that it is absolutely accurate or complete. Errors and omissions, whether typographical, clerical or otherwise, do sometimes occur and may occur anywhere within the body of this publication. Some hotels in this guide have been charged a listing fee to help defray the cost of compiling the guide.

American Hotel
& Motel Association
ALLIED MEMBER

Contents

PREFACE

For the past 20 years, I've been a travel writer and book editor covering Pacific basin countries, and it has been like having a box seat at the world's greatest magic show. So much has changed. I can truly say that nowhere else on earth has so much growth been accomplished in such a short period of time.

While there is no "Pacific" as we think of "Europe", there is a Pacific that is filled with images of Gauguin colors and flowers, white sand beaches and things exotic. But, it is also a Pacific with a mass of people who speak hundreds of languages and thousands of dialects, that sometimes boggles the mind.

Some of the countries dotting the Pacific are so small that the only way to expand is upward. Others are so ancient that temples are still being carved out of the jungle and almost-prehistoric villages are being brought into the 20th century.

The Pacific is a lot of things. It's a jam-packed bit of humanity on a Tokyo subway, or a tram ride up to the "Peak" in Hong Kong. It's handpainted umbrellas and saffron-robed priests in Bangkok, or a leisurely sampan ride for a picnic to the Sister Islands in Singapore. It's a train ride through the rubber plantations of Malaysia and the millions of sheep that dot the pastoral lands of New Zealand. It's a room with a view of the Opera House and "Coathanger" Bridge in Sydney. And now, most of all, it is one of the world's busiest traffic lanes.

Businesses have boomed and hotels in the Pacific have dramatically changed, from the "no frills" business type hotel of my 20 years ago, to some of the most sophisticated, elegant, and luxurious hotels and resorts in the world. A number of the Pacific's hotels are consistently on the "top ten" list, and many have become destinations in themselves. And where business flourishes, the quality of hotels is so competitive that even the most discriminating traveler will be delighted with the range of features from which to choose; including every possible business amenity, as well as health clubs and spas to help you get over jet lag.

Along with the influx of new and growing businesses, have come international travelers demanding international standards in restaurants. So, "variety" is the word and today there is no short supply of exciting dining experiences. Specialties are in. There's even a caviar restaurant in Hong Kong where the ambiance is devoted solely to the enjoyment of that magnificent delicacy. And that's only the tip of the iceberg when it comes to the Pacific's quest to delight you with fresh and exciting cuisine.

The Pacific has always been a place to be pampered. However, if you want it to be, it can still be an adventurous destination, as it was for the likes of Robert Louis Stevenson, James Michener, and Somerset Maugham. You can travel back to those yesteryears of romance and potted palms and stay in the same Grand Hotels that these famous adventurers once enjoyed. The Raffles Hotel in Singapore, the Oriental in Bangkok, the Peninsula in Hong Kong; elegant, palatial homes away from home for world travelers, who would move in for months at a time after traveling for weeks by ship to get there.

But, regardless of where you stay, one very special feature you will find in the Pacific is the quality of service. No other area in the world is as richly blessed with people so courteous, so intent on pleasing the visitor, so desirous of making the stranger feel at home.

While I wonder what the next 20 years will bring, one thing is for sure—I know I won't be disappointed. So, I'll continue to travel the Pacific to see, taste and enjoy the wonder of it all.

—*Lois K. Brett*

GUIDENOTES

If you are among those discerning travelers who understand that the essence of the good life is quality, this book is designed especially to enhance your travel enjoyment in the Pacific Rim area.

The hotels and resorts in this book are alphabetically sorted by country and within each country, by city. Within the U.S., we further sorted by state name. Hotels and resorts are listed in alphabetical order within each city.

In the **Room Rate** section of each hotel or resort, a code is used to indicate the latest available price range for an average double-occupancy room. The code is as follows:

> $ = Under 100 U.S. dollars
> $$ = 100-175 U.S. dollars
> $$$ = 175-250 U.S. dollars
> $$$$ = Over 250 U.S. dollars

Since rates are subject to fluctuation due to price changes and international exchange rates, be sure to call and verify exact prices when making your reservation.

This guide encompasses four types of elegant hotel accommodations. They are described as follows:

Grand Luxe Hotels: Each of these world-class hotels projects an incomparable aura of tradition and grace. A few of the services provided include superb restaurants and room service, an attentive but very discreet staff with full concierge services, and a sumptuous atmosphere of well-secured luxury.

City Center Hotels: Designed especially for the business traveler, each of these hotels offers a comfortable inviting environment where an executive may return each day to lodgings ideally appointed to satisfy business, personal and recreational needs. Special emphasis is placed upon conference facilities and services for executives.

Outstanding Resorts: The quick weekend trip within a business trip or brief resort holiday is becoming the new vacation style of the ultra-busy. From a wide range of possibilities, we have selected our resort recommendations with regard for their luxurious ambience, excellent cuisine and sporting facilities. Most also offer excellent conference facilities and are perfect for combining recreation and business meetings in beautiful surroundings.

Affordable Elegance: Though one normally expects elegant lodgings to come at higher-than-ordinary rates, we have discovered a select few that offer some of the best of both worlds: comfortable, well-appointed rooms, excellent restaurants and access to sports facilities, and many of the essential amenities associated with Grand Luxe hotels — at surprisingly reasonable prices. Please bear in mind, though, that the very top quality accommodations carry a correspondingly steep price.

In addition to what type the hotel or resort is, the *size* can also affect the atmosphere. Accommodations can vary in size, from small Grand Luxe hotels and large-scale city hotels, to intimate "hideaway" resorts. The **Number of Rooms and Suites** section can give you an idea of the size of the hotel or resort and the type of accommodations offered.

To identify the elegant hotels and resorts of the Pacific Rim, we have used the following criteria:

By "elegant," we mean decor—and also something more. If a hotel is to be one's "home away from home," its atmosphere should be like that of a fine residence. The feeling should be reflected not only in design, color and furnishings, but also in extra touches such as fresh flowers, overnight shoeshine, luxurious toiletries and oversized towels . . . all the myriad details that add up to the intangible quality we call elegance.

For us to include a particular hotel or resort, it must first have met the foregoing standards. Other factors we have kept in mind relate to the individual traveler's needs. For example ... If you conduct business while traveling, such facilities as secretarial service, translation, teleconferencing, fax and telex will be essential. Many hotels have special Business Centers catering to the many needs of a traveling executive. The **Conference Rooms/Capacity** section gives conference planners an idea of the extensiveness of the hotel's facilities.

If you are among the growing number of people to whom physical fitness is a personal must, you will be interested in the **Sports Facilities** section of each hotel. Your hotel may provide in-house facilities such as swimming pool, tennis, spa and massage room, and perhaps weight training equipment. Many of the hotels in this guide can also arrange guest privileges at private country clubs and health centers. Outside sports (such as watersports) and adventuring (such as cruises and jeep rides) can usually be arranged by the hotel.

If you are among those travelers for whom fine cuisine is a top priority, we agree completely. We have chosen our hotels with excellent dining in mind, and we sometimes include a description of a representative dinner recently served at the hotel. Some hotels have such a diversity and abundance of restaurants and bars, that we have listed several of the most popular or most elegant ones in the **Restaurant** and **Bar** sections. The description may include further information on other restaurants and bars as well.

We have noted the many services and amenities provided by each hotel in the **Services and Amenities** section of each hotel. Other services and sundries are often available. When you call to book reservations, be sure to ask whether the hotel offers those you desire.

Whether you travel for business, pleasure, or a bit of both, each elegant hotel described in this guide deserves a special place in your plans and your memories.

Every attempt has been made to be absolutely current. Some information contained in this guide has been provided by the hotels' management, and management policies may change. If you feel that anything in this book is in error or needs to be updated, please inform us so that we can make our future editions even better. We appreciate reader comments, including any hotel we have overlooked which you feel deserves to be included.

—Pamela Lanier
February 1994, San Francisco

TERRACE ADELAIDE HOTEL

Understated elegance and a cosmopolitan flair are the hallmark of the Terrace Adelaide Hotel. Ideally located for both business and pleasure, the Terrace has quickly risen to international recognition as a truly fine hotel.

All rooms feature panoramic views of either the city skyline or greenery, and are fully appointed with the luxuries guests can expect from a 5-Star hotel. The decor consists primarily of polished wood and brass. For business travelers, the Terrace offers not only proximity to the airport and downtown, but a business center complete with translation and secretarial services and fax lines connected to suites.

The Terrace is well equipped for mid-size conferences as well, with a ballroom accommodating up to 250 people and five additional function rooms. An outdoor heated pool on The Top Deck, along with sauna, spa, gymnasium and massage room, complete the picture of post-business or vacation relaxation.

The Crystal Room is the Terrace's premier restaurant, featuring modern French cuisine in an elegant atmosphere graced with silver, crystal and candlelight. The Terrace's dining options also include Gresham's Bar and Grill, serving American-style steaks, and Seafood and Spices, a Southeast Asian restaurant.

Just minutes away are the Adelaide Casino, Parliament and Government House, and a great selection of shops and entertainment.

Address: 150 North Terrace, Adelaide, South Australia 5000
Phone: (08) 217-7552, (008) 888 151, Fax: (08) 231-7572
No. of Rooms: 313 **Suites:** 21
Room Rate: $$
Credit Cards: All major
Services and Amenities: Concierge, Valet parking, Laundry, Valet service, Safe deposit fac., Luggage storage, Specialty shop, News agency, Remote ctl. TV, In-house movies, VCR, Refrigerator, ISD/STD phones, A/C, Radio, Fax sockets
Room Service: 24 hours
Restaurant: Crystal Room, Gresham's Bar & Grill
Bar: Mystics, Cascades
Business Facilities: Secretarial, Fax, Translation, Next to conven. ctr.
Conference Rooms: 6, Capacity: 300
Sports Facilities: Pool, Sauna, Spa, Massage, Gym
Location: Central Adelaide
Attractions: Adelaide Casino, Rundle Mall, Constitutional Museum

LIZARD ISLAND LODGE

Lizard Island Lodge has been called "the jewel in the Great Barrier Reef." This exclusive, 55-acre resort is located on a remote, and otherwise uninhabited, island, which is a National Park. Lizard Island is renowned for its natural unspoiled beauty. Its azure, crystal clear waters and spectacular coral reefs are teeming with brilliantly colored marine life. The Lodge's reputation for tranquility, comfort and charm attracts a sophisticated international clientele. At Lizard Island Lodge the service is gracious and unobtrusive; the focus here is on privacy, personal choice and relaxation.

Lizard Island Lodge features 32 private, air-conditioned suites, including two deluxe suites, each complete with veranda, overhead fans, king or queen-size bed, marble bathroom and stocked mini-bar. The premier deluxe suite has a separate bedroom and large living area. The private balcony boasts a magnificent view, spanning the entire length of the main beach with Cook's Look, the island's highest point, in the background.

Dining at the Lodge (meals are included in the room fee) is as inviting as the island itself. Try a Strudel of Australian Seafood served on a fresh tomato with pernod sauce, or Grilled Maori Wrasse served on a coulis of fresh peaches spiked with almond liqueur. For dessert, sample Fresh Poached Pears in a crisp shortbread pastry case set with a light caramel custard.

Lizard Island is, by all accounts, a diver's paradise. Diving and snorkeling trips are run daily to the outer and inner reefs. At the world-famous Cod Hole, divers meet face to face with Moray eels. Professional diving courses are available. Complementary activities include sail-boarding, catamaran sailing, glass-bottomed boat trips and glass-bottomed paddle skis, outboard dinghies, and tennis—and the fishing, hiking and swimming are divine.

Address: P.O. Box 2372, Lizard Island, P.M.B 40, Cairns, Queensland 4870
Phone: (03) 666-3019, (800) 445-0190 in USA, Fax: (03) 666-3939, Telex: 36971
No. of Rooms: 32 **Suites:** 2
Room Rate: $$$$
Credit Cards: AmEx, DC, DC, MC, Visa
Services and Amenities: Meals included, Gift shop, Minibar/refrigerator, Ceiling fans, Verandahs, Marble baths
Restrictions: No children under 6
Restaurant: Lizard Island
Bar: Lizard Island
Business Facilities: Fax
Sports Facilities: Pool, Archery, Tennis, Beach, Waterskiing, Sailing, Snorkelling, Diving
Location: Great Barrier Reef
Attractions: Diving/snorkeling trips to reefs, Cod Hole, fishing charters

THE BEAUFORT DARWIN

This award-winning hotel in Australia's tropical Northern Territory is only a short walk from Darwin's Central Business district and only three hours away from the "timeless land" of the Outback in Kakadu National Park. The interior of the Beaufort suits its waterside location perfectly. The lobby is decorated in blues, greens and earthtones; plants cascade down the walls from the lobby atrium, where a glass ceiling creates an ambience of warmth and spaciousness.

The Beaufort's guest rooms and suites are stylish and modern, providing excellent views of the Timor Sea. The pride of the hotel is the two-story Beaufort Suite, decorated in Perlato blue marble with magnificently elegant appointments. The upper level has a master bedroom, private lounge and a marble bathroom with spa. The lower level features a kitchen, dining room with marble banquet table, and a lounge that opens onto a large private terrace with a jacuzzi overlooking the sea.

The hotel's silver service restaurant, Siggi's, features the finest in classical European cuisine. At the streetside Cafe Esplanade, the menu showcases mouthwatering seafood and Southeast Asian cuisine. The Beaufort has put together several dinner/excursion packages. Two popular packages are "The Romantic Interlude", which includes a private champagne tour and dinner at Siggi's, and "Gone Fishing," which treats you to a full day of fishing and your catch served up to you at Cafe Esplanade when you return.

The Beaufort Darwin offers you the best of both worlds; you can catch a show at the nearby Darwin Performing Arts Center one day, and experience the adventure and natural wonders of Australia's ancient landscape the next.

Address: The Esplanade, P.O. Box 207, Darwin, Northern Territory, 0800
Phone: (089) 82 9911, Fax: (089) 81 5332, Telex: 85818
No. of Rooms: 164 **Suites:** 32
Services and Amenities: Concierge, Limousine hire, Parking, Laundry, Safe deposit fac., Currency exchange, Valet service, Barber/beauty shop, Performing Arts Ctr., TV, Turndown serv., Minibar/refrigerator, IDD/STD phone, Indiv. A/C ctl., Toaster, Coffee/tea making fac., Toiletries, Comp. fruit basket
Room Service: 24 hours
Restaurant: Cafe Esplanade, Siggis
Bar: Lobby, Raffles, Poolside
Business Facilities: Convention Center, Secretarial, Fax/telex, Translation, Copying
Sports Facilities: Pool, Sauna, Jacuzzi, Massage, Gym
Location: Harbour foreshore
Attractions: Kakadu Park, fishing, outback safaris, Katherine Gorge

HAYMAN HOTEL

Secluded on Hayman Island, the most northerly of Australia's Whitsunday Islands in the Great Barrier Reef, rests one of Australia's finest resorts. Priding itself on its friendly staff and atmosphere of relaxed elegance, Hayman Resort offers its guests thorough relaxation, a wide range of activities, fine food and excellent service.

Hayman Island is nearly 1000 acres; it is a horseshoe-shaped mountain surrounding the 200-acre flatland on which the resort was built. Thirty acres of the resort area are landscaped with exotic formal, informal, Oriental and rainforest gardens. Hayman boasts an international clientele, with approximately half the guests coming from outside Australia.

Hayman Resort offers 203 guest rooms and suites, all with balconies overlooking beach, water or gardens. The 11 Penthouse suites are each decorated in a unique style, from Art Deco or Morrocan, to an opulent, antique-filled French Provincial. All the suites have spectacular views of the Whitsundays and come complete with a personal valet.

Dining options include the classic French of La Fontaine, the casual Italian of La Trattoria or the Asian cuisines of Oriental Seafood. Guests can also choose a dinner cruise on the Sun Paradise, one of Hayman Island's luxury cruisers. Conference planners will find the resort fully equipped for meetings of 10 to 150.

You can roam the interior of the island, walking the 9 kilometers to the Dolphin Point Lookout and back, or head for the water, where extensive watersports facilities are available. If solitude is your craving, the Hayman crew will take you and a picnic by boat to a private beach.

Address: Hayman Island, Great Barrier Reef, N. Queensland, 4801
Phone: (079) 469100, Fax: (079) 469410, Telex: AA 48163 HAYMAN
No. of Rooms: 313 **Suites:** 21
Credit Cards: AmEx, DC, MC, JCB, Visa
Services and Amenities: Concierge, Laundry, Currency exchange, Barber/beauty shop, Shopping arcade, Activities desk, Babysitting, Kidz Club, TV, VCR, videos, Radio, Minibar, Phones, A/C, Ceiling fans, In-room safe, Coffee/tea making fac., Hairdryer, Bathrobes
Room Service: 24 hours
Restaurant: La Fontaine, La Trattoria, Seafood
Bar: Club Lounge, Hernandos Club
Business Facilities: Audio-visual, Secretarial, Fax, Postal
Conference Rooms: 3, Capacity: 120
Sports Facilities: Pool, Health spa, Sauna, Jacuzzi, Massage, Aerobics, Archery, Croquet, Tennis, Putting green, Windsurfing, Hobie cat sailing, Parasailing, other watersports
Attractions: Watersports, gardens

THE HOTEL COMO

If what you seek in a hotel is privacy, understated elegance, fine service and a touch of whimsy, then the "club style" Hotel Como is the place for you. Designed to cater to the top level business person, Hotel Como is so discreet it doesn't even have its name blazoned above the entrance.

Since opening in January 1989, the 5-Star Hotel Como has received many prestigious awards. Located within The Como Project development in a prestigious area of South Yarra, just 3 kilometers from Melbourne's business district, Hotel Como is graced with an impressive collection of original artwork by some of Australia's finest contemporary artists. A tapestry in the lobby woven by the Victorian Tapestry Workshop depicts the site of the hotel as it was in the early days of settlement. VIP guests who use the drive-through entrance to bypass the publicity of the lobby area will unfortunately miss this fine piece of work.

Guests can choose from 14 individually-styled suites, including split-level suites with spiral staircases, suites with Japanese terraces, or suites equipped with lockable office facilities and attached conference rooms. The hotel prides itself on ensuring each guest complete security for both business and personal needs. Complimentary evening cocktails are provided in the Lady Eyre Williams Lounge. The seventh floor of the hotel features a heated pool with a retractable roof, a sauna, spa and gymnasium.

In-suite dining and restaurant service is provided by the classic French restaurant Maxim's which, after 32 years of business, moved to a location just off the reception foyer of the Hotel Como. More casual dining is also available in the Food Court of The Como Project.

Business travelers and honeymooning couples alike will be delighted by the luxury, charm, privacy, discreetly attentive service—and the little rubber ducky in each bathroom—of Hotel Como.

Address: 630 Chapel St., South Yarra, Melbourne, Victoria
Phone: (03) 824-0400, (008) 033-400, Fax: (03) 824-1263, Telex: COMO AA 134854
No. of Rooms: Suites: 107
Room Rate: $$$
Services and Amenities: Comp. limousine, Comp. valet parking, VIP private entrance, Comp. evening drink, Child free under 14, TV, VCR, Videos, Cassette desk, Kitchen, Minibar, ISD phones, Iron & boards, In-room safe, Doonas, Robes, Spa baths, Comp. rubber duck
Room Service: 24 hours
Restaurant: Maxim's, Food court with "charge back"
Bar: Lady Eyre Williams Lounge
Business Facilities: Secretarial, Fax, Computer, Printer, Office suites
Conference Rooms: Capacity: 30
Sports Facilities: Pool, Exercise terrace, Spa, Sauna, Gym
Attractions: Melbourne attractions

THE REGENT MELBOURNE

There's no room without a view at the Regent Melbourne. The Hotel rises from the 35th floor of the Collins Place complex in the heart of Melbourne. Guest rooms start on floor 36. A spectacular 15-story atrium with mirrored galleries and a draped gold and silver curtain creates a sense of elegant airiness in this downtown locale.

The 311 rooms and 52 decorator suites all feature floor-to-ceiling windows and fresh flowers. Double glazed windows with blackout shutters make it possible to sleep comfortably any time of the day or night. Suites are equipped with fax hookups and bedside lighting and television controls. Regent Melbourne turndown service includes cold mineral water and a variety of dried fruit for a light bedtime snack.

Le Restaurant is the Regent's premier restaurant, offering an eclectic menu which incorporates Californian, Asian and Western influences. A dining experience not to be missed at the Regent is the Jazz Bruncheon, offered Sundays in Cafe La on the first, that is the 35th floor, of the Hotel. New Orleans-style jazz music and an American-style brunch featuring the Cajun flavors of southern Louisiana make for a special weekend event.

All guests are invited to take advantage of the Health Studio, which features spa, sauna, solarium and gym equipment. Gym clothes are available for your use, so no need to pack extra clothing (and no excuse not to exercise either!).

While in Melbourne, you must visit the Treasury Gardens, catch a performance at the Victoria Arts Centre, and ride the charming tram cars.

Address: 25 Collins St., GPO Box 246-B, Melbourne, Victoria, 3000
Phone: (03) 653-0000, (800) 545-4000, Fax: (03) 650-4261, Telex: AA 37724, Cable: THEREGENT
No. of Rooms: 311 **Suites:** 52
Room Rate: $$$
Services and Amenities: Concierge, Parking, Laundry, Valet service, TV, In-house movies, Stocked refrigerator, A/C, Fax socket, Coffee/tea making fac., Turndown service
Restaurant: Le Restaurant, Cafe La, Green Room
Bar: Black Swan Bar
Business Facilities: Audio-visual, Secretarial, Fax/telex/cable, Translation, Copying, Computer
Conference Rooms: 3, Capacity: 2,300
Sports Facilities: Health studio, Sauna, Jacuzzi, Massage, Gym, Solarium, Comp. use of gym attire
Location: Collins Place
Attractions: Arts Centre, Treasury Gardens, tram cars

HOTEL INTER-CONTINENTAL SYDNEY

Uniquely blending the old and the new, Hotel Inter-Continental Sydney has created a marvelous tribute both to Australia's history and to Australia's current travelers. The hotel's public rooms have been created from the restored 1851 Treasury Building, while a 28-story tower houses the 502 guest rooms.

The vaulted sandstone arcades and skylight of the Cortile bridge the old and the new at the Hotel Inter-Continental. Flowers, cane and leather, and a unique mix of traditional accessories create an atmosphere of old-style comfort in this urban locale. Guest rooms follow this motif, using colors and styles that create the feeling of an elegant 19th-century Australian home.

Business travelers are most welcome at the Inter-Continental. Three executive floors with personal valet service, and an executive lounge offering complimentary breakfast, are among the services offered. The Inter-Continental also provides an Early Arrivals Lounge for guests arriving before the check-in hour.

The hotel's formal dining room, The Treasury Restaurant, features Australian and international cuisine and an award-winning wine list. Offerings include local seafood such as Marinated Tasmanian Salmon with Colonna Virgin Olive Oil and Mixed Fresh Country Herbs, and Char-Grilled South Australian Lobster with Béarnaise Sauce, as well as other regional specialties. The Treasury Restaurant offers, as part of its regular menu, "Cuisine de Vie," innovative meals designed to address contemporary health and fine dining interests.

The hotel's fully equipped health center includes gym, indoor swimming pool, jacuzzi, private trainers and massage service. Within walking distance to most of Sydney's famous landmarks, the hotel is just a 10-minute stroll from the Historic Rocks area, the site of the original European settlement.

Address: 117 MacQuarie St., Sydney, New South Wales, 2000
Phone: (02) 230-0200, (008) 221-335, Fax: (02) 251-2342, Telex: AA 176890, Cable: INHOTELCOR
No. of Rooms: 502 **Suites:** 41
Credit Cards: All major
Services and Amenities: Concierge, Parking, Laundry, Valet service, Treasury building, Barber/beauty shop, Shopping arcade, Hotel school, Early arrival lounge, TV, In-house movies, Minibar/refrigerator, Indiv. A/C ctl., Coffee/tea making fac., Hairdryer, Harbour views
Room Service: 24 hours
Restaurant: Treasury, Cafe Opera, Cortile
Bar: Sketches Bistro, Favours
Business Facilities: Audio-visual, Fax
Conference Rooms: 10, Capacity:
Sports Facilities: Pool, Sauna, Jacuzzi, Massage, Gym, Private trainers
Location: Business district
Attractions: Royal Botanical Gardens, Sydney Opera House

THE REGENT SYDNEY

Opened in 1982 and completely refurbished in 1990, the luxurious Regent Sydney has consistently ranked among the world's top hotels.

All of the Regent's 596 rooms and suites have their own butler or floor steward who greets each guest with complimentary tea or coffee upon arrival. In each room, mirrors provide a sense of spaciousness while soft colors, tasteful wallpapers, Italian marble bathrooms and a lavish supply of Crabtree & Evelyn toiletries provide a feeling of comfort and luxury. The Regent Suite is the Regent's most spectacular offering, with two bedrooms, spacious living, dining and kitchen areas, and sunken bath in the main marble bathroom. Nightly turndown service in all rooms includes a bottle of cold mineral water, a candy and a sprig of wildflowers, all presented on a silver tray.

In addition to its luxurious accommodations and special service, the Regent also boasts the finest in "Haute Australian" cuisine. Kable's, the premier restaurant at the Regent, changes its menu daily, offering meals designed around the day's best quality local ingredients. A summertime meal at Kable's might begin with Parcels of Salmon Tartare with Seaweed Dressing, and feature Stuffed Boneless Quail with Spinach, Shallot and Garlic Puree. Dessert might be a Cointreau and White Chocolate Mille Feuille or an assortment of Australian Farmhouse Cheeses. Though elegant in its offerings, Kable's is warm and welcoming, using soft furnishings in apricot and terra cotta colors to create a comfortable environment.

Catch some Australian rays by the Regent's large, luxurious swimming pool, or go exploring. Sydney's famous landmarks are just a stone's throw from the hotel. Watersports and sailing adventures abound on Sydney's dazzling beaches.

Address: 199 George St., P.O. Box N185, Sydney, New South Wales, 2000
Phone: (02) 238-0000, (008) 022-800, Fax: (02) 251-2851, Telex: 73023
No. of Rooms: 602
Room Rate: $$$
Services and Amenities: Concierge, Limousine service, Laundry/pressing, Shopping arcade, TV, In-house movies, Radio, Stocked refrigerator, IDD phones, Full-sized desk, Coffee/tea making fac., Turndown service
Room Service: 24 hours
Restaurant: The Lobby, Kables'
Bar: Mezzanine, Club, George St.
Business Facilities: Audio-visual, Secretarial, Fax, Conf. coordinators, Personal fax machine
Sports Facilities: Pool, Sunning lounges
Location: Rocks area
Attractions: Beaches, The Opera House, Harbour Bridge, Royal Botanic Gardens, Sydney Tower

THE SEBEL TOWN HOUSE HOTEL

Sydney's Sebel Town House pampers its guests with that rare combination of European elegance and personalized, friendly service. Small enough for the staff to learn your name (if you're not already famous), and large enough to cater to seminars of 600, the Sebel Town House has earned its reputation for excellence. The decor of the hotel reflects its classic emphasis on dignified and discreet luxury. The lobby's rich wood paneling and comfortable leather chairs impart a quiet ambiance of warmth and charm.

Guest rooms are equally homey and inviting, providing luxurious amenities in an understated manner. All rooms offer queen-size beds with feather pillows, terrycloth robes and extra large towels. The Sebel Town House also provides amenities you may not have realized you'd been missing, like guest-room windows that open. Special consideration is made for women travelling on business, including business magazines, flowers, iron and ironing board in room, jewelry purse and manicure sets. The 25 Bay Suites include seven individually-designed major suites, some of which are named for the celebrity guests who frequent them. All the suites have been outfitted in uncompromising luxury.

Encore, the hotel's restaurant, serves superb international cuisine made from the freshest local ingredients; the menu features a wide range of seafood and an excellent selection of wines. The walls of the Cocktail Bar are lined with black-and-white photos of the many celebrities who stay at the Sebel Town House; a reminder that you're in good company.

The Sebel Town House is located in the elegant Elizabeth Bay area, on a hillside overlooking Sydney Harbor. From there, you're within easy reach of the City Center, and all the best that Sydney has to offer. Or, you may just want to relax by the hotel's terrific rooftop pool.

Address: 23 Elizabeth Bay Rd., Sydney, New South Wales, 2011
Phone: (02) 358-3244, (008) 222-266, Fax: (02) 357-1926, Telex: 20067 SBLHOT
No. of Rooms: 168 **Suites:** 50
Room Rate: $$$
Credit Cards: AmEx, BC, CB, DC, MC, Visa
Services and Amenities: Limousine/car rental, Laundry/dry cleaning, Barber/beauty shop, Gift shop, TV, Radio, Refrigerator, Indiv. A/C ctl.
Room Service: 24 hours
Restaurant: Encore
Bar: Cocktail Bar
Business Facilities: Fax
Conference Rooms: Capacity: 600
Sports Facilities: Pool, Sundeck, Sauna, Gym
Location: Elizabeth Bay
Attractions: Sydney Opera House, Royal Randwick Racecourse, Museum, beach

SHERATON UTAMA

Centrally located in the beautiful capital of Bandar Seri Begawan, Sheraton Utama is only fifteen minutes away from the airport and within easy reach of government and business offices. Brunei Darussalam is a land of fascinating contrasts, where magnificent mosques tower beside modern skyscrapers along the country's peaceful waterways. A Malay Muslim Monarchy whose traditions date back to before the sixth century, the discovery of oil has provided Brunei's population with the highest income per capita of any country in Asia, next to Japan.

A warm elegance permeates Sheraton Utama; marble walls and floors are accentuated by the teal and rose color scheme of the lobby's furnishings. This same color scheme is carried over into the hotel's comfortable rooms and suites. Executive suites feature a marble bathroom, stylish living room area, and meeting area with a full-sized conference table, enabling guests to hold confidential meetings or private parties. More informally, pool-side drinks or buffets can be arranged.

For casual dining, Cafe Melati serves up international favorites along with the local specialties. The Heritage Restaurant invites guests into an atmosphere of informal sophistication; its European chefs thrive on innovation and excel in the traditional. A recent offering included Mousselines of Salmon with dill sauce, Caesar Salad, Veal Medalion in pepper sauce, Black Velvet cake and Pouilly Fuisse.

Just five minutes from the hotel is Asia's largest Water Village, where local fisherman and workers live in houses with stilts on the banks of the Brunei River. A number of fascinating day excursions to the surrounding countryside and cultural sites can be arranged through the hotel.

Address: P.O. Box 2203, Bandar Seri Begawan 1922
Phone: 02-44272, 800-325-3535, Fax: 02-21579, Telex: BU 2306 UTAMA, Cable: SHERATON BRUNEI
No. of Rooms: 156 **Suites:** 13
Room Rate: $$
Credit Cards: All major
Services and Amenities: Airport transp., Limousine/car rental, Parking, Laundry/dry cleaning, Safe deposit fac., Travel arrangements, Gift shop, Babysitting, TV, In-house movies, Radio, Minibar/refrigerator, DD phones, Comp. newspaper
Room Service: 24 hours
Restaurant: The Heritage, Cafe Melati
Bar: Mallet Bar, Executive Lounge
Business Facilities: Audio-visual, Secretarial, Fax/telex, Copying, Internat'l courier
Conference Rooms: 5, Capacity: 120
Sports Facilities: Pool, Fitness center
Location: Central City
Attractions: Speed boat ride through water village, city tours

WEDGEWOOD HOTEL

It's obvious upon entering Eleni Skalbania's Wedgewood Hotel that this local businesswoman is a collector of fine antiques and art. Her 94-room hostelry reflects her personal dedication to a project that involved gutting and rebuilding an old hotel in downtown Vancouver. Opened in 1984, the Wedgewood is like an elegant home, lovingly cared for, and stressing personal services, such as complimentary shoeshine and a morning newspaper at your door. The gracious, inviting lobby is enhanced by a magnificent oriental rug, marble fireplace walls, a brass fire screen, and an assortment of period pieces. One-third of the accommodations here are suites, with tastefully coordinated furnishings. Flower-bedded balconies overlook gardens and waterfalls of Robson Square and the courthouse.

Beyond the palladian windows of the Bacchus Bar and Ristorante, diners find distinctive adaptations of regional Italian dishes—*nuovo cucina*. For an excellent opener with zest, try vongole in salsa picante. The clams are tender, and the sauce is rich in spices and fresh tomatoes. There's a prodigious variety of wines from which to choose, ranging from gems from California's boutique wineries such as a Ridge 1983 Zinfandel, to such French treats as a 1984 Pierre Ponnelle Meursault. You'll also find a nicely balanced representation from Italy, Germany, Australia, and Canada. French nouvelle cuisine, the elegance of skylights, an ornate fireplace and two garden atriums entice diners to enjoy the freshest fare in Liaisons—an elegant Banquet Room. Though a small city by world standards, Vancouver is remarkably cosmopolitan and sophisticated. Many elegant boutiques, fine restaurants, and cultural events are found nearby the hotel.

Address: 845 Hornby St., Vancouver, British Columbia, V6Z IVI
Phone: 604-689-7777, 800-663-0666, Fax: 604-688-3074, Telex: 0455234
No. of Rooms: 94 **Suites:** 34
Room Rate: $$
Credit Cards: All major
Services and Amenities: Concierge, Airport limousine, Parking, Laundry, Valet service, Currency exchange, House doctor, Babysitting, Comp. shoeshine, Cable TV, Radio, Some minibars, Indiv. climate ctl., Robes, Comp. newspaper
Room Service: 24 hours
Restaurant: Bacchus Ristorante
Bar: Bacchus Bar
Business Facilities: Audio-visual, Secretarial, Fax/telex, Translation, Copying, Teleconferencing, Message center, Full business center
Conference Rooms: Capacity: 80
Sports Facilities: Squash club privileges, health spa privileges
Location: Downtown Vancouver
Attractions: Robson Street shopping, Pacific Centre, Granville Island, Stanley Park

LAUREL POINT INN

The Laurel Point Inn occupies a beautifully landscaped six-acre peninsula extending into Victoria's inner harbor. Architect Arthur Erickson ensured that every room in the hotel would have maximum use of the view.

Guest accommodations are furnished in beige marble tones and modern furniture. All have floor to ceiling windows and large balconies with views of the water. Each bathroom has an oversized tub, separate shower stall, double sinks, TV and phone. Some split-level suites with spiral staircases have 360 degree views of the harbor.

Cafe Laurel, with its rattan furniture and profusion of plants, serves three meals daily. The Cafe faces east, enjoying sunrise over the harbor at breakfast. The Terrace Room opens to the west next to a reflecting pool and Japanese garden. A lavish Sunday brunch is presented here, and the area is perfect for banquets of 80 or receptions of up to 200. Cook's Landing, a piano lounge overlooking the Inner harbor, serves light meals throughout the day.

The Laurel Point Inn has full conference and banquet facilities. Four salons can be combined into one room that seats 200 for dinner. The hotel also offers audio-visual equipment and business services.

An indoor pool, jacuzzi, sauna, and exercise equipment are available. Guests at the Laurel Point Inn enjoy guest privileges at the Olympic View Golf Course.

The hotel offers airport transport facilities. Its location also makes it convenient to waterplane, helicopter, ferry, and high-speed catamaran services.

Address: 680 Montreal Street, Victoria, British Columbia, V8V 1Z8
Phone: 604-386-8721, 800-663-7667, Fax: 604-386-9547, Telex: 0497348
No. of Rooms: 200 **Suites:** 14
Room Rate: $$
Credit Cards: AmEx, MC, Enroute, Visa
Services and Amenities: Car rental, Free parking, Laundry, Valet serivce, Game area, Gift shop, Babysitting, Cable TV, Radio, Minibar, Phone in bath, Indiv. climate ctl., Comp. toiletries
Room Service: 24 hours
Restaurant: Cafe Laurel
Bar: Cooks Landing, Terrace Lounge
Business Facilities: Full conference fac.
Conference Rooms: 9, Capacity: 200
Sports Facilities: Pool, Whirlppol, Sauna, Aerobics, Golf privileges
Location: Inner Harbor
Attractions: Parliament buildings, Maritime Museum, Provincial Museum, Beacon Hill Park

GREAT WALL SHERATON HOTEL BEIJING

Designed to pay tribute to Beijing's impetus toward the 21st century, the Great Wall Sheraton's glass facade reflects images of the surrounding landscape and traditional Chinese architecture. Local artists crafted the stonework walls at the entry courtyard of this dramatic 1,000-room hotel. Inside, a seven-story cylindrical atrium and four glass-enclosed elevators draw attention upward. A large embroidered mural representing the Great Wall decorates the lobby.

The 1,007 guest rooms in three tower wings include 41 suites and provide impressive views of the city. The 2 Presidential Suites, located on the 18th floor, are luxuriously decorated with Chinese antiques, rosewood or lacquered furnishings and Oriental carpets. The decor of the VIP and Junior Suites is enhanced by contemporary themes and traditional Chinese artworks.

Ten restaurants and lounges provide a lively selection of dining possibilities. Le France offers classic French dining. Relish a warm scallop salad with pistachio dressing in a dining room graced by an Italian waterfall chandelier set in a stage of mirrored walls, vaulted ceilings and painted murals. Yuen Tai, 21 floors above Beijing, serves Szechuan delicacies in an atmosphere softened by burgandy woodwork and a live Chinese orchestra. Other choices range from light snacks at poolside, to the Orchid Court Pavilion buffet in the tree-lined path overlooking the traditional Chinese garden.

The Great Wall Sheraton is well-equipped for any sort of business function. Its Grand Ballroom accommodates up to 1,600 people, eight function rooms suit smaller groups, and a tiered 230-seat theatre is perfect for presentations.

With indoor heated swimming pool, tennis courts, health club, billiard room, and even a mini-golf course, the Great Wall Sheraton is equipped for pleasure and relaxation as well.

Address: North Dong Huan Road, Beijing, 100 026
Phone: (86-1) 500-5566, 800-325-3535, Fax: (86-1) 500-3398, Telex: 22002 GWHTL CN
No. of Rooms: 1,007 **Suites:** 41
Room Rate: $$
Credit Cards: AmEx, DC, MC, Visa
Services and Amenities: Parking, Laundry/dry cleaning, Currency exchange, Travel arrangements, Barber/beauty shop, Gift shop, Sundries shop, Post office, Satellite TV, Radio, Minibar, IDD phone, Indiv. climate ctl., Message light phone
Room Service: 24 hours
Restaurant: Yuen Tai, Le France, The Fan
Bar: Caravan Bar, Atrium, Cosmos
Business Facilities: Secretarial, Fax, Translation, Copying, Postal, Banquet facilities
Conference Rooms: 8, Capacity:
Sports Facilities: Pool, Health club, Billards, Gym, Bike rental, Tennis, Minigolf, nearby Golf
Location: Chao Yang District
Attractions: Great Wall, Ming Tomb, Forbidden City, Temple of Heaven

THE PALACE HOTEL

The Palace Hotel is centrally located between two main shopping streets in the Forbidden City cultural district in Beijing. The hotel was designed to balance traditional Chinese architecture with contemporary luxury. The building, with its white-tiled exterior marked by red and green highlights and pagoda styling, creates a sense of order and dignity, perfectly suited to the service the hotel provides.

Passing through the pagoda entrance, one enters a grand modern lobby, with a large white-marble staircase contrasting the dark woodwork and reflecting light from the skylights above. The 578 guest rooms demonstrate the same careful attention to design and detail, including well-chosen splashes of color, a mist-free mirror in the marble bathroom, and computerized controls for lighting and air-conditioning.

Since the vast majority of its guests are visiting China for business purposes, the hotel has created the Palace Club to cater to their special needs. Guests staying on the three Palace Club floors enjoy such luxuries as private check-in, complimentary dry-cleaning and laundry service, priority use of the 24-hour business center, and complimentary fruit, tea and cookies upon arrival. Guests staying in the Wangfujing and Presidential Suites enjoy even greater luxury, with two bedrooms, whirlpool, private elevator and an on-call butler.

A wide selection of culinary opportunities are available at the Palace Hotel, including fine French cuisine at the Champagne Room. Elegantly appointed with crystal and shining brass, the Champagne Room provides sumptuous food with attentive yet unobtrusive service. At Roma Ristorante Italiano, choose from a generous menu of gourmet Italian specialties. In addition to The Fortune Garden (Cantonese), Palace (Szechuan), and Inagiku (Japanese), the Bavaria Bierstube provides the best of Bavarian hospitality, with a wide selection of sausages and, of course, Apfelstrudel.

The Palace Hotel's health spa is a great place to unwind, as is its pool, and the alluring Forbidden City.

Address: 8 Goldfish Lane, Wangfujing, Beijing, 100006
Phone: 861-512-8899, 800-262-9467, Fax: 861-512-9050, Telex: 222696
No. of Rooms: 578 **Suites:** 80
Room Rate: $$$
Credit Cards: AmEx, Visa, MC, DC, JCB
Services and Amenities: 24 hr concierge, Limousine/car rental, Parking, Laundry/dry cleaning, Safe deposit fac., Currency exchange, Travel arrangements, Shopping arcade, Doctor on call, Babysitting, In-house movies, Minibar, Indiv. A/C ctl., Portable water supply
Room Service: 24 hours
Restaurant: Roma Ristorante, Inagiku, Fortune Garden
Bar: Club Lounge, Intermezzo Lounge
Business Facilities: Audio-visual, Secretarial, Fax, Simult. translation, Message center, Courier, Postal, Computers
Conference Rooms: 6, Capacity: 650
Sports Facilities: Pool, Health equipment, Sauna, Massage, Aerobics studio, Billard room
Location: Wangfujing
Attractions: Forbidden City

SHANGRI-LA HOTEL BEIJING

Opened in 1987, the 24-story Shangri-La Hotel is located in the western part of Beijing, close to the Negotiations Building, Exhibition Hall, and the city zoo.

Furnished in warm tones, its accommodations offer individual climate control, color television with in-room movies, a fully-stocked mini-bar and refrigerator, and multi-channel music programs. Connecting rooms are available on request, or one may wish to book a suite.

Many business travellers prefer the Shangri-La because it has a special office/residential tower in which all rooms have an adjoining, fully equipped office. Secretarial service, translation, interpreting, copying, courier service, telex and fax are available through the hotel's Business Center.

The Shangri-La's Grand Ballroom and 13 smaller function rooms can accommodate meetings and banquets of up to 1000 persons. Special sound and lighting facilities are available and simultaneous translation can be provided in up to six languages.

A heated swimming pool and full health spa with sauna, steam bath, solariums, massage, and a gym with the latest exercise equipment enhance the opportunities for relaxation at the hotel.

Live music is heard nightly in the Lobby Lounge. The Peacock Bar is the perfect place for a drink before or after dinner. And for those who wish to dance the night away, there is the discotheque Xanadu. The Shangri-La offers both Chinese and Continental cuisines. Its Shang Palace is the largest Cantonese restaurant in Beijing, seating 450. La Brasserie is a smaller restaurant serving western dishes.

Whether you are in Beijing on business, or to sightsee in the city which has been China's capital for 500 years, the Shangri-La Hotel is an excellent choice for comfort and service.

Address: 29 Zizhuyuan Rd., Beijing
Phone: (01) 841-2211, 800-359-5050,
Fax: (01) 802-1471, Telex: 222322
SHABJ CN, Cable: 1123 SHANGHTL BJ
No. of Rooms: 746 **Suites:** 40
Room Rate: $$
Credit Cards: All major
Services and Amenities: Satellite TV, Radio, Minibar, Indiv. climate ctl.
Restaurant: La Brasserie, Shang Palace
Bar: Lobby Lounge, Peacock Bar
Business Facilities: Secretarial, Fax/telex/cable, Translation, Courier
Conference Rooms: 13, Capacity: 1,000
Sports Facilities: Pool, Full health spa
Location: Haidian
Attractions: Beijing International Exhibition Hall, Beijing Zoo, Negotiations Building

GARDEN HOTEL GUANGZHOU

Ghuangzhou (Canton) has been southern China's commercial center for over 1,500 years. The Garden Hotel is located in the city's newest commercial district of Ghuangzhou and is one of China's largest and most modern hotels. Set in delightful natural gardens, the hotel's two towers house over 1,100 guest rooms and suites, 130 apartments, and more than 500 offices. Its impressive marble lobby is grandly decorated with major Chinese works of art and is the largest lobby in the world.

Spacious rooms and suites provide the utmost in comfort and modern convenience. The Presidential Suite occupies one entire wing of the hotel tower, equivalent to 19 regular room units. Lavishly appointed with Louis XIV furniture, the Suite boasts a large reception room opening onto a two-story high patio, replete with marble floors and hanging plants from wood pergola, a formal dining room and pantry, living room, spacious master bedroom and two smaller bedrooms. The generous marble bathroom suite is adorned with gold fixtures and includes a large jacuzzi.

Twelve unique restaurants and bars offer a wide range of dining delights. The hotel's finest restaurant is The Connoissor, featuring distinctive continental dishes in classic French ambience. The Peach Blossom and the Lai Wan Market offer delicious Cantonese cuisine. Northern Chinese specialties can be savored at The Ming Yuen Restaurant. Other Western restaurants include the Greenery Coffee Shop and The Cascade, both presenting a wide mix of international dishes. The English-style Tavern, modern L'Aperitif, and luxurious China Trader are popular drinking and rendezvous places.

The hotel's Executive Floor and comprehensive Business Center cater to the special needs of business travelers. The Conference Hall can hold up to 1,400.

Recreational facilities include a swimming pool and children's pool on the podium roof, fully equipped Health Center and gym, and tennis and squash courts.

The city of Ghuangzhou offers a number of choice spots for dining and entertainment. The Garden Hotel's Tour Desk is happy to assist guests planning to visit the city's many local attractions.

Address: 368 Huanshi Dong Lu, Guangzhou (Canton), Guandong Province, 510 064
Phone: (86-20) 338989, Fax: (86-20) 350467, Telex: 44788 GDHTL CN, Cable: 4735
No. of Rooms: 1,112 **Suites:** 62
Room Rate: $
Credit Cards: All major
Services and Amenities: Dry cleaning, Valet, Safe deposit fac., Currency exchange, Travel arrangements, Barber/beauty shop, Shopping arcade, Clinic, Satellite TV, In-house movies, Radio, Minibar/refrigerator, Phone, A/C
Room Service: 24 hour room service
Restaurant: Peach Blossom, Connoisseur, Ming Yuan
Bar: Lotus Pond, Tavern, Cheers
Business Facilities: Audio-visual, Secretarial, Fax/telex, Translation, Copying, Printing, Postal, Reference library
Conference Rooms: 9, Capacity: 1,400
Sports Facilities: Pool, Health club, Sauna, Jacuzzi, Gym, Sundecks, Squash, Tennis, Badminton, Snooker hall, Garden
Location: Dong Shan District
Attractions: Mausoleum of the Martyrs, Zhenhai Tower, Guangzhou Zoo, Sun Yat Sen Memorial

WHITE SWAN HOTEL

The White Swan Hotel, located on historic Shamian Island next to the Pearl River, is the centerpiece of Ghuangzhou's newest resort. The 34-story hotel faces the river on one side, and magnificent banyan gardens on the other. The White Swan is minutes away from the international airport, and is conveniently located near the Trade Fair and Cultural Park. Built around an atrium, the lobby gardens feature a pagoda poised above a waterfall that spills into a lily pond.

Elegantly appointed guest rooms and luxury suites are decorated with touches of Chinese art and feature views of either Ghuangzhou or the Pearl River. The Presidential Suite covers the entire 28th floor, enjoying spectacular views and interior gardens. Amenities on the three Executive Floors include fresh flowers, fruit and luxury soaps, complementary tea, snacks, buffet breakfast and evening cocktails, and a 50% discount on conference facilities.

The Business Center offers full secretarial services and private meeting rooms. For luxurious arrivals and departures over the hotel's private causeway, one can arrange a chauffeured Rolls Royce.

The River Garden Coffee Shop, where Chinese and Western cuisine is served, opens onto the lobby gardens and offers a wonderful view of the Pearl River. The Cantonese Room is the hotel's principal restaurant, featuring local delicacies in a luxurious atmosphere. The Song Bird Tea Lounge, on the second floor overlooking the lobby gardens, serves buffet breakfasts and lunches, and afternoon tea and cocktails. Other restaurants and lounges within the hotel offer dining delights and opportunities for private entertaining.

Two swimming pools with adjoining health club and spa, tennis courts, squash courts, and a golf driving range, provide a wide range of recreational options.

Address: 1 Southern St., Shamian Island, Guangzhou (Canton), Guandong Province, 510 133
Phone: (020) 886968, 800-223-6800, Fax: (020) 861188, Telex: 44688 WSH CN, Cable: 8888
No. of Rooms: 885 **Suites:** 62
Room Rate: $$
Credit Cards: AmEx, DC, MC, Visa
Services and Amenities: Beauty salon, Shopping arcade, TV, In-house movies, Radio, Minibar, IDD phone, Indiv. climate ctl.
Restaurant: Jade River, Hirata, Song Bird, Riverside
Bar: The Hare & The Moon, River
Business Facilities: Secretarial, Translation
Conference Rooms: 4, Capacity:
Sports Facilities: Pool, Full health spa, Sauna, Jacuzzi, Massage, Steambath, Aerobics, Squash, Tennis, Golf driving range
Attractions: Trade Fair, Cultural Park

SHANGRI-LA HANGZHOU

Uniquely located midway up the lush green Beishan Hill, the Shangri-La Hangzhou Hotel commands a full view of the city's fabled West Lake. The hotel complex, renovated and refurbished in the mid-1980's, consists of two hotel buildings, a convention center and four hillside villas for visitors who prefer a more private environment.

Of the 387 guestrooms, 17 are junior suites, 26 are one-bedroom and 4 are Presidential Suites. The most elegant of these is decorated in traditional Chinese style, with ornate furnishings, fittings and ornaments. The decor is complemented by the most up-to-date appointments, including color TV, central heating and air conditioning, and IDD telephone.

Shangri-La Hangzhou is dedicated to pleasing the most discerning of international diners. At the Lotus Pond Restaurant, indulge in indigenous Hangzhou dishes such as Beggars' Chicken, Vinegar Glazed Sweet and Sour Fish, and Braised Pork "Dong Po." In the Spring Moon grill room, enjoy two-inch thick steaks prepared by European chefs or witness a meeting of East and West in Spring Moon's delightful nouvelle-style offerings. Shang Palace "woks up" Cantonese cuisine with an aesthetically pleasing flair.

After a meal, a slow, leisurely stroll along the lake may be in order, or a visit to The Silk Shop, where an abundance of silk textiles, as well as ready-made garments, are available to dazzle you. Boating on the lake is another favorite pastime of visitors to Hangzhou.

Address: 78 Beishan St., Hangzhou
Phone: (0571) 22921, Fax: (0571) 73545, Telex: 35005/6 HOTCH CN
No. of Rooms: 387 **Suites:** 37
Room Rate: $$
Credit Cards: AmEx, DC, MC, JCB, Visa
Services and Amenities: TV, Radio, Minibar, IDD phones, Indiv. climate ctl., Balconies
Restaurant: Spring Moon, Cafe Peony, Shang Palace
Bar: Lobby, Garden
Business Facilities: Secretarial, Fax, Translation, Copying, Printing
Conference Rooms: 16, Capacity: 560
Sports Facilities: Pool, Massage, Tennis, Bicycling, Boating on lake
Location: West Lake
Attractions: Boating on West Lake, Moganshan Mountain

GARDEN HOTEL SHANGHAI

History comes alive in the Garden Hotel Shanghai. The former French Club, a fascinating architectural testimony to the international influences of the last century, forms the base of this 33-story hotel. Opened in 1989, The Garden Hotel Shanghai is set in a 28,000 square meter garden. Great expanses of marble, tall pillars topped with Corinthian capitals, sweeping Art Deco stairways and sculpture, golden mosaics, and stained glass are only a few of the decorative features that greet visitors in the hotel's public spaces. Moved from its original location, the legendary French Club, now in its third incarnation as the Garden Hotel, rests on the fashionable Huai Hai Zhong Road.

Guest rooms and suites are appointed in pastel and creme tones, featuring soft lighting, European-style furnishings and white marble bathrooms.

In keeping with its international flavor, the Garden Hotel Shanghai offers a colorful selection of cuisine. Bai-Yu-Lan serves delicious authentic Chinese fare, while Sakura and the Continental Room provide choice Japanese and European options, respectively.

After an invigorating swim in the hotel's 25-meter swimming pool, you may want to explore the fascinating city of Shanghai, with its wonderful silk and jewelry shops, and open-air Porcelain Market.

Address: 58 Maoming Nan Lu, Shanghai
Phone: (021) 433-1111, Fax: (021) 433-8866, Telex: 30157 GHSH
No. of Rooms: 478 **Suites:** 22
Room Rate: $$
Services and Amenities: Travel arrangements, Barber/beauty shop, Shopping arcade, TV, Minibar
Restaurant: Bai Yu Lan, Continental Room, Sakura
Bar: Oasis, Continental
Conference Rooms: 11
Sports Facilities: Pool, Health club

HUA TING SHERATON HOTEL

The Hua Ting Sheraton is an ultra-modern hotel in Shanghai, China's eastern gateway city. Hua Ting's magnificent lobby is decorated in rose and black granite. Stunning gold-leaf relief sculptures on the ceiling and 30 wall panels gracefully depict Chinese themes, and a spiral staircase of marble, brass and glass descends above a lotus pond.

Guest rooms are elegantly appointed with luxury amenities, including satellite TV with in-house movies, radio, mini-bar, international direct dial telephone, and individual climate control. The suites have balconies overlooking China's largest city.

The hotel's three principal restaurants offer the best in English, French, and Cantonese cuisine. Anton's, featuring French cuisine, is reknowned as one of the city's premier restaurants. Guan Yue Tai offers traditional Cantonese specialties. Seafood and grilled favorites can be found at The English Grill Room. Ka Fei Ting serves snacks around the clock, and Nicole's Disco is the hotel's night spot.

Business travellers staying at the Hua Ting will appreciate its Business Center, open 24 hours a day, providing secretarial and translation services, telex, fax, photocopying, and courier service. For conferences, the Grand Ballroom can accommodate up to 1200 theater style. Other rooms are available for smaller meetings or parties, and all are equipped with modern audio-visual facilities. One room features simultaneous translation service.

Guests at the Hua Ting may enjoy the indoor swimming pool and adjacent health club with gym, sauna, steam room, whirlpool and wonderfully relaxing massage services. The hotel also offers a tennis court, billiard room, and fully electronic ten-pin bowling alley.

There is so much to see in Shanghai. Not to be missed are the Yu-Tuan Garden, Jade Buddha Temple, the Bund, The Exhibition Hall, Sun Yat Sen's former residence, Soong Ching Ling's mausoleum, the Longhua Temple, and Longhua Pagoda.

Address: 1200 Cao Xi Bei Lu, Shanghai
Phone: 386 000, Telex: 33589SH HTH CN, Cable: 0703
No. of Rooms: 1,008 **Suites:** 33
Room Rate: $$
Credit Cards: AmEx, DC, MC, JCB, V, GW
Services and Amenities: Laundry, Valet service, Travel arrangements, Barber/beauty shop, Shopping arcade, Satellite TV, Radio, Minibar, IDD phone, Indiv. climate ctl.
Room Service: 24 hours
Restaurant: Anton's French, Luigi's, Guan Ye Tai
Bar: Lobby, Nicole's, Recreation
Business Facilities: Secretarial, Fax/telex, Translation, Copying, Courier, 24hr business center
Sports Facilities: Pool, Full health spa, Gym, Jogging, Tennis, Billiards, Bowling
Attractions: Yu-Yuan Garden, Jade Buddha Temple, Exhibition Hall, Longhua Temple

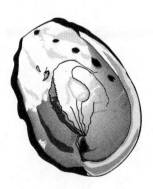

PORTMAN SHANGRI-LA

Located in the heart of Shanghai's business district, Portman Shangri-La is part of the Shanghai Center, an extensive complex which features apartment, office and retail spaces, a multi-function theater and exhibition hall. The hotel, a graceful 50-story tower, stands in the middle of the Center.

Spacious guest rooms and suites are handsomely furnished in thoroughly modern style, and feature excellent amenities. The 45th floor houses the four premier penthouse suites, affording spectacular views.

Dining pleasures at the Portman include Shanghai Jax, named after a legendary colonial figure in the early 1900's. This American grill restaurant serves thick steaks and a variety of seafood dishes. Shiki, the Japanese restaurant, features a teppan grill, sushi bar, private dining rooms and cozy tatami rooms. The Tea Garden, an international coffee shop set in an Oriental atmosphere, serves breakfast, lunch and dinner. A recent candlelight dinner at the Portman included Marinated Smoked Salmon with Caviar, Snails in Roquefort Mint Sauce Served in Puff Pastry, Beef Tournedos Topped with Goose Liver in Pink Peppercorn Sauce, served with Parisienne Potatoes, glazed Baby Carrots and Sauteed Zucchinis, and Peach Soup with Sherbet and Champagne, topped with Petits Fours.

Portman Shangri-La sports Shanghai's largest and most extensive health club. The Portman Spa encompasses three stories and includes a full range of activities including aerobic, tai-chi, karate and swimming classes. Guests can enjoy the gym, indoor and outdoor pool, exercise room, sauna and steam bath, jacuzzi, tennis, squash and racquetball courts. Massage service is also available.

Address: 1376 Nanjing Xi Lu, Shanghai, 200 040
Phone: (86-21) 2798888, 800-359-5050, Fax: (86-21) 2798999, Telex: 33272 PSH CN
No. of Rooms: 549 **Suites:** 58
Room Rate: $$
Credit Cards: AmEx, DC, MC, JCB, FC, Vs
Services and Amenities: Limousine service, Valet, Laundry/dry cleaning, Barber/beauty shop, Drugstore, Medical clinic, Babysitting, Theater, TV, In-house movies, Minibar, IDD phones
Room Service: 24 hours
Restaurant: Shanghai Jax, Tea Garden, Shiki
Bar: Long Bar, Bubbling Well Lounge
Business Facilities: Fax, Translation, Computer, Courier, Reference library
Conference Rooms: 6, Capacity: 300
Sports Facilities: Pools, Health club, Sauna, Jacuzzi, Squash, Tennis, Racquetball, Putting green

CRYSTAL PALACE HOTEL

The Crystal Palace Hotel stretches serenely alongside downtown Tianjin's beautiful lake, barely minutes away from the Tianjin Exhibition Center. Its stunning modern architecture includes a rounded reflecting glass facade that juts out from the center of the hotel's two L-shaped wings. White, black, shades of gray, and glass are apparent throughout the interior. In the high-ceilinged, airy lobby, potted trees create a feeling of ease.

All 346 rooms feature deluxe amenities, including marble bathrooms fitted with a second telephone and individual climate control. The contemporary decor features polished black furnishings, Oriental art and flower arrangements. The Presidential Suite offers guests the best in luxury accomodations, in a style that is sleek and modern.

Le Marquis, the hotel's gourmet restaurant, provides French fare in a soothing atmosphere. Shu Shang Geh is the elegant Chinese restaurant. Delicious western buffets can be enjoyed at the Terrace Cafe. TJ Bar, overlooking the lake and enlivened by music in the evening, is a cozy place for a social rendezvous.

After a day of business or touring, guests may relax at the health club, take a dip in the pool, hit a few tennis balls on the tennis court or get a great workout on the exercise equipment. Many guests rejuvenate by taking a leisurely walk along the hotel's lake or visiting the hotel shopping center.

Address: You Yi & Binshui Roads, Tianjin (Tientsin), Hebei Province, 300061
Phone: (086-022)310567, Fax: (086-022)310591, Telex: 23277 TCPH CN
No. of Rooms: 346
Room Rate: $
Services and Amenities: Parking, Bank, Shopping arcade, Satellite TV, In-house movies
Restaurant: Cafe Suisse, Le Marquis, Shu Shang Geh
Bar: TJ Bar
Business Facilities: Business center, Function rooms
Sports Facilities: Pool, Health club, Exercise equipment, Tennis
Location: Hexi District
Attractions: Tonglou shopping, recreational center, international exhibition center

THE GOLDEN FLOWER HOTEL

Known to locals as the Crystal Palace, the Golden Flower Hotel is a modern seven-story structure, clad in reflective glass. With suspended bridgeways connecting each of the six guest floors and an open semi-circular staircase leading from the ground to the seven floors, the Golden Flower presents a unique and inviting contemporary atmosphere.

Opened in 1985 with 210 guest rooms, the hotel more than doubled its capacity in 1989, adding 300 rooms and suites, a swimming pool, health center with sauna, shopping arcade and conference/banquet facilities for 250 people. The rooms are spacious and decorated in soft pastels. All rooms are equipped with color TV, coffee/tea making facilities and mini-bar. Suites offer modern furnishings with an Oriental touch, and elegant marble bathrooms.

Wan Fu Court, the Golden Flower's Chinese restaurant, serves up the fiery cuisine of Szechuan, prepared by native chefs from carefully selected local ingredients. The Jade Spring features continental cuisine prepared by European chefs, served as a spectacular buffet.

The Golden Flower provides the perfect venue from which to explore the wonders of Xi'an, including the Terracotta warriors, thousands of terracotta figures dating back 2000 years. The Hua Qing Hot Springs, rich mineral water baths where visitors can bathe just as the Emperors did, are easily accessible.

Address: 8, Chang Le Road West, Xian, Shaanxi Province
Phone: (029) 32981, Fax: (029) 32327, Telex: 70145 GFH CN
No. of Rooms: 210 **Suites:** 5
Room Rate: $$
Credit Cards: AmEx, Visa, MC, DC
Services and Amenities: Airport/city transp., Currency exchange, Travel arrangements, Shopping arcade, Babysitting, TV, In-house movies, Radio, Minibar/refrigerator, Indiv. climate ctl., Coffee/tea making fac., Comp. newspaper
Restaurant: Jade Spring, Wan Fu Court
Bar: Drunken Moon Lounge
Business Facilities: Secretarial, Fax/telex, Translation
Conference Rooms: Capacity: 20
Attractions: Ming City Wallk, Terracotta Warriors, Hua Qing Hot Springs

HOTEL BORA BORA

Bora Bora lies 150 miles northwest of Tahiti in the Leward Society Islands. The Hotel, built 25 years ago, is situated on Point Raiti, facing west southwest, 3.6 miles from the village of Vaitape.

The resort's 75 thatch-roof, Polynesian-style bunagalows, suites and villas are nestled among tropical gardens, on palm studded beaches or sitting over the lagoon. The garden and beach bungalows have 2 double beds, dressing room, shower and private lanai. The overwater bungalows have a queen and twin bed, dressing room, shower and sundeck with stairs to the lagoon. The suites and villas offer a living room, deck or terrace, and some have private swimming pools.

Casual, all-day dining is available in the Matira Terrace Restaurant overlooking the lagoon. Light lunches and refreshments are served at the Pofai Beach Bar. The Matira Terrace Bar features sandwiches and tropical beverages. Afternoon tea is served in the Matira Bar. A spectacular Sunday buffet dinner and beach barbeques provide more delectable choices for enjoying the cuisine of the gifted French chef. If you like entertainment while you dine, local musicians and Tahitian dance shows maintain the exotic atmosphere of the hotel.

There are so many outdoor and indoor activities available at this resort that you could spend a month there and never get to all of them. Snorkel among gentle fish that eat from your hand, paddle an outrigger, play tennis, scuba dive, fish for marlin, sail on a romantic sunset cruise, or attend one of the flower crown and lei making lessons. The activities desk handles all arrangements.

If your visit is also your honeymoon, be sure to ask about the special "Lovers' Paradise" packages. The deluxe version of this package provides special amenities, such as a champagne and fruit basket in your bungalow, a candlelight dinner with wine served on the terrace of your bungalow, and a private sail at sunset aboard an outrigger sailing canoe. What could be more romantic?

Address: B.P. 1, Bora Bora, Vaitape
Phone: (689) 67 70 28, Fax: (689) 67 74 38
No. of Rooms: 66 **Suites:** 17
Room Rate: $$$$
Credit Cards: AmEx, DC, MC, Visa
Services and Amenities: Car rental, Laundry, Safe deposit fac., Currency exchange, Daily activities, Shopping arcade, Medical services, Airport speedboat, 110/220 voltage, Refrigerator, coffee/tea, Fans, private bar, Coffee maker, Hairdryer, Balconies
Restaurant: Matira Restaurant
Bar: Matira Terrace, Pofai Beach
Business Facilities: Secretarial, Translation, Capacity: 40
Sports Facilities: Bike/scooter rentals, Speedboat rental, Sailing, Deep-sea fishing, Hiking, Tennis, Scuba diving, Snorkelling, Free use of paddle canoes
Location: Pointe Raititi
Attractions: Island tours, sharkfeeding, safaris, sunset sails

MOOREA BEACHCOMBER ROYAL

Only a short flight by scheduled air-taxi, ferry or helicopter charter from Tahiti, Moorea Island is one of the windward islands of French Polynesia. Here, sharp peaks overlook deep valleys, emerald lagoons teem with brightly colored fish, white sandy beaches are edged with majestic coconut palms, and 100-foot waterfalls cascade into sacred pools. In this remote vacation paradise, you'll wake to the chattering of exotic birds and fall asleep to the gentle lull of the ocean.

Sprawled out along the beach, Moorea Beachcomber Royal emanates the essence of Polynesia; tropical palms and exotic blooms grace the lobby and the local art bursts with wild, primitive color. Under the thatched canopy of the reception area, the walls have been eliminated so you can feel the gentle trade winds caressing your skin.

Accommodations can be an air-conditioned guest room in the main complex or a private fare overhanging a crystal lagoon. Here, you have the added luxury of being able to dive straight from your secluded balcony into the cool, clear water. Spacious and airy, rooms are decorated with cane furniture and Polynesian designs. Many accommodations feature views of vibrant sunsets over the volcanic peaks of Moorea.

Guests at Moorea Beachcomber Royal can savor foods at Fare Nui and Fare Hana. At Fare Nui, gourmet surprises combine with ocean views to ensure a memorable dining experience. Fare Hana offers outdoor poolside dining on fresh foods. The Motu Iti Bar provides a relaxing atmosphere in which to enjoy pool and reef views and beautiful sunsets.

Activities abound on this resort playground. Besides the tennis courts and swimming pool, the private beaches and clear ocean waters offer recreation, relaxation, and views of paradise. The South Pacific plays hostess to innumerable water activities, from parasailing, windsurfing, water skiing, sailing, scuba diving, to deep-sea fishing, pedal boating, and managing an outrigger canoe. Snorkel or scuba dive out to the reef to see schools of tropical fish. Or take a horseback ride along the beach. There are also jeep tours, helicopter tours, and breathtaking sunset or moonlight cruises.

Address: B.P. 1019, Papetoai, Moorea
Phone: (689) 56 19 19, Fax: (689) 56 18 88, Telex: 441 FP
No. of Rooms: 147 **Suites:** 98
Room Rate: $$$
Credit Cards: AmEx, DC, MC, JCB, Visa
Services and Amenities: Car rental, Valet service, Laundry, Safe deposit fac., Currency exchange, Tour desk, Mail, Helioport, TV, Video programs, Minibar/refrigerator, IDD/STD phone, A/C (exc. bungalows), Sundeck, Coffee/tea making fac., Bidet, Comp. toiletries
Room Service: Room service
Restaurant: Fare Nui, Fare Hana
Bar: Motu Iti Bar
Business Facilities: Audio-visual, Fax/telex, Postal
Conference Rooms: 1, Capacity: 100
Sports Facilities: Pool, Scooter rental, Riding, Tennis, Deep-sea fishing, Sailing, Pedal boats, Waterskiing, Parasailing, Scuba diving, Windsurfing
Attractions: Sunset/moonlight cruises, glass bottom boats, transfers to Motu, jeep tours

THE EXCELSIOR

The Excelsior's lobby, with its cool grey marble, crystal chandeliers and comfortable leather armchairs, captures the cosmopolitan elegance of this first class hotel. Ideally located in Causeway Bay, Hong Kong's diverse shopping, restaurant and entertainment area, The Excelsior is linked by air-conditioned walkway to the adjacent World Trade Center. The integrated complex offers meeting and entertainment facilities for up to 1060 persons. Each of The Excelsior's guest rooms and suites is tastefully appointed for comfort and convenience; the luxurious suites boast spectacular views of Hong Kong's bustling harbor. Complimentary continental breakfast buffet, traditional afternoon tea and evening cocktails are served in the Executive Lounge.

Causeway Bay has the highest concentration of restaurants in Hong Kong- take a stroll down "Food Street." And, in a city known worldwide for superlative food, The Excelsior's restaurants and bars enjoy an exceptional reputation. Don't miss the famous curry buffet at The Dickens Bar. At the elegant Excelsior Grill, a recent offering included: Consomme of Wood Mushrooms with Truffles and Frog Legs, baked with a Pastry Dome; and Roasted Duck Breast with a Truffle Potato Cake and Sauteed Chinese Chard in mountain honey-citrus sauce.

Relax in the penthouse lounge, with its breathtaking panoramic view of the city and harbor. No other hotel in Hong Kong offers a thousand-seat movie theater showing the latest films, or two indoor tennis courts where you can play tennis year-round. Go for a jog in nearby, beautiful 47-acre Victoria Park, or, if you like, a chauffeur-driven Mercedes Benz is available to transport you to any part of Hong Kong, Kowloon or the New Territories.

Address: 281 Gloucester Rd., Causeway Bay
Phone: 894-8888, Fax: 895-6459, Telex: 74550 EXCON HX, Cable: CONVENTION HONG KONG
No. of Rooms: 913 **Suites:** 22
Room Rate: $$$
Credit Cards: All major
Services and Amenities: Concierge, Limousine/car rental, Parking, Laundry/valet, Safe deposit fac., Currency exchange, Travel arrangements, Barber/beauty shop, Shopping arcade, Medical services, Babysitting, TV, Minibar/refrigerator, IDD phones, Indiv. A/C ctl., Desks
Room Service: 24 hours
Restaurant: Excelsior Grill, Cammino Italian
Bar: Dickens Bar, Noon Gun Bar
Business Facilities: Audio-visual, Secretarial, Fax/telex, Translation, Business center, Postal, Reference library
Conference Rooms: 8, Capacity: 1,600
Sports Facilities: Jogging track nearby, Tennis
Location: Causeway Bay
Attractions: Shopping, open air night market, Ocean Park, sightseeing

PARK LANE RADISSON

The Park Lane Radisson is ideally situated in the center of Hong Kong Island's busiest shopping, entertainment and business district: Causeway Bay. Over half of its 850 rooms overlook Hong Kong Harbor and the city's largest open area, Victoria Park.

Newly renovated, the hotel offers deluxe rooms and elegant suites. The luxurious Governor's Suite includes dining and sitting areas, a spacious lounge, marble-top desk, kitchen, and a comfortable bedroom with a king-size bed from which one has a spectacular view of the park and harbor.

The Business Center and executive floors cater to individual business travellers and groups. The hotel's Fitness Center offers a fully-equipped gymnasium and exercise room for aerobics, as well as a full health spa. Jogging trails and various sports facilities are available in Victoria Park, which is only a few minutes away from the hotel's main entrance.

The Parc 27 European Gourmet Restaurant, on the top floor of the hotel, offers superb continental cuisine. One may also relax at the end of a long day at the Gallery Bar and Lounge, or dance at the hotel's Starlight Disco.

Many Japanese department stores such as Sogo, Daimaru, and Mitsukoshi are near the Park Lane Radisson. It is also only minutes away from Hong Kong's famous "Food Street" where all types of Asian food specialties can be enjoyed.

Address: 310 Gloucester Rd., Causeway Bay
Phone: 5-890 3355, Fax: 5-767 853, Telex: 75343 PLH HX, Cable: PARKLANE
No. of Rooms: 850 **Suites:** 25
Room Rate: $$
Services and Amenities: Airport limousine Gift shop, TV, In-house movies, Radio, Minibar, IDD phone, Indiv. climate ctl., In-room safe
Restaurant: Parc 27 European Gourmet Restaurant
Bar: Lobby, Gallery
Business Facilities: Secretarial, Fax/telex/cable, Translation
Conference Rooms: 7, Capacity: 500
Sports Facilities: Full health spa, Exercise room, Gym, Jogging track
Location: Causeway Bay
Attractions: Victoria Park, Food Street, shopping district

THE MANDARIN ORIENTAL HOTEL

Located in the heart of the business and financial district, Mandarin Oriental Hong Kong is a haven of gracious service and elegant comfort. From the black marble and gold wood carvings of the lobby to the lacquered baskets of toiletries in the guest bathrooms, the Mandarin Oriental demonstrates the attention to fine details that is the essence of luxury.

All Mandarin Oriental guestrooms were refurbished during a recent extensive renovation program. The traditional highlights of the rooms have been retained using teak and burlwood panelling, Chinese porcelain lighting fixtures, beige wool carpets and "Chinoiserie" style fabric. Bathrooms feature pale pink Portuguese marble floors and walls, complemented by burgundy colored granite vanities. In addition to the modern accoutrements of TV, air-conditioning and mini-bars, most rooms have private balconies, a special treat in Hong Kong. For truly sumptuous elegance, plan to stay in the Mandarin Suite, with appointments reminiscent of the old Chinese court.

With such exquisite accommodations, only the finest of restaurants would do. Pierrot, The Mandarin Oriental's French restaurant, serves classical French cuisine in a dining room with a magnificent view of Hong Kong Harbour. Maplewood panelling and warm autumnal colors lighten the mood at this fine eating establishment. The Man Wah Restaurant appeals to visitors and locals alike, serving authentic classical Cantonese cuisine. Golden table settings and rosewood furnishings provide a rich and sophisticated atmosphere in which to enjoy a wonderful Chinese meal. The Mandarin Grill is a popular European style grill room with an extensive menu and wine list.

A full health center, with gymnasium, pool and separate spa facilities for men and women, is available for relaxation. Shopping is a breeze, whether within the hotel itself, or in nearby shopping galleries accessible by an air conditioned walkway.

Address: 5 Connaught Rd., GPO Box 2623, Central
Phone: 522-0111, 000-825-4850, Fax: 810-6190, Telex: 73653 MANDA HK, Cable: MANDARIN HONG KONG
No. of Rooms: 541 **Suites:** 58
Room Rate: $$$
Credit Cards: All major
Services and Amenities: Concierge, Car hire, Laundry, Safe deposit fac., Currency exchange, Valet service, Barber/beauty shop, Shopping arcade, Medical services, Book kiosk, TV, In-house movies, Minibar/refrigerator, IDD phone, Indiv. A/C ctl., Comp. newspaper
Room Service: 24 hours
Restaurant: Mandarin Grill, Pierrot French, Man Wah
Bar: Clipper Lounge
Business Facilities: Computer, Secretarial, Fax/telex, Translation, Copying, Courier, Postal
Conference Rooms: 6, Capacity: 300
Sports Facilities: Pool, Health center, Sauna, Massage, Gym, Solarium, nearby Tennis
Location: Central business
Attractions: Shopping, nightclubs, Tea Museum, railway, Star Ferry

HOLIDAY INN HARBOUR VIEW

Known for its distinguished service and luxurious accommodations, The Holiday Inn Harbour View offers a marvelous view of Victoria Harbour and Hong Kong Island.

Guest rooms and suites feature quality custom designed furnishings and deluxe amenities. Over fifty percent of the rooms have a panoramic view of the harbor and island. An Executive Floor is devoted to the needs of traveling business people; exclusive access is available with a special elevator key. On the top floor, just a few steps away from the rooftop Sun Court Pool & Health Center, the hotel's luxurious Presidential suite commands a premier view of the harbor and features Italian marble floors, pure wool carpets, French raw silk on the walls, a carved mahogany four poster bed with canopy, and a jacuzzi.

The Belvedere offers fine French cuisine and seasonal specialties. For the health conscious gourmet, the restaurant's chef has designed a Gourmet Health Menu. Guests can relax before dinner in the sophisticated atmosphere of The Harbour View Lounge, then dance into the wee hours of morning at the Golden Carp Bar.

The Holiday Inn Harbour View is situated in Hong Kong's busy Tsim Sha Tsui district, surrounded by a myriad of shopping arcades and commercial centers. Just beyond, ageless open air markets and rattling majong games offer a taste of old China.

Address: 70 Mody Rd., P.O. Box 98468, Tsimshatsui East, Kowloon
Phone: (03) 721-5161, 800-HOLIDAY, Fax: (03) 369-5672, Telex: HX 38670, Cable: INNVIEW
No. of Rooms: 600
Room Rate: $$$
Credit Cards: AmEx,MC, CB, JCB, DC, Vis
Services and Amenities: Limousine/car rental, Laundry, Safe deposit fac., Travel arrangements, Barber/beauty shop, Shopping arcade, Doctor/Dentist, Babysitting, TV, In-house movies, Radio, Minibar/refrigerator, IDD phone, Indiv. A/C ctl., In-room safe, Hairdryer
Room Service: 24 hours
Restaurant: Cafe Rendezvous, The Belvedere, Mistral
Bar: Golden Carp Bar, Harbour View
Business Facilities: Secretarial, Fax/telex, Translation, Pagers, Dictaphones, Cellular phones
Conference Rooms: 3, Capacity: 300
Sports Facilities: Pool, Health spa, Sauna, Massage
Location: Waterfront
Attractions: Shopping, dining, MTR railway, Star Ferry, open air markets

KOWLOON SHANGRI-LA

Upon entering the newly renovated lobby of the Kowloon Shangri-la, you will find yourself in a setting of gleaming marble, crystal chandeliers, fountains, and dramatic murals. The grand scale is well suited to this luxurious hotel, which rests on the waterfront in the heart of East Tsimshatsui, walking distance from Star Ferry and Mass Transit Railway.

In your guest room at the Shangri-la, a traditional Chinese Tea Service greets you. Each room has a bay window overlooking a view of either the city or Victoria Harbor. All rooms provide king-size or two double beds, two desks, with bedside controls of the radio, air-conditioning and drapes. "Club 21," the Shangri-la's VIP accommodations, occupies the 21st floor. "Club 21" guests are attended to by the Club's Purser, and are treated to complimentary limousine service to and from the airport, free pressing service and complimentary continental breakfast, among other special amenities.

The culinary offerings at the Shangri-la are truly special. At Margaux, you'll dine on seasonal continental cuisine in a richly colored dining room, where tables are set with Berndorf silver, Wedgwood china and Waterford crystal. Harp music and crystal chandeliers complete the romantic mood. Nadaman, a dining room reminiscent of an ancient Japanese tea house with bamboo screens and bonsai trees, specializes in Kaiseki, an authentic Japanese dinner of seven traditional entrees and two kinds of soup. For lunch, try Mini-Kaiseki. Shang Palace serves Cantonese specialties, including Dim Sum for luncheon, in a lavishly decorated red and gold setting with traditional Chinese motifs. Virtually every menu at the hotel includes items for the health-conscious diner.

The Executive Center is fully equipped to help you attend to your business needs, while the well-appointed health club provides a perfect place to wind down at the end of a busy day.

Address: 64 Mody Rd.
Phone: 721-2111, 800-359-5050, Fax: 723-8686
No. of Rooms: 719 **Suites:** 30
Room Rate: $$$
Credit Cards: AmEx, CB, AP, MC, Vs, DC
Services and Amenities: Shuttle service, Laundry, Valet service, Barber/beauty shop, Gift gallery, Cake shop, Flower shop, TV, Radio, Minibar, IDD phone, Turndown service
Room Service: 24 hours
Restaurant: Shang Palace, Nadaman, Steak Place
Bar: Tiara Rooftop Lounge, Lobby
Business Facilities: Fax, Executive centre, Convention facil.
Conference Rooms: 25, Capacity: 700
Sports Facilities: Pool, Health club, Massage, Private solarium rooms
Location: Heart of Kowloon
Attractions: Shopping, Hong Kong Cultural Centre

OMNI MARCO POLO/HONG KONG HOTELS

Located in Harbour City, one of Asia's shopping and commercial centers, the 17-story Omni Marco Polo Hotel provides a special ambience for contemporary business and leisure travelers who demand first-class service and accommodations. The hotel is a short walk from the celebrated Star Ferry and underground railway, and is within easy reach of the airport and financial districts. Gleaming brass handrails and lush tropical plants line the approach to the sparkling glass doors at the entrance. The marble-floored lobby's computerized check-in and check-out system reflects the hotel's modern efficiency, while the Information Counter and Guest Relations Service preserve the personal touch.

Guest rooms and suites are decorated in pastel hues and designs, fusing ceilings, walls, curtains, coverings, and furniture into a soothing and elegant ensemble.

Experience fine provincial French cuisine at La Brassierie, a re-creation of a traditional Parisian Brasserie in the heart of Hong Kong. The rich wood and bevelled glass create a pleasant and unpretentious atmosphere for romantic dining and business entertainment. On weekends, La Brasserie features a delicious steak luncheon. Slip into the Coffee Mill for morning coffee or choose from their lavish array of hot and cold Oriental and Western specialties. In the mood for Scotch after dinner? Then stop by the Tartan Bar, decorated in true Scottish motif to create the atmosphere of a pub in the Highlands.

For recreation, guests have access to the 6th floor open-air pool at the neighboring Omni Hongkong Hotel and the jogging track at lush Kowloon Park.

The Omni Marco Polo offers many facilities for the business traveler. Two function rooms can accommodate up to 80 people for intimate gatherings, banquets, business meetings, and presentations. A full executive business center is located just off the lobby.

Harbour City is a haven for shopping and nightlife. Visit the Space Museum or enjoy one the various performances at the Hong Kong Cultural Centre.

Address: Harbour City, Kowloon
Phone: (3) 736-0888, Fax: (3) 736-0022, Telex: 40077 OMPHK HX, Cable: OMNIMP
No. of Rooms: 439 **Suites:** 55
Room Rate: $$
Credit Cards: AmEx, DC, JCB, MC, Visa
Services and Amenities: Limousine service, Valet parking, Laundry/dry cleaning, Safe deposit fac., Currency exchange, Guest relat. officer, Barber/beauty shop, Gift shop, Doctor, Babysitting, Shoeshine service, TV, In-house movies, Radio, Minibar/refrigerator, IDD phone, Indiv. A/C ctl., Executive desk
Room Service: 20 hr room service
Restaurant: La Brasserie, Coffee Mill, Patisserie
Bar: Tartan Bar
Business Facilities: Audio-visual, Secretarial, Fax/telex/cable, Translation, Copying, Printing, Courier, Postal, Reference materials
Conference Rooms: 2, Capacity: 70
Sports Facilities: Pool in Omni The Hong Kong Hotel.
Location: Harbour City
Attractions: Tsimshatsui area, theaters, Space Museum, Cultural Center, shopping, restaurant

THE PARK HOTEL

The Park Hotel, a 16-story highrise in the center of Kowloon's shopping district, offers service and convenience at reasonable prices. Opened in 1961 and recently renovated, the Park's rooms are large and comfortable, offering all the finest amenities.

Authentic Chinese cuisine and Dim Sum, prepared by master chefs, are offered at The Chinese Restaurant. The Coffee Shop on the ground floor serves continental and Chinese specialties in a cozy and relaxed atmosphere. The Poinsettia Room, next to the bar, specializes in European cuisine, fine wines, and friendly service.

A rooftop banquet room accommodates 80 persons, and can be divided into smaller meeting rooms.

The Assistant Manager is on duty 24 hours and the hotel is happy to arrange cots for infants, baby-sitters, medical services, same day laundry service, parcel and postage service, and a host of other conveniences.

The Tour Desk in the lobby can guide you to such tourist attractions as the Museum of History, the Jamia Masjid, or the Space Museum. Barely fifteen minutes from Kai Tak International Airport by air-conditioned hotel transport, close to the Cross Harbor Tunnel, and within walking distance of the MTR subway which gives rapid access to both sides of the harbor, the Park Hotel is a home away from home in Hong Kong.

Address: 61-65 Chatham Rd. South, Kowloon
Phone: 3-661 371, Fax: 3-739 7259, Telex: 45740 PARK HX, Cable: PARKHOTEL
No. of Rooms: 410 **Suites:** 41
Room Rate: $
Credit Cards: AmEx, MC, DC, OTB, Visa
Services and Amenities: Airport limousine, Valet service, Safe deposit fac., Currency exchange, Beauty salon, Gift shop, Medical services, TV, Radio, Refrigerator, IDD phone, Indiv. climate ctl.
Room Service: 24 hours
Restaurant: Poinsettia Room, Park Chinese Restaurant
Bar: Marigold Bar
Business Facilities: Secretarial
Conference Rooms: 4, Capacity: 80
Location: Tsim Sha Tsui
Attractions: Kowloon shopping district, Jamia Masjid, Museum of History, Space Museum

THE PENINSULA HOTEL

Kowloon's Peninsula Hotel, flagship of the Peninsula Group, is one of the top five hotels in the world according to a survey by Institutional Investor magazine.

Built in 1928, the Peninsula offers colonial elegance and every modern convenience. A fleet of Rolls Royces is available to whisk the traveller from airport to hotel, and chauffeur him or her to appointments. But why meet those appointments elsewhere?

The Peninsula's distinctive lobby features soaring columns, gilded ceilings, and sculpted figures of gods and angels. Clark Gable, Princess Margaret, and President Ronald Reagan are among those who have signed the Peninsula's guest register.

Recent renovations have narrowed the hallways and enlarged the sitting areas of the impeccable guest accommodations. All have luxurious marble baths. Superior suites overlook the center courtyard and deluxe suites have harbour views.

Afternoon tea in The Verandah Lounge, accompanied by music, is a tradition. Five other restaurants within the Peninsula offer superb dining. Gaddi's is known as one of the finest French restaurants 'East of the Suez'. The Edwardian-style Verandah Grill serves continental cuisine and has a private dining room, the Salon Royale. Chesa, a rustic alpine enclave, has a Swiss menu. The Spring Moon Chinese Restaurant specializes in exquisite Cantonese dishes. This split-level restaurant has three function rooms on the upper level, providing guests with spacious venues for private functions. The Inagiku Japanese Restaurant, operated by the internationally renowned Inagiku Group, offers sushi, teppanyaki and tempura bars on its ground floor, and elegant a la carte dining and private function rooms on its upper level.

Comfort, convenience, and personal service at The Peninsula Hotel are *sans pareil*.

Address: Salisbury Rd., Kowloon
Phone: (3) 666 251, Fax: (3) 722-4170, Telex: 43821 PEN HX, Cable: PENHOTE HK
No. of Rooms: 189 **Suites:** 21
Room Rate: $$$
Credit Cards: All major
Services and Amenities: 24hr concierge, Airport limousine, Beauty salon, Shopping arcade, Satellite TV, Radio, Minibar, IDD phone, Indiv. climate ctl.
Room Service: 24 hours
Restaurant: Gaddi's, Verandah Grill, Chesa, Inagiku
Bar: Verandah
Business Facilities: Secretarial, Translation
Conference Rooms: 1, Capacity: 16
Location: Tsim Sha Tsui
Attractions: Shopping, Star Ferry, public transportation

RAMADA RENAISSANCE HOTEL

The Ramada Renaissance is located in Sun Plaza, a sparkling new development in the heart of Tsimshatsui, Hong Kong's major tourist and commercial district. Step outside and you will find shops, boutiques, department stores and major company offices. The Ramada Renaissance is also centrally located near the ferry, underground railway, and airport.

Guest rooms are decorated in subdued peach and salmon, or pink and lilac color combinations with mahogany wood trim. The bay window sitting area, with sofa, easy chair and breakfast table, is perfect for admiring the harbor view. Three telephones, electronic safe, and fully marbled bathroom with deep tub and cotton robe are just several of the room amenities. There's even a relaxing bathroom jacuzzi in every suite.

Ramada Renaissance houses the renowned Italian restaurant, Capriccio. Accented by Italian frescoes and oil paintings, Capriccio offers gastronomic delights such as Wild Boar Ham with Mushroom Salad, as well as an extensive Italian wine cellar. Those interested in innovative seafood cuisine can visit The Bostonian for a creative blend of American seafood based on California, New England, and select Cajun/Creole dishes. The T'ang Court Chinese Restaurant offers the best in Cantonese cuisine in a traditional Chinese setting.

The Business Centre is another well-equipped area of the hotel, with the latest computerized and audio-visual equipment. The ballroom and 4 meeting rooms can accommodate up to 450. Parlor offices can also be rented. Secretarial services are available in English, Japanese and Chinese.

After a day of business, shopping, or attractions, return to the hotel to revitalize. On the Hotel's top floor, you'll find an excellent health club. There's a squash court, fully-equipped gym with sauna, massage and solarium as well as an outdoor heated pool for guests' use. Ramada Renaissance helps you enjoy Hong Kong as you should—refreshed, invigorated, and in style.

Address: 8 Peking Rd., Kowloon
Phone: 852-375-1133, 800-228-9898, Fax: 852-375-6611, Telex: 45243 RRHK HX
No. of Rooms: 474 **Suites:** 27
Room Rate: $$$
Services and Amenities: Limousine/car rental, Valet parking, Laundry, Valet service Gift shop, Doctor, Nonsmoking areas, In-house movies, Radio, Minibar/refrigerator, IDD phones, Indiv. A/C ctl., In-room safe, Jacuzzi, Desk, Hairdryer, Account status on TV
Room Service: 24 hours
Restaurant: Cariccio Italian, Tang Court, Sun's Cafe
Bar: Bostonian, Lobby, Poolside
Business Facilities: Audio-visual, Offices, Fax/telex/cable, Translation, Notary, Copying, Computers, Laser printing, Reference materials
Conference Rooms: 4, Capacity: 120
Sports Facilities: Pool, Health club, Sauna, Massage, Solarium, Squash
Location: Tsimshatsui area
Attractions: Shops, boutiques, offices, major modes of transportation

REGAL MERIDIEN HOTEL HONG KONG

The Regal Meridien Hotel Hong Kong is a bit of France set in Kowloon. Opened in 1982, it is conveniently located in the city center, a few blocks from the train station and about 15 minutes from the airport by hotel limousine.

All rooms at the Regal Meridien have satellite TVs, VCRs, radios, and mini-bars. There are 33 suites, including the Presidential Suite, a luxurious two-bedroom duplex decorated in cool pastels with bleached teak and pale marble fittings. French Empire furniture, French contemporary art and delightful Chinoiserie complete the decor.

Le Restaurant de France is a taste of Paris, featuring fine French wines to accompany every dining adventure.

The Hotel's three main function rooms are located on the third floor. The Versailles Ballroom has a capacity of 350 for cocktails. Luxembourg and Longchamps each accommodate about 80 at a reception. All are decorated in Louis XVI Empire-style in beige and gold, and can be subdivided into smaller rooms if desired. Four other rooms on the second floor—Montparnasse I,II,III, and IV—are available for small meetings and conferences. Secretarial and translation services can be arranged. After a busy day in Hong Kong, guests at the Meridien can unwind at Le Rendezvous, enjoy the discotheque, or take advantage of the health spa.

Address: 71 Mody Rd., Tsimshatsui East, Kowloon
Phone: (3) 722-1818, Fax: (3) 723-6413, Telex: 40955 HOMRO HX, Cable: HOMRO
No. of Rooms: 590 **Suites:** 33
Services and Amenities: Airport limousine Gift shop, Satellite TV, VCP, Radio, Minibar, Indiv. climate ctl.
Restaurant: Le Restaurant de France
Bar: Le Rendezvous
Business Facilities: Secretarial, Translation
Conference Rooms: 7, Capacity: 350
Sports Facilities: Full health spa
Location: Tsimshatsui East

THE REGENT HONG KONG

Situated on the Kowloon waterfront, The Regent Hong Kong has time and time again been singled out as one of the top hotels in the world. What guests remember is the spectacular view! Standing 17-stories high and clad in red granite, the hotel's interior features polished granite, marble and glass walls which provide a nearly frameless view of the harbour. Through the vast glass walls, guests can view the open skies, the soaring Hong Kong skyline, and the ceaseless activities of the harbor. As dusk descends, Hong Kong Island transforms into a dazzling jewel of multicolored lights.

Guests are met at the airport by chauffered limousine, and greeted at the hotel by white-liveried doormen. Room butlers provide 24-hour service. Guest rooms and suites offer deluxe amenities. The Regent's signature luxury is its bathrooms—each is fitted in Italian marble with large sunken bathtub and separate glass-enclosed shower unit.

The Regent houses six outstanding restaurants and lounges, which all afford spectacular views. Plume is The Regent's premier restaurant, offering innovative European cuisine. At Lai Ching Heen, savor the finest traditional Cantonese delicacies and "New Hong Kong Cuisine". Exquisite jade, silver and ivory accents adorn each table.

For a truly indulgent experience, spend some time in the health spa. Each of the six private, self-contained units encloses a hot tub, steam bath, sauna, solarium and massage facilities lined in Brazilian marble. The Regent also boasts the largest outdoor pool in Hong Kong, set in luxuriant gardens, with a track along the causeway for jogging.

Business travelers will also find The Regent perfect for gatherings. The Regent Ballroom, the largest ballroom in Hong Kong, can accommodate 1,900 for cocktails. Nine harbour-view meeting rooms, along with a complete business center, can service any function.

It would be tempting to never leave The Regent. Insulated in lavish surroundings, yet somehow involved in the life of the harbour, one could easily spend many days savoring the different cuisines, exercising, shopping and pampering it offers.

Address: Salisbury Rd., Kowloon
Phone: 3-721-1211, Fax: 3-739-4546, Telex: 37134 REG HX
No. of Rooms: 602 **Suites:** 90
Room Rate: $$$
Credit Cards: All major
Services and Amenities: Concierge, Limousine service, Butler service, Laundry/dry cleaning, Valet service, Beauty salon, Gift shop, TV, In-house movies, Radio, Minibar/refrigerator, IDD phone, Executive desks, Fax sockets, Bathrobes, Comp. paper, Hairdryer, Arrival fruit basket
Restaurant: Plume, Lai Ching Heen, Steak House
Bar: Lobby, Mezzanine
Business Facilities: Audio-visual, Secretarial, Fax/telex/cable, Simult. translation, Copying, Printing, Portable phones, Reference materials
Conference Rooms: 9, Capacity: 1,500
Sports Facilities: Pools, Health spa, Jacuzzis, Massage, Sun terrace, Facials
Location: Tsim Sha Tsui
Attractions: Shopping, dining, entertainment, access to New World Center

GRAND HYATT HONG KONG

The sophistication and elegance of a bygone era has found a waterfront home in Grand Hyatt Hong Kong. When you arrive, you pass through a striking modern exterior of polished marble and silvered glass, into the ornate opulence of the 1930's-style Art Deco lobby. The boldness of this contrast marks the drama of Grand Hyatt.

More than 70 percent of the hotel's 575 rooms command spectacular views of Victoria Harbor, while the remaining rooms overlook Victoria Peak and other parts of the island. The rooms are furnished in warm, earth-tone colors and rich, luxurious fabrics. Bathrooms feature marble baths and showers, with gold fixtures. The Regency Club, Hyatt's "hotel within a hotel," comprises four floors of executive accommodations and three floors of specialty suites, all of which are serviced by two private elevators. Regency Club rooms are luxuriously appointed with elegant furnishings and a full home-entertainment system. The Presidential Suite is a model of luxury, with a grand piano, views from every angle, and a bathroom the size of a guest room, complete with an oversized jacuzzi. In addition to complimentary use of two boardrooms and a private lounge, Regency Club guests have access to a private, rooftop, outdoor swimming pool.

Dining is no less dramatic at Grand Hyatt. One Harbour Road, the premier restaurant of the hotel, has been described as an elegant re-creation of the terrace of a taipan's Peak mansion during the 1930's. The two-level restaurant serves traditional Cantonese cuisine, no foreign or nouvelle influences, beneath a glass roof with expansive views of the harbor. A lily pond, trees, and tables set with crystal and silver complete the exquisite scene. On the second floor of Grand Hyatt, Grissini offers authentic Milanese cuisine in a casually chic setting reminiscent of a stylish New York bistro. A large baking oven at the entrance of Grissini greets diners with the sumptuous aroma of freshly baked bread.

If you go for a stroll or jog through Victoria Park, you are likely to come across the peaceful sight of the city's older residents practicing their daily Tai Chi exercises. Causeway Bay offers fabulous shopping, dining and entertainment options. Boat tours of the beautiful harbor are also available.

Address: 1 Harbour Rd., Wanchai
Phone: (5) 861-1234, 800-233-1234, Fax: (852) 861-1677, Telex: 68434 GHHK
No. of Rooms: 575 **Suites:** 35
Room Rate: $$$$
Credit Cards: All major
Services and Amenities: Airport limousine, Valet parking, Laundry, Valet service, Multilingual staff, Barber/beauty shop, Babysitting, London taxi shuttle, TV, Radio, Minibar, IDD phone, Indiv. A/C ctl., In-room safe, Alarm clock, Hairdryer
Room Service: 24 hours
Restaurant: One Harbour Road, Grissini, Tiffin
Bar: Champagne Bar, Cascades, JJs
Business Facilities: Audio-visual, Secretarial, Fax, Simult. translation, Reference materials
Sports Facilities: Pool, Health spa, Jacuzzis, Exercise rooms, Jogging track, Tennis, Golf driving range
Attractions: Causeway Bay shopping, Ocean Park, Victoria Peak, boat tours

THE LEELA KEMPINSKI BOMBAY

Surrounded by cultivated parkland in a quiet yet central location, The Leela Kempinski Bombay welcomes visitors to India's largest seaport. The hotel has the most enviable of all things in Bombay: space. Spread over 9 acres, 6 acres of which are landscaped lush flora, the 15-story hotel is a veritable oasis in the city, yet just a 5-minute drive from the airport and a 45-minute drive from downtown.

The lobby is the mirror of Leela's philosophy, merging Indian ornate resplendence with European polished grace. Beautiful bronzes are attractively offset by lacy latticework.

Guests have a variety of cuisines to choose from. Indian specialties can be found at the Indian Harvest, Chinese cuisine at the Great Wall, Italian favorites at Fiorella. The Waterfall, a cafe with views of gently cascading waterfalls, serves international fare 24 hours a day. Bonaparte's Bar exudes the comfort of a royal Indian chamber with European touches.

The Leela Kempinski offers a multitude of recreational facilities. The Fitness and Squash Centre contains jacuzzis, sauna, turkish bath, gymnasium, tennis courts, squash court, and badminton court. The beautiful landscape can be seen along the jogging track, or, guests can take a cool dip in the inviting blue lagoon swimming pool.

Ideal halls, technical equipment, and complete business center assure the success of meetings and conventions. The Grand Ball-room is Bombay's largest ballroom, comfortably accommodating up to 3,000 guests.

Leela Kempinski Bombay has become popular among tourists and business travelers who want to avoid the wear and tear of traffic snarls and congested city environs. Come see why many heads of state from abroad have preferred to stay at The Leela while in Bombay.

Address: Sahar, Bombay, Maharashtra, 400 059
Phone: (91-22) 6363636, Fax: (91-92) 6360606, Telex: 011-79236/79241 KEMP
No. of Rooms: 430 **Suites:** 38
Room Rate: $$
Credit Cards: AmEx, DC, AP, MC, JCB
Services and Amenities: Airport transfer, Barber/beauty shop, Shopping arcade, Satellite TV, Radio, Minibar, IDD/STD phone, A/C
Room Service: 24 hours
Restaurant: Orchid, Waterfall, Indian Harvest
Bar: Fiorella, Bonapartes, Emerald
Business Facilities: Secretarial, Fax/telex
Conference Rooms: 12, Capacity: 2,000
Sports Facilities: Pool, Fitness center, Sauna, Jacuzzi, Gym, Jogging, Squash, Tennis, Turkish bath

OBEROI TOWERS BOMBAY

Bombay, India's pulsating business capital, is as cosmopolitan as it is a fascinating mosaic of cultures. The Oberoi Towers, rising 35-stories high, is located at Nariman Point and commands a magnificent view of the Arabian sea.

Each of the 600 rooms and suites reflect exquisite attention to detail. Decorated in soothing pastels and elegantly furnished, rooms offer superb amenities. By sheer height of the hotel, many rooms afford splendid views of the metropolis and the Arabian Sea. Suites have individual themes and are decorated in regional and hand-crafted Indian furnishings.

Guests have many opportunities to experience the flavors of faraway lands. Cafe Royal is reputed for its French cuisine and vintage wines: meals begin with an exquisite salmon mousse, compliments of the house. The Outrigger is the only Polynesian restaurant in the city. Amid bamboo decor and strains of a guitar, South Sea cuisine and exotic cocktails create an enchanted evening. Mewar, the gourmet Indian cuisine, brings guests the finest Indian culinary experience, with a subtle serenade from the restaurant's musicians. Samarkand, overlooking the busy Marine Drive promenade, is the hotel's 24-hour restaurant. The Cellar is a swanky discotheque that accepts members, their guests, and hotel residents only.

As one of Bombay's leading hotels, The Oberoi Towers is very much a part of the social and business life of the city. Meeting planners will appreciate the audio-visual aids, simultaneous translation in four languages, and secretarial support.

For moments of rejuvenation, the swimming pool, a well-equipped health club with a modern gymnasium, sauna, turkish baths, beauty salon and barber shop are all available to guests. Those inclined to shop will enjoy the hotel's shopping arcade, with over 200 shops.

Address: Nariman Point, Bombay, 400 021
Phone: 2024343, Fax: 2043282, Telex: 84153, 84154 OBBY IN, Cable: OBHOTEL
No. of Rooms: 600
Room Rate: $$
Services and Amenities: Car hire, Bank, Travel agency, Barber/beauty shop, Shopping arcade, TV, Radio, Minibar/refrigerator, DD phone, Indiv. A/C ctl.
Restaurant: Cafe Royal, Outrigger, Samarkand, Mewar
Bar: Bonaparte's Retreat, Lancers
Business Facilities: Audio-visual, Secretarial, Fax, Simult. translation
Conference Rooms: 6, Capacity: 2,000
Sports Facilities: Pool, Health club Sauna, Gym, Turkish baths

TAJ MAHAL INTER-CONTINENTAL

The Taj Mahal Inter-Continental stands facing the Arabian Sea. Best known for its ornate architecture, Taj Mahal is comprised of the original palatial structure and a more modern 24-four story tower. First opened in 1904, the hotel has been one of Bombay's best known landmarks ever since.

All of the Taj Mahal's guest accommodations have air conditioning, TVs, radios and mini-bars. About 60% of its rooms have balconies overlooking the sea and the city's most famous landmark, The Gateway of India, which is just outside the gates of the hotel. There are 48 suites, the three most famous being the Rajput, decorated in Rajasthani style; the Bell Tower, a European duplex; and the Presidential, with a bedroom terrace overlooking the sea.

The hotel houses several restaurants. The Golden Dragon serves fine Chinese cuisine; Shamiana is a 24-hour coffee shop; and Tanjore offers Indian regional delicacies. Rooftop Rendezvous, the European restaurant, is said to provide the finest continental fare in Bombay. In addition, special poolside barbecues are offered in season. The chic Apollo Bar, 24-stories above Bombay, offers a beautiful view of the city nightscape. There is also a separate discotheque, The 19 Hundreds, a club open to members and hotel guests only.

The Taj Mahal's Ballroom accommodates 2,500 persons at a reception, or 500 persons seated. There are nine other function rooms which can serve small conferences of 12 or groups of up to 350. The business center is well equipped to handle all executive needs.

Situated in the heart of downtown Bombay, The Taj is at the heart of the city's commercial, shopping and entertainment areas. It is within walking distance to the Grand Prince of Wales Museum, the University, the High Courts and the Rajabhai Clock Tower. One excursion not to be missed is the ferry ride to the famous Elephanta Caves, leaving from the harbor just outside the hotel.

Address: Apollo Bunder, Colaba, Bombay, 400 039
Phone: (022) 202-3366, Fax: (022) 287-2711, Telex: 11-2442 TAJB IN
No. of Rooms: 650 **Suites:** 48
Room Rate: $$
Credit Cards: AmEx, DC, MC, Visa
Services and Amenities: Car rental, Parking, Laundry, Valet, Safe deposit fac., Currency exchange, Travel arrangements, Barber/beauty shop, Shopping arcade, Art gallery, TV, Radio, Minibar, A/C
Room Service: 24 hours
Restaurant: Tanjore Indian, Golden Dragon, Shamiana
Bar: Apollo Bar, Harbour Bar
Business Facilities: Secretarial, Fax/telex/cable, Translation, Copying, Newswire, Courier, Postal, Reference library
Conference Rooms: 10, Capacity: 500
Sports Facilities: Pool, Health club, Massage
Location: Apollo Bunder
Attractions: Gateway of India, Grand Prince Wales Museum, Elephanta Caves

OBEROI GRAND

Calcutta, India's largest city and former capital of the British Raj, is a sprawling megalopolis, so varied it's beyond description. In the commercial center of this city stands The Oberoi Grand. The historic 5-story hotel has deliberately maintained its Victorian architecture, and the interior decor mirrors this, as well. Old-fashioned elegance exudes from every niche of the hotel. Victorian furnishings, dark wood trim and panels, muted colors, and cream-colored walls forego flashy grandeur for an understated and very appealing Old World warmth and charm. The hospitality at the hotel is just as gracious.

Each of the Oberoi Grand's 250 rooms and suites have been individually designed for luxury and relaxation. Colors are soft, and hand-crafted furniture and Victorian period decor are arranged throughout. Suites are spacious, with plenty of room to entertain or work. All accommodations are fully air-conditioned and fitted with refrigerators.

The Oberoi Grand houses four exclusive restaurants. The Rotisserie offers refined Continental dining; Ming Court serves savory Chinese cuisine; the Moghul Room features exotic Indian cuisine; the Garden Cafe is a casual place for informal dining. A popular meeting spot is the Chowringhee Bar, which boasts a cozy, den-like atmosphere, conducive for business or pleasure.

Recreational facilities, fortunately, depart from the Victorian theme. Guests can enjoy the outdoor pool and the fully equipped modern health club, complete with a weight and fitness room, sauna, massage and a beauty salon.

Meetings can be arranged for groups of twenty or less, right up to large formal banquets for 1,000. Audio-visual aids, secretarial support and other business services are available in the 24-hour business center.

The popular sights in Calcutta are St. Paul's Cathedral, the Victoria Memorial, and the Botanical Gardens with an extraordinary trunkless banyan tree. Many travelers like to visit the New Market and test their bargaining skills for silks and unusual items.

Address: 15, Jawaharlal Nehru Rd., Calcutta, West Bengal, 700 013
Phone: 033-29-2323, 033-29-0181, Fax: 033-29-1217, Telex: 5919, 5937, 5971, Cable: OBHOTEL
No. of Rooms: 250 **Suites:** 30
Room Rate: $$
Credit Cards: All major
Services and Amenities: Car rental, Laundry/dry cleaning, Safe deposit fac., Currency exchange, Travel arrangements, Barber/beauty shop, Babysitting, TV, In-house movies, Radio, Minibar, IDD/STD phone, Indiv. A/C ctl., Balconies
Room Service: 24 hours
Restaurant: La Rotisserie, Moghul Room, La Brasserie
Bar: Chowringhee, Pink Elephant
Business Facilities: Audio-visual, Secretarial, Fax/telex, Copying
Conference Rooms: 3, Capacity: 1,000
Sports Facilities: Pool, Health club, Gym
Attractions: Victoria Memorial, Marble Palace

MALABAR HOTEL

The Malabar Hotel, located at the tip of Willingdon Island, faces the Malabar Coast of southern India. The location affords views of the beautiful backwaters of Cochin Harbor and picturesque scenery. Watching the rice boats float by, you feel you have left urban life far behind. Though the hotel may feel remote, it is only a 10-minute drive from the Cochin Airport, and a 3-kilometer walk from the Cochin Railway Terminus.

The meeting facilities include their own separate registration area, check room, restroom, and kitchen. For an extra charge, the hotel can obtain vans, decorative services, entertainment, a photographer, and audio-visual equipment.

Two restaurants at the Malabar Hotel offer a choice of cuisines. At the Rice Boats Restaurant, continental and Indian specialties are served inside an actual rice boat. The Sao Gabriel bar, decorated in a nautical motif, is a comfortable place to relax and sip a cocktail. For casual outdoor dining, the hotel also holds barbecues on the lawn.

For recreation, one can enjoy the hotel's swimming pool. Around Chochin, interesting sights include the Saint Francis Church and the Dutch Palace. The more adventurous might consider a boat trip to the harbor, Allepey, and the Periyar Game Sanctuary.

Address: Willingdon Island, Cochin, Kerala, 682 009
Phone: 0484 6811, Telex: 885 6661 MLBRIN, Cable: COMFORT
No. of Rooms: 37 **Suites:** 2
Room Rate: $
Services and Amenities: Car rental, Laundry, Safe deposit fac., Currency exchange, Doctor on call
Room Service: 24 hours
Restaurant: Rice Boats, Jade Pavilion, lawn service
Bar: Sao Gabriel
Business Facilities: Audio-visual, Secretarial, Copying, Postal
Conference Rooms: 2, Capacity: 300
Sports Facilities: Pool, Boat rental
Location: Willingdon Island
Attractions: Dutch Palace, Saint Francis Church, Kerala, Allepey, tea plantations, Hindu temples

LEELA BEACH GOA HOTEL

Overlooking the aquamarine waters of the Arabian Sea and River Sal, festooned by hundreds of swaying palms and edged by powdery white sands, is Leela Beach Goa, one of the most spectacular holiday resorts. The hotel's 60 tropical acres combine the atmosphere of a beach resort with understated colonial elegance.

Resort accommodations are a collection of peach-painted Portuguese villas, set amid groves of coconut palms, verdant greens and all interconnected by a gentle, blue lagoon. Villas are spacious, airy, and appointed with beautiful European-style colonial furniture, baths, walk-in-showers, and bidets. Wood doors open up to a private balcony, which is a perfect area for leisure breakfasts or sunset drinks.

The cuisine is rich and varied. La Gondola features Italian cuisine. The Riverside Wharf serves seafood specialties on an outdoor deck overlooking the River Sal. The Ocean Terrace, situated on the seafront, offers savory barbecue delicacies.

For relaxation and recreation, one can't help being immediately drawn to the fabulous stretches of unspoiled white sand beaches. For meetings, the Conference Room can host up to 800 people and offers all modern conference facilities and audio-visual aids. The Business Centre can help executive travelers with secretarial services and much more.

A host of exciting water sports, such as parasailing and scuba, helps you enjoy the warm sea waters. Resort facilities include tennis and squash courts, a health spa, two swimming pools, and a putting green. For the shopping inclined, there are plenty of boutiques to browse through in the shopping mall. Guests at Leela Beach Goa are never bored!

The city of Goa has more than its fair share of natural beauty and historic sites. What could be more relaxing than dividing up your time between beaches, resort activities, museums, mosques, shopping, and wildlife sanctuaries? Leela Beach Goa is the perfect getaway spot to bask in the charm and relaxed spirit of Goa.

Address: Mobor, Goa
Phone: 00-91-8342-6363, 00-91-8342-6350, Fax: 00-91-8344-6352, Telex: 81-196-258 KEMPIN
No. of Rooms: 180 **Suites:** 3
Room Rate: $
Credit Cards: All major
Services and Amenities: Airport transport, Car rental, Safe deposit fac., Beauty parlor, Shopping arcade, Babysitting, TV, Minibar, DD phone, A/C, Coffee/tea making fac.
Restaurant: La Gondola, Waterfall, Riverside Wharf
Bar: Library Bar, Sea Lounge
Business Facilities: Secretarial, Fax/telex
Conference Rooms: 3, Capacity: 800
Sports Facilities: Pool, Steambath, Sauna, Jacuzzi, Massage, Gym, Squash, Tennis, Putting green, Watersports, Fishing
Attractions: Beautiful beaches, watersports, museums

AGUADA HERMITAGE HOTEL

Built on a hillock on the ramparts of a 16th Century Portuguese fortress, the 20 deluxe villas of The Aguada Hermitage overlook beautiful Calangute Beach. Each villa is luxuriously outfitted, featuring its own private lawn and garden, and a fabulous uninterrupted view of the sea, lush greenery and village below.   All facilities are shared with Fort Aguada Beach resort. These include The Anchor Cafe and Bar, open from 7:30 a.m. till midnight, and The Sea Shell Restaurant, serving Continental and Goan cuisine for lunch and dinner. A mouthwatering meal from The Sea Shell Restaurant might begin with Stuffed Crabs and Moules Marinerire, Langouste Thermidor with Bouguetiere of Vegetables or Steamed Rice, and for dessert, Gateu Moules au Chocolate.

The conference facility at Fort Aguada Beach Resort has a capacity of 140 seated auditorium-style, or 250 at a reception. Audio-visual equipment and secretarial services are available at a charge.

Regular car service between the Hermitage and Fort Aguada makes all the facilities easily accessible. Poolside service is available at the freshwater swimming pool. The resort offers facilities for boating, windsurfing, parasailing, waterskiing, tennis, volleyball, badminton and squash.

Take a tour of Old Goa; known as the Rome of the East, its beautiful 15th Century Churches were built by the Portuguese. Visit the famous Temples of Goa, or explore Goa's many exotic beaches. At the end of the day, you can luxuriate in the seclusion of your own seaside villa.

Address: c/o Fort Aguada Beach Resort, Sinquerim, Goa, 403 519
Phone: (091) 832 7501, Telex: 194291 TAJ IN, Cable: FORTAGUADA, GOA
No. of Suites: 20
Credit Cards: AmEx, DC, MC, Visa, Bob
Services and Amenities: Car rental, Airport transfer, Parking, Laundry, Valet, Safe deposit fac., Currency exchange, Travel assistance, Shopping arcade, Doctor on call, Bank, TV, Radio, Indiv. A/C ctl.
Room Service: Room service
Restaurant: Sea Shell, poolside service
Bar: Anchor Bar
Business Facilities: Secretarial, Telex/cable, Translation, Copying, Postal
Conference Rooms: 2, Capacity: 250
Sports Facilities: Pool, Volleyball, Badminton, Squash, Tennis, Watersports
Location: Coastal
Attractions: Panjim (capital), 15-century Portuguese churches, temples, beaches

THE RAMBAGH PALACE

A former residence of the Maharaja of Jaipur, the Rambagh Palace is a royal abode turned hotel. Set admist beautifully landscaped lawns, the two-story hotel still feels very much like a palace, even today. The hotel's Rajasthani architecture, with its seemingly endless archways and delicate cupolas, evoke the romance of India.

All rooms are decorated in the colorful Rajasthani style. Amenities include air-conditioning and a TV. In the special suites, precious art pieces adorn the suites. The Moghul and the Sangaⁿ-ner, garden suites on the second floor, have raised living-room areas overlooking the beautiful Moghul garden. The Amber, a deluxe suite, has a living room and bedroom overlooking the marble fountain in the lawns. Most elegant are the four royal suites: the two Maharaja suites, the Maharani, and the Princess.

The palace dining room, Suvarna Mahal, is elegantly decorated in French 18th-century decor. It serves three meals a day, offering Indian, continental, and Chinese cuisine. Sometimes there is traditional Indian music at dinner. The Maharaja's love of polo is commemorated in the Polo bar, where you can enjoy a refreshing cocktail.

For relaxation, you can swim in His Highness' indoor pool. The hotel has a health club with gym, sauna and massage. You can also opt for a walk among the Rambagh Gardens, which is beauti-fully-tended by 12 gardeners. While visiting Jaipur, capital of Raja-sthan, be sure to visit the City Palace, the Museum, and the Observatory. An elephant ride up the steep hill to the old Amber Palace is an experience not to be missed. When the elephant first rises from his knees, you may feel a long way from the ground, and as he starts up the hill, perhaps a bit uncertain, rocking slowly with every shift of the animal's immense weight. But confidence soon increases, and you will become imbued with the regal dig-nity of Rajasthan, an experience which actually began back at your hotel, the Rambagh Palace.

Address: Bhawani Singh Rd., Jaipur, 302 005
Phone: 0141 75141, Telex: 365 254 RBAG IN, Cable: RAMBAGH
No. of Rooms: 110 **Suites:** 15
Room Rate: $$
Credit Cards: AmEx, DC, V, MC, Bob, And
Services and Amenities: Parking, 24hr laundry, Valet, Safe deposit fac., Currency exchange, Travel assistance, Barber/beauty shop, Shopping arcade, Doctor on call, Bank
Room Service: 24 hours
Restaurant: Dining room
Bar: Polo Bar
Business Facilities: Audio-visual, Secretarial, Telex/cable, Copying, Courier, Postal, Newswire
Conference Rooms: 4, Capacity: 300
Sports Facilities: Pool, Gym, Steam room, Sauna, Whirlpool, Massage
Attractions: City Palace, Museum, Observatory, Amber Palace

TAJ COROMANDEL HOTEL

The Taj Coromandel Hotel, located on the road leading to Madras's Marina Beach, is a white high-rise hotel with all the modern amenities. In the center of busy Madras, Taj Coromandel is especially suited for the business traveler. In contrast to the modern exterior, the hotel's interior reflects a native decor. A terra-cotta horse, hand-carved wood, an ancient temple lamp, and other touches echo Madras style.

Its 240 rooms all have TVs, refrigerators, and air-conditioning. Suites are provided with personalized guest stationery, fruit baskets, Indian and foreign newspapers and magazines, monogrammed bath towels, bathrobes, scales, exercise cycles, soap baskets and shaving kits.

Mysore Restaurant delights the palate with delectable Indian dishes from different regions. In the evening, classical Indian dance performances also delight the eye. The Golden Dragon features Szechuan cuisine, and the Pavilion, a European cafe, serves savory snacks 24 hours a day.

The hotel is well equipped for conferences. The Taj's Ballroom can seat 800 persons auditorium-style. At poolside, 300 can be seated for a function. Either space can accommodate up to 1,500 persons for a reception. There are also five other smaller function rooms. In addition to extensive audio-visual equipment, the hotel offers simultaneous translation into French and German. The business center can cater to every business request.

The hotel is happy to help arrange tours of Madras and local entertainment.

Address: 17 Nungambakkam High Road, Madras, 600034
Phone: 044 474849, Fax: 044 470070, Telex: 417194 TAJM IN, Cable: HOTELORENT
No. of Rooms: 240 **Suites:** 27
Room Rate: $$
Credit Cards: AmEx, DC, V, MC, And, Bob
Services and Amenities: Car rental, Parking, Laundry, Valet, Safe deposit fac., Currency exchange, Travel assistance, Barber/beauty shop, Shopping arcade, Doctor on call, Bank, TV, Refrigerator, A/C
Room Service: 24 hours
Restaurant: Pavilion, Mysore Indian, Golden Dragon
Bar: Fort St. George
Business Facilities: Audio-visual, Secretarial, Fax/telex/cable, Newswire, Copying, Courier, Postal, Reference library
Conference Rooms: 4, Capacity: 1,500
Sports Facilities: Pool, Health club, Sauna, Massage

HYATT REGENCY DELHI

The Hyatt Regency Delhi is beautifully situated atop a small hill in the green belt area of New Delhi, overlooking the Cama Gardens and close to the diplomatic enclave. Even with the Hyatt standard of efficiency and modernity, the hotel's atmosphere still retains its Indian air, as demonstrated by the architecture, which was inspired by the Golden Gupta period in India. Located in New Delhi's exclusive residential and commercial district, the Hyatt Regency Delhi is known as one of India's best hotels. The hotel is only ten minutes from the airport, and another ten minutes to the city center.

Decorated with the touches in the Indian motif, the guest rooms are modern and comfortable, and offer all the amenities. The three premier suites, all split level, are The Victorian, with European decor, and the Rajasthani and the Kalamkari, each with an Indian theme.

From the hotel's spacious marble lobby, one steps down to the Cafe Promenade, a landscaped area where one can have a casual snack or leisurely meal at any hour. The Cafe overlooks an outdoor pool, shaped like a Victoria Cross, and surrounded by Moghal style gardens with fountains. Three restaurants offer a variety of cuisine. Aangan serves classic North Indian food during lunch and dinner. Authentic Sichvan and Haka dishes are prepared at Pearl's. Valentino's, with art deco decor, features Italian delicacies and live music in the evening. For an evening of dancing, visit the Oasis Discotheque, where one can dance on a unique glass dance floor over the water.

The Hyatt Business Center provides extensive secretarial services, and translation services can be arranged. The hotel has seven conference rooms, ranging in capacity from 18-250. The Regency Club, an executive floor with its own concierge service and private lounge, has an elegant conference room.

The hotel boasts two tennis courts and a thoroughly-equipped fitness center that features a nine-station workout setup. Also, the staff can arrange other types of instruction, including yoga classes.

Address: Bhikaiji Cama Place, Ring Rd., New Delhi, 110 066
Phone: 60 9911, Fax: 60 9880, Telex: 031-61512 HYT IN
No. of Rooms: 512 **Suites:** 23
Credit Cards: AmEx, Bob, DC, And, Visa
Services and Amenities: Airport limousine Shopping arcade, TV, Radio, Minibar, Indiv. A/C ctl.
Restaurant: Aangan Indian, Pearls, Valentino's
Bar: Piano Bar
Business Facilities: Secretarial, Translation
Conference Rooms: 7, Capacity: 250
Sports Facilities: Pool, Full health spa, Gym, Tennis
Location: near Diplomatic Enc.
Attractions: Indian State Emporia, Red Fort, Old Fort, Qutab Minar, Asoka Pillar

LE MERIDIEN, NEW DELHI

Rising 20 stories, Le Meridien stands in the shape of a glass curtain wall. The hotel is located in the heart of the city, near Government offices, Rashtrapati Bhawan and the bustling Connaught District. Le Meridien's location proves to be perfect for both tourists and jet-set business travelers, alike.

The hotel brings French style refinement and grace to India. Its spectacular atrium lobby is over 200 feet high and graced with refreshing waterfalls and trees. Glass and brass capsule elevators rise from the atrium to restaurants and guest floors.

Each room, decorated in light pastels, has air-conditioning, a minibar stocked with mineral water and beer, as well as French phones with direct dial facility. For travelers who delight in different settings, the hotel boasts thematically-designed luxury suites, such as the Rajasthani Suite and French-era suites.

Le Meridien has an eatery for every taste. Pierre, decorated in the cozy richness of French classical interiors, is the perfect rendezvous for connoisseurs of French cuisine. Other cuisine options include Mughlai, Tandoori, Continental, Indian, and Cantonese cuisines. The Aloha Bar is a unique Polynesian-style bar, complete with lamp-lit cabanas and thatched huts. Henri's Bar commands a breathtaking view of the prestigious Rajpath.

Executive travelers will find Le Meridien well-equipped for business. The Napoleon Hall can accommodate up to 1000. The Business Centre provides state-of-the-art meeting facilities, secretarial, photography, translation and other services.

For recreation, the hotel has a bowl-shaped swimming pool and health club with exercise equipment, jacuzzi, chill pool, Turkish and sauna bath, and massage rooms. Tennis, golf, and polo can be arranged on request.

Delhi has a host of sites and activities. For a historical excursion, sign up for a 3-hour tour of Old or New Delhi. Shopping can be found at Connaught Place and Palika Bazaar. In the middle of all the bustle of Delhi, Le Meridien provides French elegance and style, and service with a smile.

Address: Winsor Place, Janpath, New Delhi, 110 001
Phone: 383960, Telex: 63076 HOME IN, Cable: MERIDHOTEL
No. of Rooms: 375 **Suites:** 57
Services and Amenities: Laundry, Valet service, Safe deposit fac., Currency exchange, Bank, Barber/beauty shop, Shopping arcade, Doctor on call, Babysitting, CC TV, Radio, Minibar/refrigerator, IDD/STD phone, Indiv. climate ctl.
Room Service: 24 hours
Restaurant: Le Belvedere, Golden Phoenix
Bar: Henri's, Aloha, La Terrace
Business Facilities: Audio-visual, Secretarial, Fax/telex, Translation, Copying, Offices
Conference Rooms: 4, Capacity: 900
Sports Facilities: Pool, Health club, Sauna, Whirlpool, Jogging track, arrangements for Golf, Tennis, and Polo
Attractions: Parliament House, Rashtrapati, Bhawan, Connaught Place

THE OBEROI NEW DELHI

Opened in 1965, The Oberoi was India's first modern hotel. Conveniently located 20 minutes from the airport and 15 minutes from Connaught Place, New Delhi's main shopping and commercial area, the hotel is well suited for both the business and leisure traveler. Upon entering the Oberoi, you'll notice a fine collection of artwork adorning the interior.

The guest rooms are decorated in pastels, and feature, among all expected amenities, a minibar and a luxurious bathroom in polished granite. Rooms overlook either the lush Delhi Golf Course or the historic tomb of Moghal emperor Humayun. Every floor has its own personalized butler service. There are 30 suites, the most elegant being the Presidential Suite on the 8th floor. The suite features Indian decor with traditional artifacts in the bedroom and lounge.

Five restaurants within the hotel cater to a variety of tastes, both Western and Oriental. The principal restaurant is La Rochelle, serving French delicacies and a fine selection of French wines. The Taipan serves some of the best Szechuan dishes in India. The two bars, The Club and The Connaught, provide spirits, dancing and entertainment in the evening. The Connaught Bar commands a magnificent view of the Delhi skyline.

The Oberoi has eight conference rooms, the largest accommodating up to 600 people. A complete Business Center provides secretarial and other support services necessary for a conference.

For relaxation options, a pool, health club, and shopping arcade are all available at the Oberoi. The Delhi Golf Course, located nearby, is also a popular place for Oberoi guests.

Other attractions in New Delhi include Connaught Place, India Gate, the President's Estate, and the Qutab Minar. Janpath, about 5 kilometers away, offers shopping for Indian arts and crafts.

Address: Dr. Zakir Hussain Marg, New Delhi, 110 003
Phone: 363030, Fax: 360484, Telex: 74019 OBDL IN, Cable: OBHOTEL
No. of Rooms: 258 **Suites:** 33
Room Rate: $$
Services and Amenities: Butler service, Shopping arcade, TV, Radio, Minibar, Indiv. climate ctl.
Restaurant: La Rochelle French
Bar: Club Bar, Connaught Bar
Business Facilities: Secretarial, Business center
Conference Rooms: 8, Capacity: 600
Sports Facilities: Pool, Health club, Golf
Attractions: India Gate, Connaught Place, President's Estate, Humayun's Tomb, Qutab Minar, Red Fort, Janpath

TAJ MAHAL HOTEL

Behind the facade of hand-chiseled sandstone, the 16-story Taj Mahal Hotel New Delhi offers all the modern amenities, yet still retains an Indian atmosphere. Upon entering the lobby, you feel you are in a great Moghal court. The lobby is adorned with stretches of white marble. An elevated, formal sitting area is accentuated with three majestic domes of blue, red, and gold. In a second lobby, marble railings grace the grand staircase, brass planters hang from above, and the ceramic lattice-work window screens scatter the sunlight.

The spacious guest rooms are extremely comfortable, featuring handsome teak furniture with brass fittings and deluxe amenities. Each of the deluxe suites are individually designed. Offering views of the city and pool, luxury suites are equipped with refrigerator, soft drink trolley, Indian and foreign newspapers and magazines, and personalized stationery. A valet is available on request. Bathrooms feature VIP toilet kit, initialled towels, bathrobe, and soap basket.

The hotel has several restaurants. Casa Medici, the rooftop restaurant, offers Italian meals and breathtaking views of the city. The House of Ming serves Cantonese and Szechuan specialties. The Haveli dining room offers kadai specialties from Peshawar. Indian musicians and dancers perform in the evening. The 24-hour Machan serves international favorites. For breakfast as well as drinks, guests visit the Captain's Bar.

The hotel has a health club offering sauna, massage, yoga, gymnasium and steam baths. The pool is set in a beautiful garden-like setting.

The hotel's business center is open 24 hours a day. The Taj Mahal has four conference rooms, the largest accommodating 1000 reception-style. In addition, there are beautiful outdoor areas. Two poolside lawn areas are available for barbecues and receptions.

The Taj Mahal hotel is within walking distance to Raj Path, shopping areas, government offices and sights.

Address: #1 Mansingh Road, New Delhi, 110011
Phone: 011 301 6162, Fax: 011 301 7299, Telex: 031-66874 TAJD IN, Cable: TAJDEL
No. of Rooms: 322 **Suites:** 28
Room Rate: $
Credit Cards: AmEx, DC, Bob, MCh, Visa
Services and Amenities: Car rental, Parking, 24hr laundry, Valet, Safe deposit fac., Currency exchange, Travel assistance, Barber/beauty shop, Shopping arcade, Bank, Doctor, TV, In-house movies, Refrigerator, Indiv. climate ctl.
Room Service: 24 hours
Restaurant: House of Ming, Haveli, Casa Medici
Bar: Captain's Cabin
Business Facilities: Secretarial, Fax/telex/cable, Translation, Copying, Courier, Postal, Reference library
Conference Rooms: 5, Capacity: 1,000
Sports Facilities: Pool, Full health spa, Sauna, Massage
Attractions: Tours of New Delhi and Old Delhi, Cottage Emporium, Janpath

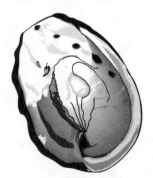

TAJ PALACE HOTEL- NEW DELHI

Situated on six acres of landscaped gardens in the diplomatic enclave of New Delhi, The Taj Palace Intercontinental is a palatial hotel. It is well-equipped for the business traveler, as evidenced by the hotel's separate convention center. The airport and commercial center of New Delhi are just 10 minutes away.

Polished marble is used extensively in the grand lobby. Expansive canopies cover the ceiling. During the day, the colorful gardens and pool can be viewed from the lobby. In the evening, melodious sounds can be heard from the lobby's three-piece ensemble.

All guest accommodations at the Taj Palace have climate control, TV, refrigerators, fresh fruit and daily newspapers. There are 32 suites, including two presidential suites. Additional suite amenities include daily flowers, personalized stationary and bathrobes. All accommodations have cold, purified drinking water.

The restaurants at Taj Palace are among the best known restaurants in New Delhi. Most famous is the Orient Express, a real dining car, modeled after an elegant dining car of the Orient Express train. European splendor and posh elegance exude from this restaurant which seats only 35 people at tables and 40 at the bar. The Tea House of the August Moon, the hotel's Chinese restaurant, is set in a serene courtyard and serves many specialties, including dim sum. The Isfahan, open 24 hours a day, serves delectable dishes that combine Persian and Indian cuisines. For respite from the noise of the day, visit the aptly named lounge, Quiet Place, which overlooks a peaceful garden.

For relaxation, guests may enjoy the swimming pool, visit the full health spa, or visit the shopping arcade.

Taj Palace offers some of the best convention facilities in India. The Taj Convention Center features a separate conference entrance, mini-theater, an exhibition hall, and outdoor reception areas. The business center can cater to any executive request.

Delhi's main shopping area, Connaught Place, is only a 10-minute drive away. In addition, Malcha Marg, a shopping center, is only a short walk away. Many New Delhi attractions are easily accessible from the hotel.

Address: 2 Sardar Patel Marg, Diplomatic Enclave, New Delhi, 110 021
Phone: 3010404, Fax: 011 301 1252, Telex: 3162756 TASJ IN
No. of Rooms: 500 **Suites:** 24
Room Rate: $$
Credit Cards: AmEx, DC, MC, Visa
Services and Amenities: Car rental, Parking, 24hr laundry, Valet, Safe deposit fac., Currency exchange, Travel assistance, Barber/beauty shop, Shopping arcade, Doctor, TV, In-house movies, DD phone, Indiv. climate ctl.
Room Service: 24 hours
Restaurant: Handi, Orient Express, Tea House
Bar: Quiet Place
Business Facilities: Secretarial, Fax/telex/cable, Translation, Copying, Courier, Postal, Reference library
Conference Rooms: 10, Capacity: 5,000
Sports Facilities: Pool, Health club
Location: Diplomatic Enclave
Attractions: New Delhi, Old Fort, Jama Masjid, Qutab Minar

WELCOMGROUP MAURYA SHERATON

Amidst the kaleidoscope of old and new in Delhi stands Welcomgroup Maurya Sheraton. An imposing 10-story sandstone facade edifice, the hotel's ambiance and architecture is a tribute to the age of India's first dynasty—the mighty Mauryans.

At the entrance, you are warmly welcomed by a doorman in traditional attire. The Mauryan theme continues in the lobby, where wood and stone soar to reproduce a "chaitya" or Buddhist hall of worship. The austerity of the "chaitya" is enriched by the sweep of arches, artistic creations, and glowing murals on the ceiling.

The guest rooms are luxurious, especially the suites. All accommodations have climate control, closed-circuit television and telephones. The Presidential and Luxury suites are named after a famous person in Mauryan history. These theme suites are elaborately decorated to re-create the splendor of the old Orient and Persia. Along with the suites there are the special Tower Service rooms and executive rooms.

Dining options abound at the Welcomgroup Maurya Sheraton. Bali Hai is an unique combination of a rooftop night club and a Chinese restaurant. Shatranj's buffet spread is an opportunity to feast on delectable vegetarian and non-vegetarian fare created from recipes unique to various Indian regions. At Bukhara, immerse yourself in the atmosphere of India's rugged frontier region, while enjoying barbecued or tandoori meats, served hot and succulent off the skewer. Takshila serves exotic French cuisine. After hours, visit Ghungroo; designed by Juliana's of London, it is one of the classiest clubs and discotheques in town.

Welcomgroup conference venues offer up-to-date facilities. The main hall can accommodate up to 1,200 people. The landscaped Nindiya Gardens provide a perfect setting for outdoor parties. The business center has a Board Room, Executive offices, and complete secretarial services. The Executive Club provides executive club rooms and business amenities and services catered for business travelers.

For recreation there's a swimming pool, tennis courts, health club and Yoga Center. Golf and riding can be arranged on request.

Address: Diplomatic Enclave, New Delhi, 110 021
Phone: 301-0101, Fax: 301-0908, Telex: 031-61447 WELH IN, Cable: WELCOTEL
No. of Rooms: 500 **Suites:** 13
Room Rate: $$$$
Services and Amenities: Limousine service, Laundry/dry cleaning, Safe deposit fac., Currency exchange, Travel counter, Barber/beauty shop, Shopping arcade, Doctor on call, TV, Radio, Phones, Indiv. climate ctl., Butler service
Room Service: 24 hours
Restaurant: Bukhara, Bali-Hi, Takshila, Shatranj
Business Facilities: Secretarial, Fax/telex, Copying, Dictaphones
Conference Rooms: 4, Capacity: 1,200
Sports Facilities: Pool, Health club, Yoga center, Jogging track, Tennis, Golf on request

THE LAKE PALACE

Over three centuries old and formerly a maharani's summer residence, The Lake Palace is one of the most dramatic hotels in the world. The white marble palace is situated in the middle of Pichola Lake, and is truly a spectacular sight. The hotel is only accessible by boat.

Since none of the accommodations have climate control, one must keep the climate in mind. The hottest months of the year are March to October, when temperatures range from 25-38 degrees C. (77-100 degrees F.). July and August are monsoon months. November to February are the winter months with temperatures ranging from 7-25 degrees C. (44-77 degrees F.).

In favorable weather, a visit to the Lake Palace can be an extraordinary experience, especially if one books a deluxe suite. The Sandhya are two small suites with Rajasthani decor and beautiful sunset views. The Sajjan Niwas also enjoys a sunset view and has a private terrace overlooking the garden. Sarvaritu adjoins the pool, and also has a boat landing. Kushmahal has a large living room-cum-bedroom decorated in Rajasthani style. The marble entrance of Kamal Mahal leads to a large living room-cum-bedroom and three small rooms. It enjoys south and west views. The Maharana is a modern suite with a large terrace overlooking the pool.

There is one function room in the hotel, accommodating about 55 people.

The hotel's main restaurant, Neel Kamal, serves excellent European and Indian cuisine. There is also a terrace cafe, Jalkiran, and a regal-style bar, Amritsagar Bar.

Recreational opportunities include a swimming pool shaded by mango trees and a stroll along the beautiful lily pond in the courtyard. An open air theater entertains guests with Rajasthani folk dances, puppet shows, and music. Other activities include bird watching, water sports, fishing, sailing, and picnics to recreation islands. There are also many sights to see in and around the city of Udaipur.

Address: Pichola Lake, Udaipur, 313 001
Phone: 0294 23241-5, Telex: 33 203 LPAL IN, Cable: LAKEPALACE
No. of Rooms: 80 **Suites:** 9
Room Rate: $$
Credit Cards: AmEx, DC, MC, Bob, And, Visa
Services and Amenities: Laundry, Safe deposit fac., Currency exchange, Bank, Travel arrangements, Shopping arcade, Doctor on call
Room Service: 24 hours
Restaurant: Neelkamal European, Jalkiran Cafe
Bar: Amritsagar
Business Facilities: Telex/cable, Postal
Conference Rooms: 1, Capacity: 55
Sports Facilities: Pool, Massage, Watersports
Location: Pichola Lake
Attractions: Eklingji Temple, Rajsamand Lake, Jaisamand Lake, Temple of Shiva, City Palace

NUSA DUA BEACH HOTEL

Located on the beautiful beach of Nusa Dua on the southern peninsula of Bali, Nusa Dua Beach Hotel combines beach resort atmosphere with Balinese elegance. Set on 850 acres of landscaped tropical parkland, this four-story hotel is only 10 minutes from the Ngurah Rai International Airport, 30 minutes from the bustling capital of Denpasar and within easy reach of popular attractions.

In the airy lobby, a complex structure of timber beams supports a vaulted roof of tile and thatching, sandstone frescos and intricate wood carvings. Brickwork, paintings, fountains, and rattan furniture adorned with fine batik, create on aura of relaxed elegance.

All 450 air-conditioned rooms are tastefully decorated in Balinese decor. Appointed with beautiful batiks, terracotta murals, traditional hand-painted panels, wood carving and teak parquet flooring, each room also has its own private balcony, bathroom, and telephone. Two stunning Presidential Suites additionally feature their own private swimming pool and personal staff in attendance.

Eating options are as varied as they are delicious. Warung Bali Coffee Shop offers air-conditioned comfort or open-terraced dining for European, Indonesian and Oriental specialties. Kertagosa Restaurant is a romantic spot, enhanced by beautiful traditional Wayang-style Balinese paintings, for the best of Oriental and Continental cuisine. Lumba-Lumba Seafood Restaurant offers delicious charcoal-grilled seafood. The swim-up Jukung Bar serves thirsty in-pool and poolside guests. The hotel offers weekly cultural entertainment and theme nights, such as Ramayana Ballet, Legong dancing, Italian buffets, and seafood buffets.

A 500-person capacity conference room, complete with the latest audio-visual equipment, is available for meetings.

Recreation opportunities abound. Beach activities and water sports, such as sailing and windsurfing, take advantage of the beach location. Hotel recreational facilities include the health center, tennis and squash courts, jogging track, swimming pool, and pitch-and-putt golf.

The Balinese live in perfect harmony with their island. Theirs is a culture filled with color, pageantry, and hospitality. Let Nusa Dua Beach Hotel show you a slice of Bali you'll always remember.

Address: P.O. Box 1028, Denpasar, Bali 51161
Phone: (361) 71210, (361) 71220, Fax: (361) 71229, Telex: 35206 NDBH IA
No. of Rooms: 450 **Suites:** 14
Room Rate: $$
Services and Amenities: Bank, Barber/beauty shop, Shopping arcade, Cultural entertnmt., TV, In-house movies, Radio, Refrigerator, IDD phone, Central A/C, Hairdryer
Room Service: 24 hours
Restaurant: Kertagosa, Lumba-Lumba, Pizzeria
Bar: Kertagosa, Bale Banjar, Jukung
Business Facilities: Audio-visual, Fax, Copying, Photographer
Conference Rooms: 3, Capacity: 500
Sports Facilities: Pool, Health center, Sauna, Massage, Gym, Jogging track, Squash, Tennis, Dance lessons, Putt golf, Snorkeling, Sailing, Scuba diving, Windsurfing

THE OBEROI BALI

If you are looking for a small, luxury hotel with plenty of Balinese atmosphere, your destination is The Bali Oberoi. Once an exclusive club on the site of an ancient Balinese Village, The Bali Oberoi is now an international hotel set on 30 acres of tropical gardens with native artifacts, along a mile-long private beach. Just 15 minutes from the airport, the hotel is intimate, hosting at most 150 guests, enough to be fun but never crowded.

The club-style hotel consists of an ethnic coral stone building, thatch roof cottages and villas. All accommodations are suites with balcony, minibar, air-conditioning, refrigerator and telephone. The Private Villas also include a sunken bath, garden courtyard and private balcony overlooking the beach. Accommodations are spacious and airy, tastefully decorated with Balinese crafts, cane and carved-wood furniture, tiled floors, Balinese rugs and batiks, and poster beds. The tranquil atmosphere is enhanced by soft sea breezes wafting floral fragrances throughout the cottages.

The Kura Kura Restaurant offers Indonesian, Indian and Continental delicacies. Their celebrated entree is lobster with mango and coconut sauce. The open-air Frangipani Cafe on the beach front is ideal for light snacks and iced fruit drinks. In the Amphitheatre Restaurant, enjoy a candlelit dinner while watching intricate Kecak, Legong and Ramayana dancing.

The conference rooms offers the perfect venue for meetings or private functions. Audio-visual, secretarial services, and translators are available. Conference planners should be sure to obtain valid permits for conferences held in Indonesia.

Recreation and relaxation is the key to Oberoi Bali. There are miles of empty beaches to stroll, a warm inviting sea to splash in, and beautiful sunsets to admire. At the hotel, there is a garden pool with poolside bar, a chess hut, pool table, lighted tennis courts, and health club with sauna and massage. Rent a bicycle, motorcycle or jeep for exploring nearby temples and villages. Arrangements can be made for diving lessons and 18-hole highland golfing.

Just a 5-minute drive away lies Legian Village, Bali's most exciting shopping area for antiques, leather, local ceramics, jewelry and summer clothes. Excursions to Tanah Lot Sea Temple and Monkey Forest are less than an hour's drive away.

Address: Box 351, Legian Bch, Jl. Kayu Aya, Denpasar, Bali
Phone: 62-361-51061, 62-361-53044, Fax: 52-361-52791, Telex: 35125/35352 OBHOTL
No. of Rooms: 60 **Suites:** 15
Room Rate: $$
Credit Cards: AmEx, AP, MCh, DC, Visa
Services and Amenities: Free transp. to Kuta, Laundry/dry cleaning, Barber/beauty shop, Gift shop, Radio, Minibar/refrigerator, DD phone, Indiv. A/C ctl., Balconies
Room Service: 24 hours
Restaurant: Kura-Kura, Frangipani
Bar: Kayu
Business Facilities: Audio-visual, Secretarial, Fax, Translation
Conference Rooms: 1, Capacity: 60
Sports Facilities: Pool, Health club, Massage, Tennis, 18-hole Golf, Table tennis, Surfing
Attractions: Shopping, Legian Village

TANDJUNG SARI HOTEL

Located in the busy Sanur Beach area, the Tandjung Sari is a walled compound of thatched-roof cottages set in luxuriant foliage. A hotel limousine carries guests the 17 kilometers from the airport to the reception pavilion, which is decorated with carved stone animals. Religious statuary appears throughout the gardens.

The ground floor of each bungalow has a private courtyard and air conditioned living area, while the upstairs bedroom is screened and cooled by traditional overhead fans. Tiled floors, sunken baths, and antiques contribute to the ambiance.

Marble tables and antiques grace the Tandjung Sari terrace restaurant, where Indonesian buffets are served to the strains of Balinese music. The Tandjung Sari Bar faces the beach. There is a small fresh-water pool for those who do not want to swim in salt water.

This small, traditional hotel with family service is appreciated by the vacationer who would eschew the large resorts.

Address: P.O. Box 25, Denpasar, Bali, 80001
Phone: 361 8441, 361 8442, Telex: 35157 TANSRI IA
No. of Rooms: 25 **Suites:** 1
Services and Amenities: Airport limousine, Minibar, IDD phone, Indiv. A/C ctl.
Restaurant: Tandjung Sari Restaurant
Bar: Tandjung Sari Beach Bar
Sports Facilities: Pool, Sailing
Location: Sanur Beach

BALI PADMA HOTEL

"Padma" means "lotus flower" and symbolizes the exotic beauty of Bali. Welcome to Bali Padma Hotel, a beach resort on Legian Beach, just 20 minutes from the airport and close to bustling Kuta, yet far away from the hustle. At Bali Padma, all one sees are miles of sandy beach and the ever-changing vistas of the Indian Ocean.

Situated among landscaped grounds, tropical flowers, and lily-filled ponds, one-story chalets are clustered like a local village. However, the village exteriors are contrasted by the elegant interiors, boasting cool colors, polished woods and beautiful, carved Balinese panels.

Each of the 400 rooms is equipped with air-conditioning, IDD telephone, satellite TV, mini-bar, and large private balcony. Balinese wall decorations and statues grace the rooms, complementing local cane furniture and parquet floors. Tropically-inspired fabrics add a touch of vibrant color. A special feature of all accommodations is the private garden-style bathrooms, bringing nature's beauty indoors.

A gourmet heaven awaits you at Bali Padma. Nautilus Seafood Restaurant delights guests with the freshest catch of the day and breathtaking sunsets. The poolside Pizzeria tempts guests with pizzas and pastas. Japanese food can be savored at the Kurumaya Restaurant, where culinary preparation is a feast for both eyes and stomach. The Balinese Open Theater is not to be missed. Colorful dance performances accompanied by a gamelan orchestra entertain guests as they enjoy international fare.

Meeting facilities are thoroughly elegant and modern. Bali Padma can accommodate 500 guests for cocktails and 300 for dinner. The business center can assist executive travelers with all their needs.

Recreation abounds on the beach and at the resort. Watersports and beach activities are popular at the neighboring Legian and Kuta beaches. The resort offers gymnasium, tennis and squash courts, and a 45-meter swimming pool. Guests can relax after their workout with a steambath, sauna or the outdoor massage hut by the beach.

Outside the resort, explore the surrounding countryside scenery and sculpted rice-terraces, or experience the temple ceremonies the Balinese are so famous for. At day's end, the setting sun is another sight to behold.

Address: Box 1107, Jalan Padma No. 1, Legian Beach, Bali
Phone: 0361-52111, 0361-51723, Fax: 0361-52140, Telex: 35624 PADMA IA
No. of Rooms: 380 **Suites:** 220
Room Rate: $$
Credit Cards: AmEx, DC, MC, Visa
Services and Amenities: Car rental, Parking, Laundry, Safe deposit fac., Currency exchange, Shopping arcade, Doctor on call, Babysitting, TV, In-house movies, Minibar, IDD phones, Taped music, Bedside ctl. panel
Room Service: 24 hours
Restaurant: Nautilus Seafood, Open Air Theatre
Bar: Barong, The Pub
Business Facilities: Audio-visual, Secretarial, Fax/telex, Copying, Postal
Conference Rooms: 3, Capacity: 500
Sports Facilities: Pool, Fitness center, Sauna, Steambath, Massage, Gym, Aerobics, Squash, Tennis, Watersports
Attractions: Kuta Beach, Bali sights

HOTEL PUTRI BALI

Hotel Putri Bali means "Balinese Princess Hotel," and a royal resort it is. Opened in 1985, this 4-story building is based on Balinese architecture. Each room has a private balcony facing either lush gardens or the magnificent Nusa Dua Bay. All accommodations are individually air-conditioned, and feature satellite TV, radio, mini-bars, direct dial telephones, and modern Balinese decor.

There are one- and two-bedroom suites, two presidential suites, standard cottages, and deluxe cottages.

The resort's location, right on the beach, allows ample opportunity for water sports. Pizza lovers will appreciate the Pizzeria Beach Bar. There is also a marvelous swimming pool featuring the sunken Samudra Pool Bar.

For those who want a quick snack or a full meal, Le Pau Coffee Shop is open 24 hours. The Semeru Rotisserie is the Putri Bali's main restaurant, offering grilled items. Samudra Seafood Restaurant specializes in delicacies from the sea. The Kahyangan Supper Club takes full advantage of the beautiful panoramic view of Nusa Dua Beach. A sumptuous international buffet with entertainment provided by a gamelan orchestra and Balinese dancers is offered at the Ambara Open Stage. Those who wish to dance to modern rhythms will enjoy the Oasis Disco Club.

Full conference facilities are available at the Hotel Putri Bali, which is located only 7 miles from Ngurah Rai International Airport. The Bale Banjar function hall can accommodate 500 for a banquet, 600 for a meeting, or 800 for a reception. Five other rooms provide attractive venues for smaller groups.

There is plenty to enjoy in the tranquil resort setting of the Hotel Putri Bali, but for those who wish to explore there are excursions to temples and villages. The towns of Kuta and Sanur with their restaurants and night life are only about 20 minutes away.

Address: P.O. Box 1, Nusa Dua, Bali, 80363
Phone: 71020, 71420, Fax: (062-0361) 71139, Telex: 35247 HPB DPR, Cable: NUSABALI
No. of Rooms: 384 **Suites:** 41
Services and Amenities: Limousine service, Parking, Laundry/dry cleaning, Travel arrangements, Barber/beauty shop, Gift shop, Drugstore, Bank, Satellite TV, Radio, Minibar, DD phones, Indiv. climate control.
Room Service: 24 hours
Restaurant: Kahyangan, Semeru, Samudra, Ambara
Bar: Lobby, Paseban, Samudra
Business Facilities: Audio-visual, Secretarial, Fax/telex/cable, Translation, Photography
Conference Rooms: 6, Capacity: 500
Sports Facilities: Pool, Health club, Squash, Tennis, Windsurfing, Waterskiing, Scuba diving, Snorkelling, Sailing
Location: Nusa Dua
Attractions: Excursions to Art Village, Besakih Temple, Monkey Forest, Royal & Sea Temples

MELIA BALI SOL

Melia Bali Sol is a perfect place to bask in island luxury. On the Nusa Dua beach at the southern end of Bali, Melia Bali Sol is set amidst lush tropical gardens, a small complex of low buildings, trees and a swimming pool that extends before you like a small lake.

The design of this modern paradise takes its cue from traditional Balinese architecture, beginning with the airy lobby, a tropical-feeling room with narrow wooden pillars that draw attention upward to a tiered ceiling painted with murals of island life. An open staircase seems suspended over a small pool in the lobby's center. Guest rooms are equally inviting, with cheerful colors and airy textures complementing the many luxurious amenities. One hundred duplex suites are available, with bedroom lofts. Two presidential suites offer living room, dining room, kitchenette, two bedrooms and private balcony.

Culinary options range from the gourmet tastes of the Pavilion restaurant, to the Chinese delicacies of Lotus, to the Indonesian specialties served at the Sateria, the beach restaurant. Enjoy Gado-Gado for a poolside lunch, and dine on Seafood Gratin Papaya and Veal Steak Chartreuse in the garden for dinner. The Banji coffee shop serves breakfast, lunch and dinner.

Conferences and incentive trips are well provided for at Melia Bali Sol. In addition to well-equipped meeting rooms with a capacity of 400, Melia Bali Sol has suggestions for itineraries and traditional entertainment that are certain to contribute to the success of any business trip. Whether you spend your days taking off on excursions to the island's temples and volcanoes, or taking advantage of the hotel's Health Center and many recreational facilities, a visit to Melia Bali Sol is sure to please.

Address: P.O. Box 1048, Tuban, Nusa Dua, Bali
Phone: (0361) 71510, Fax: (0361) 71360, Telex: 35237
No. of Rooms: 388 **Suites:** 112
Room Rate: $$
Services and Amenities: Car rental, Parking, Laundry/dry cleaning, Safe deposit fac., Currency exchange, Travel agency, Barber/beauty shop, Shopping arcade, Doctor, Babysitting, Radio, Minibar/refrigerator, IDD phone, Indiv. A/C ctl., Welcome drink
Room Service: 24 hours
Restaurant: Banji, Pavilion, Lotus, Sateria
Bar: Piano Bar
Business Facilities: Audio-visual, Secretarial, Simult. translation, Pagers, Courier, Postal, Security
Conference Rooms: 7, Capacity: 500
Sports Facilities: Pool, Sundeck, Aerobics, Sauna, Steam room, Massage, Gym, Jogging track, 3 Tennis courts, 2 Squash courts, Volleyball, Bicycling, arrang. for Golf
Attractions: Nusa Dua Beach, Kintamani, Kehen Temple

BALI HYATT SANUR

Surrounded by 36 acres of landscaped gardens and the beautiful white sands of Sanur Beach, the Bali Hyatt is a true tropical paradise. A hotel limousine transports you to and from the airport, which is 20 minutes away. The Balinese architecture of the hotel blends harmoniously with the beauty of the natural surroundings. The open air lobby has a soaring thatched roof.

The Balinese decor of the guest rooms incorporates intricately carved teak and bamboo furniture, grass matting, temple hangings, and hand-blocked batiks. Every room has a private balcony with views of the gardens, the golf course, the water, or Bali's sacred volcano Gunung Agung. Regency Club is a separate part of the hotel for those who require the very highest level of extra services. These include express check-in and check-out, and attentive service from a Regency Club butler.

Five restaurants, four bars and Bali's most famous discotheque provide a variety of gastronomic delights, tropical libations, and entertainment. Spice Islander Restaurant serves excellent Indonesian and continental cuisine. The outdoor Purnama Terrace offers authentic Indonesian dinners and Balinese dances under the night sky. The Ming Cafe, open 24 hours, offers light snacks and full meals. And located right on the beach, the Pizzeria serves pizzas and pastas. The Matahari Bar and Discotheque is an elegant place to sip drinks and dance.

The hotel has two function rooms, complete with audio-visual equipment. Rinjani Hall, with its thatched roof in traditional Balinese architecture, accommodates up to 200 persons auditorium-style.

There is a host of recreational activities at the Bali Hyatt. Walkers and joggers will enjoy the jogging track that winds through the landscaped gardens and Sanur Beach. Water activities include windsurfing, sailing, waterskiing, fishing, and exploring the nearby coral reefs. Sightseeing tours of the island are available in air-conditioned taxis. Or, guests can board one of the hotel's pleasure cruisers for a trip around the outlying islands. Of course, you can always stroll along the beautiful beach, or contemplate the sky, as seen through whispering palms.

Address: P.O. Box 392, Sanur, Bali, 80001
Phone: (62) 361 8271, Fax: (62) 361 71693, Telex: 35127 HYTDPR IA
No. of Rooms: 387 **Suites:** 11
Room Rate: $
Credit Cards: AmEx, DC, MC, JCB, BCA, V
Services and Amenities: Laundry/dry cleaning, Safe deposit fac., Travel arrangements, Beauty salon, Shopping arcade, House doctor, Drugstore, TV, Minibar/refrigerator, IDD phone, A/C
Room Service: 24 hours
Restaurant: Spice Islander, Fisherman's, Purnama
Bar: Piano, Lobby, Beach
Business Facilities: Audio-visual, Secretarial, Fax/telex, Translation, Copying, Photography
Conference Rooms: 3, Capacity: 400
Sports Facilities: Pool, Sauna, Massage, Jogging track, Tennis, 3-hole golf, Watersports, Deep sea fishing, Children's playground
Location: Sanur Beach
Attractions: Art center at Ubud, Gold/silver jewelry making at Celuk, Kuta craft shops

AMANDARI

High on a cliff above the Ayung river in Central Bali, Amandari is a true celebration of Bali's culture and mystical beauty.

The resort was designed in the style of a traditional Balinese village. Amandari's grand balais has been modeled after a Balinese community meeting place and contains the resort's open air lobby, bar and restaurant. Guests are greeted there in traditional Balinese style; young girls in temple sarongs shower them with fragrant frangipani blossoms. A manager assigned to each guest makes sure all their needs are met.

Thatched roofs crown each of the 27 individual suites. The suites' carved stone walls are made of paras, a volcanic stone unique to Bali. Here, privacy is assured. Furniture of local hardwoods and rattan rest on elegant Javanese marble floors. Sliding panels of teak and glass open to a private, walled Balinese garden with a sunken, outdoor marble bathtub. Four of the suites have their own private swimming pool.

Eating at the Amandari is an undisputed delight. The menu features both Indonesian and European food. A recent offering by Chef Richard Jenn included: Bodor Bayam, a creamy coconut and Balinese spinach soup; Gadon, a shrimp and glass noodles mousse wrapped in a banana leaf and steamed; and Ikan Kakap Baker, char-grilled fish with a rich samal of lemon grass and chili; topped off with a delicious desert of Pisang Goreng, deep-fried banana served with vanilla ice cream.

Everything about the resort's terraced landscape, even its saltwater pool, echoes the gentle harmony of surrounding rice terraces and verdant hills. The slopes above the Ayung River are ideal for picnics, and the river is wonderful for swimming and fishing. One of the world's top 100 golf courses, which has the distinction of being in the crater of an extinct volcano, is just an hour away by taxi.

Address: P.O. Box 33, Kedewatan, Ubud, Bali
Phone: (0361) 95333, Fax: (0361) 95335
No. of Suites: 27
Room Rate: $$$$
Credit Cards: AmEx, DC, JCB, MC, Visa
Services and Amenities: Personal manager, Comp. airport trans., Welcome fruit basket, Minibar, IDD phone, A/C, Indoor shower, Outdoor marble bathtub, Pvt. Balinese garden
Restaurant: Verandah Restaurant
Bar: Poolside Bar
Sports Facilities: Salt water pool, Tennis court, Tour/trekking guides, Fishing nearby, Gardens, Library, Art gallery
Attractions: Kedewatan Village, Ubud, beaches, volcanoes, shrines

HOTEL ISTANA GRIYAWISATA

Just ten minutes from the airport, Hotel Istana Griyasata is situated on each side of the Jalan Lembong road in Bandung. The Astoria Wing, which is slightly more expensive, is the southern wing. The northern part of the hotel is called the Wisata Wing.

All rooms are outfitted in true Indonesian elegance and offer air-conditioning, TV, radio, mini-bars, and 24-hour room service. Deluxe Suites feature handsomely carved teak beds, with touches of Indonesian fabric. The lovely fruit basket and cookies in the suites are delicious!

Western cuisine can be enjoyed at the hotel's Continental Restaurant. Cafe d'Orientale offers Indonesian specialties, such as Nasi Goreng (Indonesian fried rice), Soto Bandung (a special local soup) and Ayam Rica Rica (spicy chilly chicken). Relax in the intimate atmosphere of The Baku Dapa Lounge, or, you may prefer to take your refreshments by the pool.

The hotel is located within walking distance of Braga, the main shopping area in Bandung. Sometimes called Flower City, Bandung has lush tropical foliage. Surrounding the city is a beautiful mountainous area, and excursions to the Tangkuban Perahu Crater, 29 kilometers to the north, are popular. At Saung Angkling, you can hear traditional music played on bamboo instruments. Sari Ater, a hot water spring in the tea plantation area half an hour from the hotel, offers the ideal opportunity to restore and refresh yourself.

Address: Jalan Lembong 21-44, Bandung, 40111
Phone: (022) 430351, (022) 433025, Telex: 28409 GHCHIB IA
No. of Rooms: 88 **Suites:** 3
Services and Amenities: Laundry, Valet service, Travel arrangements, TV, Radio, Minibar, Phone
Restaurant: Cafe D'Orientale, Continental Restaurant
Bar: Bakudapa
Conference Rooms: Capacity: 300
Sports Facilities: Pool
Attractions: Braga shopping area, excursions to Tangkuban Perahu Crater, Saung Anklung

HOTEL BOROBUDUR INTER-CONTINENTAL

Deep in the bustling center of Jakarta, Hotel Borobudur Inter-Continental is a tropical oasis that offers travelers a haven from busy city life. Set on 24 landscaped acres, the hotel is an impressive tower of marble, crystal and teak, which incorporates Indonesia's lush natural beauty with the luxury of a full-scale country club.

In the hotel's striking interior, rich teak, local marble, traditional Indonesian carvings and batiks create an ambiance of timeless beauty and serenity. This unique Javanese decor is carried over into the hotel's guest rooms, where comfortable teak furnishings and marble bathrooms lend an added touch of elegance to deluxe amenities. Guest rooms feature two independent telephone lines with a private voice mail system. For the health minded, the eleventh floor has been designated as a no-smoking area. Long-stay guests will find that the 140 Garden Wing apartments provide all the comforts of home.

The hotel is well equipped for business meetings and conventions. The business center can supply everything from instant translation services to private offices. There are nine conference and meeting rooms, the largest of which can accommodate 4,000 people. The ballrooms are very elegant.

Overlooking the landscaped gardens, Toba Rotisserie offers sumptuous European specialties and a unique international wine list from its private cellar in an atmosphere of sublime sophistication. A recent meal featured Panfried Veal Sweetbreads with caramelized citrus sauce. In the Keio Japanese Restaurant, classical and modern Japanese cuisine are served in authentic style. Pendopo Lounge features a weekday 'Executive Power Breakfast,' and live New Orleans jazz at their Sunday brunch. The Music Room, a truly cosmopolitan discotheque with all the ambiance of a private club, is open to guests on Saturday and Sunday afternoons.

Recreational facilities at this world class hotel include the only olympic-sized hotel swimming pool in Jakarta, six outdoor and two indoor tennis courts, seven squash courts, badminton and racquetball courts, mini golf, jogging track and a fully equipped gymnasium.

Address: Box 1329, Jl. Lapangan Banteng Sel., Jakarta, 10710
Phone: (62-21) 370 333, (62-21) 370 108, Fax: (62-21) 3809595, Telex: BDO JKY 44156, Cable: BOROBUDUR JKT.
No. of Rooms: 860 **Suites:** 305
Room Rate: $$$
Services and Amenities: Laundry, Valet service, Banks, Travel arrangements, Tropical gardens, Shopping arcade, Childrens playground, Satellite TV, In-house movies, Radio, Minibar, IDD phone, Indiv. A/C ctl.
Room Service: 24 hours
Restaurant: Toba Rotisserie, Keio, Nelayan, Bogor
Bar: Pendopo, Music Room, Lisoi
Business Facilities: Audio-visual, Secretarial, Fax/telex/cable, Translation, Copying, Computers, Postal, Business library
Conference Rooms: 9, Capacity: 1,200
Sports Facilities: Pool, Fitness center, Jogging track, Squash, Tennis, 9-hole minigolf, Racquetball, Badminton, Volleyball
Location: Jakarta Pusat
Attractions: Street markets, shopping, Fantasyland, National Monument

HYATT ARYADUTA JAKARTA

"Aryaduta" is an old Javanese word meaning ambassador. The newly renovated and extended Hyatt Aryaduta Jakarta stands as an ambassador to the business world, offering outstanding facilities in central Jakarta.

All rooms have central air-conditioning, satellite TV, radio, mini-bars, hairdryers in the bathrooms, and other amenities. There are 28 suites, including the spacious presidential suite, Cendena, located on the hotel's top floor with a panoramic view of the city of Jakarta. Some rooms have terraces opening onto the Balinese Pool. Food and beverage service is available at the pool, and the nearby Fitness Center offers two squash courts, sauna, and massage. A variety of restaurants serve the international clientele. In the lotus garden of the hotel is beautiful Cafe Teratai, serving local dishes. Continental cuisine is featured at Le Parisien on the hotel's mezzanine level. Shima is renowned for its Japanese dishes. The Tavern is the place to unwind, throw a few darts, and enjoy some pub food while watching a sports video in the afternoon or a band at night. For a more formal drink with a business associate, try the Ambassador Lounge off the main lobby.

The airport limousine can whisk you to the Hyatt Aryaduta in about 35 minutes. The hotel is conveniently located near the Monas Monument, Keris Gallery, Sarinah, and Ratu Plaza shopping centers. Bogor Botanical Garden is about 45 minutes away.

Address: P.O. Box 3287, Jl. Prapatan 44-48, Jakarta, Java, 10110
Phone: (021) 376008, Fax: (021) 349836, Telex: 46220 JKT, Cable: ARYADUTA
No. of Rooms: 340 **Suites:** 28
Services and Amenities: Limousine service Gift shop, Satellite TV, Radio, Minibar, Indiv. A/C ctl.
Restaurant: Le Parisien
Bar: Ambassador Lounge, Tavern Bar
Business Facilities: Secretarial, Translation
Conference Rooms: 4, Capacity:
Sports Facilities: Pool, Squash
Location: Central city
Attractions: Shopping centers: Keris Gallery, Sarinah, Ratu Plaza

MANDARIN ORIENTAL JAKARTA

Situated in the heart of Jakarta's financial and diplomatic district, Mandarin Oriental boasts an ideal location for business travelers. The 27-story hotel is completely modern, yet retains the beauty of Indonesia. All public areas, restaurants, rooms and suites are richly decorated with fine batiks, woods, antiques and exotic curios.

Guest rooms offer every amenity and are decorated in Indonesian teak furniture, tasteful pastel colors and batiks. Mandarin Oriental's Executive Deluxe Rooms additionally feature floor valets. In the luxurious suites, marble bathrooms, antiques, and original works of art create an ambience of relaxed splendor.

Distinguished French and Continental cuisine can be savored at the award-winning Club Room. Its varied menu, fine wines, posh atmosphere, and attentive service create an unforgettable dining experience. The Spice Garden offers celebrated Szechuan-style Chinese cuisine. Crimson and gold colors, exquisite wood carvings and batiks surround guests as they choose from a remarkable menu offering nearly 200 gourmet specialties. More informal dining can be found at The Marquee, where Western fare and Indonesian specialties are served. The Captain's Bar is a handsome gathering spot for business lunches and early evening cocktails. Musical entertainment is featured nightly, often with Indonesian and international stars.

Mandarin Oriental offers exceptional convention and banqueting facilities. The luxuriously-appointed Grand Ballroom can accommodate 1,000 people for a reception or 450 for dinner. Equally beautiful smaller rooms are also available. Since the international business day never ends, the Executive Business Centre is open 24 hours a day. All business services, along with a knowledgeable staff, help make doing business a breeze.

The Fitness Centre is fully equipped with state-of-the-art exercise apparatus, sauna, and expert fitness instructors. The swimming pool and two squash courts are also popular venues for workout or relaxation.

During free moments, take a sightseeing tour, or visit the City Museum, the Wayang (puppet) Museum, or the Bharata Theatre. Artifact collectors will want to visit Jalan Surabaya and test their bargaining skills.

Address: Box 3392, Jalan M.H. Thamrin, Jakarta
Phone: (62-21) 321-307, 800-448-8355, Fax: (62-21) 324-669, Telex: 61755 MANDA IA, Cable: MANDAHOTEL
No. of Rooms: 462 **Suites:** 19
Room Rate: $$$
Credit Cards: All major
Services and Amenities: Car hire, Airport transfers, Parking, Laundry, Valet service, Safe deposit fac., Sightseeing & tours, Barber/beauty shop, Shopping arcade, Medical services, TV, In-house movies, Radio, Minibar/refrigerator, IDD phones, Indiv. A/C ctl., Comp. newspaper
Restaurant: Club Room, Spice Garden, Marquee
Bar: Captain's, Clipper
Business Facilities: Audio-visual, Secretarial, Fax/telex, Translation, Copying, Postal, Computers
Conference Rooms: 2, Capacity: 1,000
Sports Facilities: Pool, Health club, Sauna, Massage, Squash
Attractions: City Museum, Art & Painting Museum, Bharato Theatre, Bogor

AMBARRAKMO PALACE HOTEL

The Ambarrukmo Palace Hotel is set in lush tropical gardens in a suburban area about four miles from downtown Yogyakarta. It is less than five miles away from the local airport, and about 50 miles from the world famous Borobudur Temple.

Guest rooms are comfortably appointed with deluxe amenities, which include satellite TV, VCR, radio, minibar, and central air conditioning. Many of the rooms feature balconies with views of the surrounding, picturesque mountains. In the spacious Presidential Suite, guests may enjoy their own whirlpool.

At the hotel's Borobudur Theater Restaurant, you can feast on Lumpia and other Indonesian delicacies. Be sure to try the Putri Hijau Pudding for dessert. The Aneka Sari Bar features live entertainment and a dance floor.

There are 11 function rooms at the Ambarrukmo Palace, ranging in size from small meeting rooms to a ballroom that accommodates up to 800 for a reception. Secretarial and translation services are available on request.

Guests can revitalize in the hotel's swimming pool, tennis and volleyball courts, and jogging track. Excursions to Borobudur Temple, Prambanan Temple, Sultan's Palace, and the Water Castle are available. Indonesian handicrafts can be purchased in the hotel gift shop and other local stores.

Address: P.O. Box 10, Jl. Laksda Adisutjipto, Yogyakarta, 55281
Phone: 062 0274 88488, Telex: 25111 APHYK IA
No. of Rooms: 248 **Suites:** 14
Services and Amenities: Gift shop, Satellite TV, Radio, Minibar, A/C
Room Service: 24 hours
Restaurant: Borobudur Theater Restaurant, Dagi Hill
Bar: Aneka Sari
Business Facilities: Secretarial, Translation
Conference Rooms: 11, Capacity: 800
Sports Facilities: Pool, Jogging track, Tennis, 18-hole golf, Volleyball, Children's playground
Attractions: Borobudur Temple, Prambanan Temple, Sultan's Palace, Water Castle

ANA HOTEL HIROSHIMA

Opened in 1983, the Ana Hotel Hiroshima is a 22-story luxury hotel situated in the business and entertainment center of the city.

All rooms are handsomely outfitted with modern amenities, and feature panoramic views of Hiroshima, including Peace Memorial Park, Hiroshima Castle, and Miyajima Island.

The hotel's three restaurants offer a variety of cuisine. The Castle View restaurant, located on the top floor with views of the city, specializes in grilled fare. Chinese delicacies are available at Tao Li. For Japanese food, explore the taste treats at Unkai, which is open for breakfast and lunch. The Star Dust Bar is an ideal place to meet for a casual drink, while you are entertained by live music.

The hotel's ten function rooms can host a variety of functions. As an international hotel, the hotel provides many business services, including simultaneous translations in four languages.

The hotel's swimming pool and fully equipped health spa offer the perfect place to unwind after your busy day of sightseeing or business. The world-famous Peace Memorial Park is a short walk away. Its museum chronicles the effects of the atomic bombing of Hiroshima in 1945. Also available are day and evening inland sea cruises from Hiroshima port.

Address: 7-20 Naka-machi, Naka-ku, Hiroshima, 730
Phone: (082) 241-1111, Telex: 652751 ANAHIJ J
No. of Rooms: 431 **Suites:** 4
Room Rate: $$
Credit Cards: All major
Services and Amenities: TV, Radio, Minibar, Indiv. climate ctl.
Restaurant: Castle View Grill, Unkai Japanese, Taoli
Bar: Star Dust
Business Facilities: Simult. translation
Conference Rooms: 10, Capacity: 1,000
Sports Facilities: Pool, Health club, Gym, Sauna
Location: Downtown
Attractions: Peace Memorial Park, Hiroshima Castle, Hijiyama Park

MIYAKO HOTEL

Celebrating its 100th anniversary in 1990, the Miyako Hotel is cherished for its distinguished history and world-renowned guests. The Miyako is situated on a wooded hillside in the midst of Kyoto's seasonally-changing landscape, and consists of the historic Main Building, the New Building with its comfortable meeting facilities, and the Japanese annex. The recently-constructed New East Wing continues the tradition of international quality and service. Public areas are graced with polished marble and streamlined furnishings, creating a brightly lit, open, and uncluttered atmosphere.

You can choose from Japanese- or Western-style rooms. Both styles are luxurious. Western-style rooms are decorated in light wood furnishings, pale grays and soothing pastels. Amenities include minibar and television. The Japanese annex, "Kasui-en", captures the spirit of traditional Japanese architecture with traditional Sukiya style rooms. Situated in peaceful, manicured gardens, the Kasui-en is a display of aesthetic purity and restfulness.

Miyako Hotel offers an abundance of restaurants. The French restaurant Espoir is most prominent. Guests savor French specialties such as Sauteed Duck with Red Wine Sauce and Goose Liver with Truffles. The Grandview Restaurant commands a sweeping view of the 1,000-year-old city, set against the Higashiyama Mountains. Kunugi serves teppanyaki, where beef and fresh seafood are roasted in front of you. Shisen (Chinese Szechuan), Hamasaku (Japanese) are other dining options. In the evening, relax in the Moonlight Lounge Bar for live music and fine liquors.

Meeting facilities are varied and extensive, with different style conference rooms available for all types of meetings. The Convention Staff Room is specially designed for the role of secretarial control center. Business services include simultaneous translation, secretarial, and audio-visual.

The hotel's recreational facilities offer fitness club, pool, gymnasium, health-counseling staff, tennis, and jogging course.

Kyoto is the cultural capital of Japan, and a stroll through this ancient city will reveal some of its soul. Visit nearby Nanzenji Temple, Heian Shinto Shrine, museums, festivals, and other cultural and scenic attractions. Shopping can be found at the Kyoto Handicraft Center, Inaba Cloisonne and Mikimoto.

Address: Sanjo Keage, Kyoto, 605
Phone: (075) 771-7111, Fax: (075) 751-2490, Telex: 5422-132 MIYAKO J
No. of Rooms: 366 **Suites:** 40
Room Rate: $$$
Credit Cards: AmEx, DC, CB, MC, Visa
Services and Amenities: Parking, Shopping arcade, Satellite TV, Radio, Minibar, Indiv. climate ctl.
Restaurant: Espoir, Grand View, Kunugi, Hamasaku
Bar: Moonlight, Seven Stars, Lobby
Business Facilities: Audio-visual, Secretarial, Fax, Simult. translation, Convention staff rm.
Conference Rooms: 18, Capacity: 2,000
Sports Facilities: Pool, Fitness center, Gym, Jogging course, Tennis, Health-counseling staff
Location: Higashiyama
Attractions: Kinkakuji and Ginkakuji Temples, Heian Shrine, Nijo Castle

HOTEL OKURA TOKYO

Internationally recognized as one of the world's top hotels, The Hotel Okura is centrally located in the quiet, exclusive neighborhood of the American Embassy. The hotel's unique architecture is a graceful testament to ancient and contemporary design, surrounded by exquisite classical Japanese gardens. Rich wood paneling and subdued lighting in the lobby create an ambiance of warmth and intimacy.

Guests rooms feature classic decor, a tasteful blend of European elegance and traditional Japanese beauty. Plush deluxe suites have been adorned in dignified opulence; guests will appreciate the superb comfort and style. And, in a hotel designed to meet the needs of top level executives and visiting dignitaries, the service and amenities go far beyond the ordinary.

Superior convention facilities accommodate from 15 to 2600 people; the hotel can provide a music or entertainment program to enhance any program. Hotel Okura's restaurant and bars offer a wide range of outstanding food; from authentic Cantonese and Japanese fare to gourmet French dining. The Bar Highlander is a true Scottish pub, where guests can order from over 200 Scotch labels.

Hotel Okura's Health Club boasts an expert staff, indoor and outdoor swimming pool, gymnasium, sauna and massage service. Next door to the hotel is the Okura Shuko-kan Museum, where the display of fine art includes national treasures. Just minutes away are Tokyo's business district, Imperial Palace and the famed Ginza shopping sector.

Address: 2-10-4 Toranomon, Minato-Ku, Tokyo 105
Phone: 03-3582-0111, Fax: 03-3582-3707, Telex: 22790 HTLOKURA J
No. of Rooms: 884 **Suites:** 64
Room Rate: $$$$
Credit Cards: All major
Services and Amenities: Free parking, Travel arrangements, Barber/beauty shop, Shopping arcade, Doctor/dentist, Babysitting, Satellite TV, In-house movies, Minibar/refrigerator, IDD phone, Fax or computer avail., Slippers, Japanese robe
Room Service: Room service
Restaurant: Orchid Room, Yamazato, La Belle Epoque
Bar: Starlight, Orchid, Highlander
Business Facilities: Audio-visual, Secretarial, Fax/telex, Simult. translation, Copying, Printing, Courier, Postal, Computers
Conference Rooms: 34, Capacity: 3,000
Sports Facilities: Pools, Sauna, Massage, Gym, Traditional garden, Tea ceremony room
Attractions: Ginza shopping area, business district, Imperial Palace

HOTEL SEIYO GINZA

In the exciting district of Ginza, Tokyo's financial, fashion and cultural hub, stands the Seiyo Ginza Hotel. Rumors still abound that Seiyo Ginza is the most exclusive hotel in the world, an intimate hideaway for the rich and famous. Upon entering the discreet entrance, the staff welcomes you like an old friend. The hospitality is lavish: every preference and dislike is kept on hotel file to make the rest of your stay and future stays like being in a luxurious "home away from home".

The Seiyo Ginza has very little public space; the guest rooms are the heart of the hotel. Elegantly appointed with the finest furnishings, upscale bedding, and draperies, each of the 80 individually-designed suites emanates the feel of a sumptuous private residence. All accommodations have televisions, VCRs, individual climate and humidity controls, stocked bars, separate vanity areas, and walk-in closets. Bathrooms at the Seiyo Ginza are the biggest in Japan, featuring deep tubs, separate showers, televisions, and telephones. The most notable amenity is your own personal secretary, whose job is to see that your every request (business need, travel arrangement, or assistance) is quickly fulfilled.

Pastorale, the hotel's gourmet establishment, offers delectable French nouvelle cuisine and a magnificent wine list. Guests sit in the atmosphere of a posh drawing room and savor such delights as Pheasant with Truffles and Pigeon with Caviar. Attore is considered to serve some of the best Italian food outside of Italy. Kitcho, the Japanese restaurant, is famous both in Japan and overseas. Cafe Intra is an American-style cafe, offering light meals and pop food in a high-tech atmosphere. Members' Bar G1, open only to guests and private members in the evening, is an exclusive nightspot.

For relaxation outside your suite, visit the fitness room and massage facilities. Arrangements can be made for other sports at nearby fitness clubs.

The Salon la Ronde, featuring a foyer, bar, and banquet room, houses private meeting and banquet facilities up to 120 persons. Posh private dining rooms are available for smaller gatherings.

The Seiyo Ginza, offering personal service and luxurious surroundings, prides itself on being a personal sanctuary for travelers who find themselves in the bustling city of Tokyo.

Address: 1-11-2 Ginza, Chuo-Ku, Tokyo, 104
Phone: (03) 3535-1111, Fax: (03) 3535-1110, Telex: 2523118 HSYG J
No. of Suites: 80
Room Rate: $$$$
Services and Amenities: 24hr Concierge, Limousine/car rental, Laundry, Currency exchange, Ticket services, Helicopter charters, 3 TVs, VCR, video lib., Fax, Private bar, Kitchen, 3 phones, Indiv. temp/humidity, In-room safe, Steambaths, Bathrobes, Hairdryer, Personal secretary
Room Service: 24 hours
Restaurant: Pastorale, Attore, Kitcho, Cafe Intra
Business Facilities: Secretarial, Fax, Copying, Printing, Courier
Conference Rooms: Capacity: 75
Sports Facilities: Fitness center, Arrangements for other activities

IMPERIAL HOTEL

Since the Imperial Hotel first opened it's doors over 100 years ago in 1890, it continues the tradition of entertaining and lodging foreign dignitaries and travelers from around the world.

Guest rooms reside in the main building and the newer Imperial Tower. In Japan, where space is a precious commodity, the guest rooms are quite spacious. Each room offers views of Tokyo Bay or the Palace Gardens and Hibiya Park. Decorated with cleanly-styled furnishings and impeccably in order, the individually-styled rooms provide all the expected amenities as well as crisp cotton yukata kimonos.

Being an international hotel, the Imperial offers a variety of world cuisines in its 13 restaurants and 4 bars. The newest of the restaurants is Eureka, featuring a California-style menu of world cuisines, the freshest ingredients, and a generous selection of California wines. Les Saisons Restaurant has been recognized worldwide and offers an elegant setting for Western foods with Japanese accents. The award-winning Fountainbeau serves haute French cuisine in a very elegant setting. Other restaurants serve traditional Japanese cuisine, sushi, as well as continental-style cuisine. The hospitable Rainbow Room presents over 40 international dishes on its buffet table. Several lounges and bars provide places to relax. There are also three tea chambers, where guests may enjoy a traditional Japanese tea ceremony.

The impressive meeting facilities at the Imperial Hotel can easily accommodate international conferences, wedding banquets and other large scale events. From cozy to expansive, there is a meeting room to suit every gathering. A full service business center caters to executives' every need.

The hotel has a swimming pool and sauna for relaxation.

The Imperial is within walking distance to many wonderful sights Tokyo has to offer, including Ginza, the business district of Marunouchi, the government offices in Kasumigaseki, and of course, the Imperial Palace. It's not necessary to leave the hotel grounds to shop, however. The Imperial Plaza shopping complex occupies four floors of the hotel tower and includes an array of international designer shops.

Address: 1-1, Uchisaiwai-cho 1-C, Chiyoda-Ku, Tokyo 100
Phone: (03) 3504-1111, Fax: (03) 3581-9146, Telex: 222-2346 IMPHO J, Cable: IMPHO TOKYO
No. of Rooms: 984 **Suites:** 74
Room Rate: $$$$
Credit Cards: All major
Services and Amenities: 24hr concierge, Limousine/car rental, Valet parking, Laundry/Valet, Safe deposit fac., Currency exchange, Travel arrangements, Barber/beauty shop, Shopping arcade, Medical services, Babysitting, Wedding chapel, Remote ctl. TV, Desks, Radio, Minibar/refrigerator, Phones, Indiv. climate ctl., In-room safe, Kimono, Robes, Hairdryer, Newspaper
Room Service: 24 hours
Restaurant: Les Saisons, Eureka, Nadaman, Peking
Bar: Old Imperial, Rendez-vous
Business Facilities: Audio-visual, Secretarial, Fax/telexc, Translation, Copying, Postal, Computer stations
Conference Rooms: 25, Capacity: 3,000
Sports Facilities: Pool, Sauna, Massage, Tea ceremony pavilion
Attractions: Ginza, Imperial Palace, theaters, shopping

KEIO PLAZA INTER-CONTINENTAL HOTEL

An imposing skycraper hotel, Keio Plaza Inter-Continental Hotel is located in the Shinjuko area of Tokyo, close to shopping, entertainment, the New Metropolitan Center, and the train station (5 minutes walk away).

This ultra-modern hotel has 1,500 guest rooms and 23 suites, three of which are Japanese style. All guest rooms have large windows, which afford panoramic views of Tokyo and Mount Fuji. Amenities include satellite TV, mini-bar, yukata nightgowns, slippers, hot servers, and telephone receivers in the bathrooms.

The Keio Plaza has 19 international restaurants and ten lounges, offering a wide variety of cuisine and entertainment. You will find continental haute cuisine at the Sky Restaurant Ambrosia, along with beautiful views of the city; delicious Cantonese cuisine at Nan-En; seafood specialties at Prunier; steaks at Medallion. There are also five Japanese restaurants, serving different types of Japanese cuisine in different atmospheres.

Thirty function rooms offer as much variety in meeting and private entertainment space. The fifth floor Convention Complex, with its enormous Concord Ballroom and Eminence Hall, boasts marvelous lighting, audio-visual facilities, cargo lift, and multi-channel simultaneous interpretation services. The hotel's Executive Service Center is open for business six days a week. The hotel can also arrange closed-circuit broadcasts for groups.

There is an outdoor pool on the 7th floor garden terrace, with an adjacent sauna. The health club across the street provides use of an indoor track, gymn, pool, and squash, at a special discount rate.

Once the western gateway of Tokyo, the Shinjuko area is now its center. The main street, Shinjuko-dori, stretching from the east exit of the train station, becomes a pedestrian mall after 3 pm on weekends. This boulevard and the maze of side streets off it are key attractions for visitors to Tokyo, all within walking distance from the Keio Plaza Inter-Continental.

Address: 2-2-1, Nishi-Shinjuko, Shinjuku-ku, Tokyo, 160
Phone: (03) 344-0111, Fax: (03) 344-0247, Telex: 26874 J
No. of Rooms: 1,500 **Suites:** 23
Room Rate: $$
Credit Cards: AmEx, CB, DC, JCB, Visa
Services and Amenities: Airport limousine, Travel center, Shopping arcade, Medical/dental, Satellite TV, Radio, Minibar, IDD phone, Indiv. climate ctl.
Restaurant: Ambrosia French Restaurant
Bar: Sky Bar Polestar
Business Facilities: Secretarial, Fax/telex/cable, Translation, Postal, Reference library
Conference Rooms: 32
Sports Facilities: Pool, Sauna
Location: Shinjuku

MANDARIN ORIENTAL MACAU

Opened in 1984, the Mandarin Oriental stands at the seawall of Macau's Outer Harbour on the southeastern coast of China, some 40 miles from Hong Kong. The imposing 17-story hotel is within five minutes walking distance from the jetfoil terminal, and only 20 minutes by car from the border of China.

Craftsmanship and attention to detail by famous artisans of Portugal and China are evident throughout the Mandarin Oriental. The stately lobby, showcasing a carved teak grand staircase and Portuguese replicas, is reminiscent of a Portuguese Palacio.

Each guest room has been decorated in soft pastels, with natural teak furnishings and delightful Portuguese fabrics. All rooms are fully equipped with modern amenities and marbled bathrooms. Rooms also afford uninterrupted views of the South China Sea or the wooded hillside crowned by the 17th century Guia Fortress.

Cafe Girassol overlooks the sea and features Portuguese and Continental specialties in a rustic village setting. The Bar da Guia embodies the theme and excitement of the annual Macau Grand Prix with paintings of historic racing cars. The top-notch Grill Restaurant, in elegant Portuguese decor, offers succulent grills, roasts and renowned fresh seafood. The Dynasty serves classic Cantonese cuisine in a stylish setting.

Three function rooms and business support, such as secretarial and translation services, make the Mandarin Oriental an ideal location for a meeting in Macau.

After a day of working or sightseeing, one may press on to a game of tennis or squash, relax in the pool, or renew oneself in the health spa at the hotel. The hotel's exclusive casino is one of the most popular in the city.

If one should happen to be in Macau on the third weekend in November, which is the annual date of the Macau Grand Prix, a room at the Mandarin Oriental may offer a grandstand view, as the hotel is right next to the race's starting grid. Other nearby attractions include the ruins of St Paul's, the Jai-Alai Stadium, colorful dragon-boat races in June, and the Barrier Gate, Macau's only crossing point into China.

Address: Box 3016, 956 Avenida Da Amizade, Macau
Phone: (853) 567888, Fax: (853) 594589, Telex: 88588 OMA OM, Cable: ORIENTAL
No. of Rooms: 406 **Suites:** 32
Room Rate: $$
Credit Cards: All major
Services and Amenities: Concierge, Car hire, Parking, Laundry/dry cleaning, Safe deposit fac., Currency exchange, Shuttle bus, Beauty salon, Gift shop, Medical services, Casino, TV, Radio, Minibar/refrigerator, IDD phone, Indiv. climate ctl.
Room Service: 24 hours
Restaurant: Cafe Girassol, The Grill, The Dynasty
Bar: Bar da Guia
Business Facilities: Secretarial, Fax/telex/cable, Translation, Offices
Conference Rooms: 3, Capacity: 480
Sports Facilities: Pool, Health center, Sauna, Jacuzzi, Massage, Gym, Jogging, Squash, Tennis, Table tennis
Location: Outer Harbour
Attractions: Macau Grand Prix, China, Taipa Island horse racing, Barrier Gate, Guia Fortress

HYATT REGENCY MACAU

The Hyatt Regency Macau at Taipa Island Resort is considered to be one of the best venues in Asia for business or leisure. Macau is located 50 minutes by jetfoil from Hong Kong. A hotel limousine can meet you at the Macau Pier and transport you over the bridge to Taipa Island, a journey of about 10 minutes. The Taipa Island Resort, built in traditional Portuguese style with tiled terraces, archways, a beautiful circular pool, and winding paths, is set in three acres of lush gardens.

The hotel accommodations, furnished in soft tones, offer every sort of luxury. Many suites have large balconies overlooking the South China Sea. The Regency Club floor has complimentary continental breakfast, all day tea and coffee service, and complimentary cocktails and canapes every evening in the Regency Lounge.

A variety of restaurants cater to every taste. Many restaurants offer low-calorie meals for guests concerned with physical fitness. O Pescador serves gourmet Portuguese specialties. A Pousada Cafe offers a buffet in a stylish atmosphere. Authentic teppanyaki cuisine can be savored at Kamogawa, the Japanese restaurant. The Flamingo, located in the center of the recreational complex, prepares Macanese and Portuguese dishes in an open kitchen.

Well-appointed function rooms equipped with the latest in audio-visual equipment, and a complete range of secretarial and business services, make this an ideal place for a conference. A multi-lingual staff is at your service, ready to help with arrangements. The second floor atrium connects you to the most extensive health and recreational complex in Macau. Facilities include a large free-form pool with swim-up whirlpool bar, a state-of-the-art fitness center, a sports medicine center offering individual consultations and programs, and a beauty clinique. In addition, the resort has facilities for tennis, golf putting and driving, jogging, squash, volleyball, badminton, and basketball. A jai alai is held every night. For less physical recreation, there is, of course, the hotel's 24-hour casino.

Although there is a great deal to enjoy at the hotel, you might also wish to savor some of the great sightseeing that Macau offers as one of Asia's oldest European settlements.

Address: 2 Estrada Almirante Marques Espart., P.O. Box 3008, Taipa Island
Phone: 32-1234, Telex: 88512 HYMAC OM, Cable: 008 2288
No. of Rooms: 353 **Suites:** 20
Room Rate: $
Services and Amenities: Laundry, Valet, Safe deposit fac., Currency exchange, Tour desk, Beauty salon, Gift shop, Medical services, Babysitting, TV, Radio, Minibar, DD phones, Indiv. climate ctl.
Restaurant: Alfonso's, A Pousada, Flamingo, Kamogawa
Bar: Greenhouse Bar
Business Facilities: Secretarial, Telex/cable, Translation
Conference Rooms: 7, Capacity: 300
Sports Facilities: Pool, Full health spa, Sports shop, Gym, Jogging track, Squash, Tennis, Putting green, Driving range, Croquet lawn, Badminton, Volleyball
Location: Taipa Island
Attractions: Ruins of St. Paul

CARCOSA SERI NEGARA

Carcosa Seri Negara lies on 40 acres of landscaped gardens, just five minutes from Kuala Lumpur's city center. Both the Carcosa and Seri Negara mansions were built in traditional style at the turn of the century for the Governor of the Malay States and his honored guests. In October 1989, following Elizabeth II's stay at Carcosa, both mansions were opened for guests from around the world.

All of the eight suites in the Carcosa and the six in the Seri Negara are air-conditioned, furnished with a minibar, television, writing desk, video player and stereo. Each suite differs in size and decor, some offering large terrace, jacuzzi and separate dining and living rooms. Suites are identified by their own name, derived from names of the Malaysian States.

The Mahsuri Restaurant serves classical Continental dishes and original recipes using Malaysian herbs and spices. The adjoining bar is furnished in its original colonial style. The Titiwangsa, adjacent to the Mahsuri, is designed in traditional colonial fashion with cane chairs and a long bar. Curry tiffin and lawnside barbeques are prepared each week or upon request. The Seri Negara Drawing Room & Verandah offers a light menu and High Tea, served daily, while the Cini Poolside Terrace offers drinks and snacks.

There are six main function rooms for conferences, meetings, seminars, banquets, luncheons, dinners and receptions, which can accommodate from 12 to 200 people. Business equipment is available.

Sports activities are endless. There is a fresh water swimming pool, two tournament-size, hard-surface, floodlit tennis courts, two sauna rooms, massage rooms, gym with treadmills, cycles and weights (instructor on-site).

Kuala Lumpur is five minutes away, with The National Art Gallery, The National Mosque and Bukit Nanas, a virgin lowland jungle right in the center of the city. Some of the best shopping is in the renovated Central Market, with galleries and stalls devoted entirely to cotton craft, paintings and food from around the world.

Address: Taman Tasik Perdana, Kuala Lumpur, 50480
Phone: (03) 2306766, Fax: (03) 2306959, Telex: 30504 CACOSA
No. of Suites: 13
Room Rate: $$$$
Credit Cards: AmEx, DC, MC, Visa, Acces
Services and Amenities: Airport limousine, Car rental, 24hr personal butler, TV, VCP, Stereo, Minibar, IDD phone, A/C, Morning tea, Fruit and chocolates, Toiletries, Mono-grammed bathrobe
Room Service: 24 hours
Restaurant: Mahsuri Restaurant, Drawing Room, Garden
Bar: Poolside Terrace
Business Facilities: Secretarial, Fax, telex, Translation, Copying, Computers, Pagers, 24hr business center
Conference Rooms: 5, Capacity: 200
Sports Facilities: Pool, Health center, Sauna, Whirlpool, Weights, Gym, Jogging track, 2 Tennis courts
Attractions: National Museum, Tunku Abdul Rahman Street, mosque, jungle tours

THE REGENT KUALA LUMPUR

Soaring skyward in a wall of reflecting glass, the Regent Kuala Lumpur occupies one of the prime business and shopping districts of the capital, the Golden Triangle. Upon entering the lobby, the cool greenery, sweeping marble stairway, and glass-walled elevator rising from a pool of cascading water, all create a sense of grandeur, matched only by the high international standard of service.

Guest rooms have been designed to meet the needs of the discerning business traveler. Practical, spacious, and furnished in brass, woods and warm fabrics, guest rooms have executive desk, hands-free dual line IDD phones, and views overlooking the business district or the Genting Highlands. Marble bathrooms feature exclusive toiletries, toweling robes, deep soaking tubs and separate glass-enclosed shower. Each floor has a butler who introduces himself to the guest whilst offering a welcome cup of Chinese tea. The ultimate in luxury is the Regent Suite, encompassing three floors and containing its own private bar, billiard room, private sun terrace and swimming pool.

The Brasserie, for informal dining, offers a variety of light meals, some with a distinct local flavor. The Grill specializes in Western cuisine in an atmosphere of relaxed luxury, enhanced by the subtle glow of mahogany, leather and soft lighting. Edo Kirin features Japanese chefs who skillfully prepare traditional Japanese dishes with expert flourishes against a backdrop of traditional Japanese decor. A singular gastronomic experience awaits you at Lai Ching Yuen. Delicate creations are served on Chinese place settings of jade and pure silver.

The Regent provides for every executive need. The 24-hour business center is fully-equipped and staffed by personnel fluent in English, Malay and Chinese. The Ballroom has banquet seating capacity for 300, and the Boardroom can seat a maximum of 18 around an imposing center granite table.

Recreation and relaxation can be found in the health spa. Sensations of glowing health abound as one soaks up the marble splendor of the Roman Baths. The gym complex includes squash courts and body massage. The landscaped terrace, sun deck, and impressive free-form pool also help soothe tensions.

Address: 160 Jalan Bukit Bintang, Kuala Lumpur, 55100
Phone: 03-241-8000 800-545-4000, Fax: 03-242-1441, Telex: MA 33912 REGKL
No. of Rooms: 452 **Suites:** 17
Room Rate: $$$
Services and Amenities: Concierge, Limousine service, Laundry, Valet service, Barber/beauty shop, TV, In-house movies, Radio, Minibar, IDD phones, Executive desk, Comp. newspaper, Robes, Hairdryer, Butler service
Room Service: 24 hours
Restaurant: The Brasserie, Lai Ching Yuen, Terrace
Bar: Lobby Lounge, Bar, Pool Bar
Business Facilities: Audio-visual, Secretarial, Fax/telex/cable, Translation, Offices, Pagers, Courier
Conference Rooms: 8, Capacity: 500
Sports Facilities: Pool, Health club, Saunas, Jacuzzis, Massage, Gym, Squash, Arrangements of Golf, Tennis, and Watersports
Location: Golden Triangle

PENANG MUTIARA BEACH RESORT

The Penang Mutiara, meaning "Pearl of Penang", is a self-contained resort located on 18 acres of lush tropical gardens along the finest beachfront on Penang Island. The resort provides limousine service from the airport, 45 kilometers away. Opened in 1988, the 12-story Penang Mutiara is contemporary in design, with a distinctive Malaysian flavor. The lobby, surrounded by glass, provides beautiful views of the gardens and ocean. The polished white marble floor is a beautiful contrast to the colorful Malay rugs and Malaysian gold-embroidered fabrics.

Each guest room faces the sea and has its own balcony to enjoy the beautiful sea views. The rooms are luxuriously-furnished with hardwood floors, wooden chairs, wicker furniture, and ceiling fans. The bathrooms feature oversized tubs. There are also 32 suites, including one duplex facility with roof garden terrace, jacuzzi, library, and video room.

La Farfalla, the elegant main restaurant with crystal chandeliers and silk panels, specializes in delicious continental dishes. The Garden Terrace serves meals outdoors or inside gazebos 24 hours a day. The House of Four Seasons, a Chinese restaurant, serves Oriental cuisine in a luxurious setting. Five other food and beverage outlets offer a wide variety of refreshments. There is entertainment at the Puppetry Bar and dancing at the cozy Study Discotheque, which is run by Juliana's of London.

The Mutiara offers meeting and banquet facilities for up to 750 people, and its Business Center can help arrange conferences.

A swimming pool, full health club and courts for tennis, squash, badminton, netball and volleyball offer plenty of opportunity for exercise in this tropical paradise. Deep-sea fishing and para-sailing are available from the Mutiara's marina. For families vacationing with children, there is a children's entertainment park.

The hotel can also help guests arrange excursions to the Penang Batik Factory, the Penang Butterfly Farm, Forest Reserve Park, and a typical Malaysian fishing village.

Address: 1 Jalan Teluk Bahang, Penang, 11050
Phone: 04-812828, Fax: 04-803470, Telex: 40829 PMBR MA
No. of Rooms: 431 **Suites:** 48
Room Rate: $$
Services and Amenities: Beauty salon, Shopping arcade, TV, Radio, Minibar, DD phone, Indiv. A/C ctl.
Room Service: 24 hours
Restaurant: La Farfalla Continental
Bar: The Puppetry
Business Facilities: Secretarial, Translation, Business services
Conference Rooms: 6, Capacity: 750
Sports Facilities: Pool, Full health club, Volleyball, Squash, Tennis, Badminton, Deep-sea fishing, Parasailing
Location: Teluk Bahang
Attractions: Penang Batik Factory, Butterfly Farm, Forest Reserve Park, fishing villages

SHANGRI-LA INN PENANG

The Shangri-La Hotel is strategically located in the commercial hub of Georgetown City, providing easy access to Penang's State and Federal Government offices, and to shops, department stores, banks and historical places of interest.

This modern highrise has 447 guestrooms, all appointed with features like IDD telephone, tea/coffee-making facilities and individually controlled air-conditioning.

The Brasserie is a cozy place to dine, where excellent Continental cuisine is coupled with an impressive wine list. Shang Palace serves authentic Cantonese food prepared by Hong Kong masterchefs and specializes in Dim Sum, a must for Chinese food lovers. The Coffee Garden offers light snacks, savory Asian favorites, as well as Continental fare at all hours. Lobby Lounge promises a repertoire of live music as you relax or rendezvous.

On a sundeck overlooking the city, a big swimming pool with poolside bar provides relaxation or workout. Guests will find a gym, sauna and massage at the health center. Golf and squash can easily be arranged. If you long for a day on the beach, hop on board the shuttle bus, which will take you to any of Shangri-La's three sister hotels along the famed Batu Ferringhi beaches and enjoy cross-signing facilities at the other hotels.

The Shangri-La is also Penang's main convention center, with a ballroom hosting up to 900 for a banquet. Supported by a full range of audio-visual equipment, simultaneous translation, a modern business center and catering, the ballroom is the biggest function hall of the entire city. Seven other function halls cater to smaller meetings.

On this colorful little island of Penang, memories of Britain, Portugal, and China mix and blend. From modern city center to palm-fringed sunny beaches and cool hilltops, Penang enchants all who come to visit.

Address: P.O. Box 846, Jalan Magazine, Penang, 10300
Phone: (04) 622 622, Fax: (04) 626 526, Telex: MA 40878
No. of Rooms: 442 **Suites:** 16
Room Rate: $$
Credit Cards: AmEx, AP, DC, JCB, MC, Vs
Services and Amenities: Limousine service, Laundry, Valet service, Tour & travel desk, Barber/beauty shop, Drugstore, Babysitting, TV, In-house movies, In-room safe, Coffee/tea making fac., Hairdryer
Room Service: 24 hours
Restaurant: The Brasserie, Shang Palace
Bar: Lobby Bar, Poolside Bar
Business Facilities: Audio-visual, Fax, Simult. translation
Conference Rooms: 8, Capacity: 1,200
Sports Facilities: Pool, Health center, Sauna, Massage, Golf (20 min.)
Attractions: Downtown, department stores, historical sites

SHANGRI-LA KUALA LUMPUR

Kuala Lumpur, the capital city of Malaysia, is truly a city of contrasts, where the fantastic domes of the Railway Station conjure images of 'Arabian Nights' and modern highrises stand beside minarets. In the center of Kuala Lumpur business district, The Shangri-La Hotel welcomes guests with the gracious elegance for which these hotels are known the world over.

Stylish and charming, all of the Shangri-La's rooms have been designed with a commanding view. The rooms are attractively appointed with modern amenities; garden fresh flowers add a personal touch. Luxury suites are located on the higher floors, offering a panoramic view of the city. Decorated with the finest fittings, suites include a dining room for 16 people and large bathroom with jacuzzi. Seven specialty suites take their theme from Asian nations. On the Horizon Floor, guests are treated to a host of special luxuries, including unpacking of bags by housemaid, 24-hour butler service and personalized telephone service.

The Coffee Garden offers a lavish buffet, Continental cuisine, plus a wide range of Malay, Chinese and Indian favorites. Set in the tranquil style of 16th century Japan, the 150-year old Nadaman Restaurant serves superior Japanese cuisine. Restaurant Lafite specializes in exquisite Continental and innovative cuisine. A recent meal featured Baked Tiger Prawn glazed with Sea Urchin Mousse and tarragon sauce, with Broccoli Souffle, with a Crepe filled with Tropical Fresh Fruits on Warm Kiwi Coulis, for dessert. Kuala Lumpur is itself a gourmet's dream; exceptional restaurants and open-air stalls are found all over the city. Avid shoppers can catch a night market and shop by lantern or take a stroll through Chinatown for great bargains. Cultural and modern entertainment are unlimited, and just outside the city limits are quaint Malay villages and cool hill resorts.

Address: 11 Jln. Sultan Ismail, Kuala Lumpur, 50250
Phone: (03) 232-2388, 800-457-5050, Fax: (03) 230-1514, Telex: SHNGKL MA 30021
No. of Rooms: 685 **Suites:** 35
Room Rate: $$$
Services and Amenities: 24hr Concierge, Limousine service, Laundry, Valet service, Currency exchange, Travel office, Barber/beauty shop, Shopping arcade, Medical clinic, Babysitting, TV, In-house movies, Radio, Minibar/refrigerator, IDD phone, A/C, Comp. breakfast
Room Service: 24 hours
Restaurant: Lafitte, Nadaman, Shang Palace
Bar: English Pub, Lobby, poolside
Business Facilities: Audio-visual, Secretarial, Fax/telex/cable, Simult. translation, Postal, Courier, 24hr business center, Reference library
Conference Rooms: 13, Capacity: 2,000
Sports Facilities: Pool, Health club, Sauna, Hydropool, Massage, Gym, Squash, Tennis, Golf
Location: Golden Triangle
Attractions: Local cuisine, shopping, entertainment, cultural attractions

HOLIDAY INN DAMAI BEACH

A number of years have gone by since pirates and headhunters roamed this land. Today, Sarawak is a country of friendly people and untouched forests with vibrant fauna and flora. A 40-minute drive from Kuching, the Holiday Inn Damai Beach sits astride the white sandy beaches of Teluk Bandung, amid the exotic and beautiful rainforest of Borneo beside the warm waters of the South China Sea.

Sprawled over 90 acres of unspoiled land, the Holiday Inn Damai Beach is a low-rise tropical resort of 202 rooms, consisting of chalets, studio units and individual guest rooms. All rooms have shower, long bath, hot and cold water and hairdryer. Room facilities include air-conditioning, IDD phone, color TV with in-house video and radio.

There are two restaurants, the air-conditioned Cafe Satang which features Malay, Chinese and Western cuisine and the open-air Mango Tree Terrace, serving a variety of local and international cuisine. The Santubong Bar features live entertainment by the resident band. Cocktails can also be enjoyed at the other two bars, the swim-up bar at the pool and the Sunset Bar.

For the business travelers and convention organizers, there are up-to-date facilities to meet every need. The two meeting rooms can each cater up to 240 people. Special theme parties can be arranged for groups.

Recreational activities abound at this beach resort, which offers 2 squash courts, 2 tennis courts, mini-golf, swimming pool, whirlpool, spa pool, fitness center with Finnish sauna, aviary, and a children's playground. The adventurous can go jungle trekking up the beautiful Santubong Mountain. Guests can also relax on Teluk Bandung Beach, directly in front of the hotel, or try their hand at fishing, water skiing, windsurfing, sailing, canoeing, water pedal-cycling, knee-board skiing and water scooter. There are excursions to Turtle Island, and river cruises to Kuching. Bicycles and motorbikes can be rented to explore nearby local villages. To top it off, the 18-hole championship golf course is the newest addition to this recreation-oriented resort.

Address: P.O. Box 2870, Kuching, Sarawak, 93756
Phone: (082) 411777, Fax: (082) 428911, Telex: MA 70081 DAMAI
No. of Rooms: 280
Room Rate: $
Credit Cards: All major
Services and Amenities: Laundry/dry cleaning, Safe deposit fac., Tour desk, Barber/beauty shop, Gift shop, Nurse on call, Child care ctr., Aviary, Cultural village, TV, In-house movies, Radio, IDD phone, Indiv. A/C ctl., Hairdryer
Room Service: 24 hours
Restaurant: Cafe Satang, Mango Tree, Poolside
Bar: Santubong, Swim-up, Sunset
Business Facilities: Audio-visual, Secretarial, Fax, Copying
Conference Rooms: 2, Capacity: 240
Sports Facilities: Pool, Fitness center, Sauna, Shuffleboard, Gym, Jogging track, Squash, Tennis, Golf, Watersports, Fishing, Bicycles, Jet skiing
Attractions: Museums, mosques, open-air markets, festivals, river safaris

HOLIDAY INN KUCHING

Kuching is the captivating capital of Sarawak, a city of contrasts where skyscrapers and stilt villages surround the warm, muddy waters of the Sarawak River, and where stately mosques stand side by side with architectural reminders of the "White Rajah" colonial past. Located on the banks of the picturesque Sarawak River, the lifeline of Kuching, Holiday Inn Kuching is only minutes away from the old city center and 20 minutes from the airport.

The 12-story high-rise houses 320 air-conditioned rooms and suites, all with private bath, over-sized beds, IDD phones, color TV with in-house movies, tea and coffee-making facilities, radio, and minibar. Most accommodations have panoramic views of the busy Sarawak River.

The hotel's food and beverage outlets provide a wide range of fine foods. The Serapi Restaurant features international cuisine. Szechuan and Cantonese delights are served at the Meisan Szechuan Chinese Restaurant. A popular rendezvous spot is the Rajang Bar that overlooks the river and features a nightly band. The Poolside Pavilion serves snacks daily and a poolside barbecue lunch every Sunday and holiday.

Overlooking the Sarawak River, the swimming pool is the perfect location to bask in the sun while watching the passing parade of fishing boats in the river. More recreation can be found at the health center with its Finnish sauna, or the floodlit tennis court next to the hotel. Squash and golfing can be arranged. Guests whose favorite form of recreation is shopping, will enjoy the shopping center with over 100 shops located next to the hotel.

The Holiday Inn Kuching has extensive convention and banqueting facilities for up to 800 people. To meet the needs of the busy executive, there is a Business Centre with secretarial services, telex, and telefax services.

Many sights and adventures lie outside the hotel. There are museums, mosques, temples, traditional shop-houses, and open-air markets. Beyond Kuching, the sense of adventure increases: long houses, river safaris, national parks, rain forests, stone age caves and seaside villages. However, even in Borneo, time doesn't stand still. Modernity is creeping in and some of things you can still see today may disappear before your next visit.

Address: Box 2362, Jalan Tunku Abdul Rahman, Kuching, Sarawak 93100
Phone: 082-423111, Fax: 082-426169, Telex: MA70086
No. of Rooms: 320
Room Rate: $
Credit Cards: All major
Services and Amenities: Car rental, Parking, Laundry, Valet service, Safe deposit fac., Travel arrangements, Drugstore, Shopping arcade, Medical/dental, Babysitting, Childrens playground, TV, In-house movies, Radio, Minibar, IDD phone, Indiv. A/C ctl., Coffee/tea making fac., Hairdryer, Safe treated water
Room Service: 24 hours
Restaurant: Serapi, Meisan Szechuan, Orchid Garden
Bar: Rajang Bar, Poolside Pavilion
Business Facilities: Secretarial, Fax/telex/cable, Postal, Reference library
Conference Rooms: 5, Capacity: 800
Sports Facilities: Pool, Fitness center, Finnish sauna, Tennis, Arrangements for Golf & Squash
Location: Sarawak River bank
Attractions: Sarawak Museum, mosques, shop-houses, open-air markets, festivals, river safari

LAS HADAS

It's been a long time since Bo Derek and Dudley Moore frolicked at luxurious Las Hadas in the movie "10." Nonetheless, after a major face-lift and under new management by Camino Real Hotels, it's still one of the world's most exotic tropical playgrounds.

Nestled on a cove on Bahia de Manzanillo, the gleaming white jig-saw of minarets and onion domes spill down a lush hillside overgrown with bougainvillea, hibiscus and mimosa. Part-Moorish Spain, part-Arabian, and part-Disney, it twists and turns, looking like a palace ordered by Aladdin from a genie.

Rooms are airy with white stucco walls, white marble floors and brightly screened Mexican fabrics. Each has a private patio and views of the seemingly limitless sea, the yacht harbor and lagoons, or the surrounding jungle.

Your palate won't be ignored, for Antenor Patino's architect included five bars, restaurants and a disco in his 220-room Xanadu. The new management stresses sophisticated Mexican specialties and seafood served in a variety of ways.

Playing is the name of the game here, and everything possible is offered. There is an immense swimming pool, done in circles with swim-up bars serving pina coladas. Waterskiing, speedboats, sailing, and snorkeling are all popular. Manzanillo is known as the "Sailfish Capital of the World", and you're likely to get hooked. There are two clay and eight hard-surface courts (lit for night play) for tennis buffs, and a marina to accommodate visitors who pop in by boat. La Mantarraya, the championship golf course, is spectacular in its layout. The name comes from the final hole, just a few feet from the ocean: if one's ball doesn't make the green, it will be devoured by the sting ray waiting in Las Hadas Bay.

Address: P.O. Box 158, Peninsula de Santiago, Manzanillo
Phone: 333-30000, Telex: 62506
No. of Rooms: 220 **Suites:** 38
Room Rate: $$
Credit Cards: AmEx, CB, DC, MC, Visa
Services and Amenities: Concierge, Airport transfer, Parking, Laundry, Valet service, Currency exchange, Barber/beauty shop, Library, Medical services, Babysitting, Fresh flowers, Balconies, Radio, Minibar, Phone in bath, Indiv. A/C ctl., Bidet, Comp. toiletries, Robes, Comp. newspaper
Room Service: 24 hours
Restaurant: Legazpi, Los Delfines, El Palomar
Bar: Oasis, Plaza Dona Albina
Location: Mexico's Gold Coast
Attractions: Shopping for handicrafts, sailing, deep-sea fishing, sunset cruises

HOTEL VILLA DEL SOL

Villa Del Sol is located in a sheltered picturesque bay on Mexico's Pacific Coast. Builder-owner-director Helmut Lewis, a Munich engineer, became enchanted with the sleepy fishing village of Zihuatanejo and its glistening ocean beach in 1969. Today his vision of an intimate beachfront inn, framed by lush tropical gardens, is a reality, and 36 tastefully appointed suites, with masterful design, comprise the bungalow-style Villa Del Sol. More like minisuites, the Mediterranean Mexican fashioned rooms are highlighted by expansive canopied beds, augmented by comfortable and attractive built-in sitting areas. Private terraces, fans, and hammocks add to the relaxing Villa lifestyle.

Each deluxe room affords stunning views of the beautifully landscaped courtyard, the ocean, a winding man-made stream, or the eye-catching South Seas Palapa (thatched roof) which artistically shades and covers the impressive sunken dining and bar pavilion. Mexican and European chefs combine their talents to prepare the finest international cuisine for your rate-inclusive breakfast and dinner, (Nov. 15th–Apr. 1st) as Mexican drinkmasters blend exotic libations, including their famed Margaritas. Feast on shrimp and grapefruit salad, fresh seafood, peppered loin of lamb, or any one of a number of perfectly prepared entrées. Top it off with poached pears with Sabayon sauce over cinnamon ice cream.

Be as active as you desire, enjoying beach and water sports, tennis, parasailing, fishing, touring the small, timeless mountain villages, or simply relax and savor the tranquil beauty of this Mexican West Coast paradise.

Address: Playa La Ropa, P.O. Box 84, Zihuatanejo, Gro. 40880
Phone No.: 0-11-52-753-4-22-39
0-11-52-753-4-32-39
FAX: 0-11-52-753-4-27-58
Telex: 16224 HVDS-ME
Rates: $$$
Credit Cards: Visa, MC, AmEx
No. of Rooms: 30 **Suites:** 36
Services and Amenities: Valet service, Library, Barber and beauty shops, Car rental, Parking, Currency exchange, Babysitting service, Laundry, Game area, Gift shop, Individual air conditioning, Complimentary toiletries
Restrictions: No pets; children under age 14 not accepted during winter season
Concierge: 9:00 a.m.-7:00 p.m.
Room Service: 8:30 a.m.-10:30 p.m.
Restaurant: Villa Del Sol, 8:30 a.m.-11:00 p.m., Dress Code
Bar: Villa Del Sol, 8:30 a.m.-11:00 p.m., Orlando's Bar, 4:00 p.m.-11:00 p.m.
Business Facilities: Message center, Secretarial service, Translators, Copiers, Audio-visual, Telex
Conference Rooms: Capacity 35
Sports Facilities: Outdoor swimming pool, lighted tennis courts, 18-hole golf course nearby, riding, waterskiing, sailing, parasailing, scuba diving, snorkelling, 3 whirlpools, massage
Location: Playa La Ropa beach resort; 10 mi. from airport; 140 mi. north of Acapulco on Mexico's Pacific coast; 6 mi. south of Ixtapa
Attractions: Country and mountain tours, one-day tours to Mexico City, Guadalajara, overnight to Cuernavaca

HYATT AUCKLAND

Just a three-minute walk from the city center, the Hyatt Auckland towers over beautiful Waitemata Harbor and Albert Park, adjacent to Auckland's central business, shopping and entertainment district. The lobby' Italian granite floor, pastel decor and rounded pillars set a tone of sophisticated relaxation for the entire hotel.

Newly refurbished guest rooms and suites capture the residential style of boutique hotels in Europe, with an emphasis on comfort, fine furniture and charm. The new decor features an attractive blend of ceramics, wrought iron and mixes of timbers. All rooms have either a harbor or park/city view. Three floors of the hotel are devoted to Regency Club rooms, which feature a deluxe range of imported bathroom amenities, fruit bowl, concierge service, and complimentary evening drinks, canapes, and continental breakfast in the Club Lounge.

Hyatt's Top of the Town Restaurant is three-time winner of the prestigious "New Zealand Restaurant of the Year" and voted Best Restaurant for 1989 and 1990 by New Zealand Diners club. Top of the Town boasts spectacular panoramic views of the city and harbor, excellent gourmet cuisine, and one of New Zealand's best wine lists. Clouds Cafe's buffet offers guests local and international dishes in a relaxed, friendly environment, along with a tempting array of fresh desserts from the hotel's patissier. The restaurant takes its name from its distinctive decor; soft, fluffy clouds against a background of pale indigo have been subtly airbrushed on the ceiling, creating a realistic image overhead of a sunset sky. Guests can purchase tickets to attend New Zealand's leading Maori Cultural Show, held at the Hyatt Auckland every Sunday evening. The evening includes an extensive New Zealand Buffet and entertainment by Te Roopu Manutaki, who perform Maori action songs, intricate stick and poi dances, armed combat fights and the famous fierce Maori war dance.

Address: Box 3938, Princes & Waterloo Quad., Auckland
Phone: (64 9) 366-1234, 800-228-9000, Fax: (64 6) 303-2932, Telex: NZ 2298
No. of Rooms: 275 **Suites:** 47
Room Rate: $$
Credit Cards: All major
Services and Amenities: Airport limousine, Valet parking, Laundry/dry cleaning, Safe deposit fac., Currency exchange, Barber/beauty shop, Gift shop, Doctor, Babysitting, Satellite TV, In-house movies, Radio, Minibar/refrigerator, IDD phone, Indiv. A/C ctl., Desk, Coffee/tea making fac.
Room Service: 24 hours
Restaurant: Top Of The Town, Clouds Cafe
Bar: Lobby, Champs Videotheque Bar
Business Facilities: Secretarial, Fax/telex, Translation, Copying, Courier, Dictaphones
Conference Rooms: 7, Capacity: 800
Sports Facilities: Jogging track, near Squash, Tennis, Beaches, Golf, Sailing, Windsurfing
Attractions: Harbor/island cruises, Auckland Museum, underwater aquarium

THE REGENT AUCKLAND

The 332-room Regent of Auckland is an international luxury hotel situated in the center of New Zealand's financial and business district. The hotel is just a minute's walk from Waitemata Harbour and the central shopping area of Queen Street. Rising 11 floors, The Regent is modern in decor, polished and streamlined. The service is impeccable as well.

Guest rooms are large and furnished in relaxing pastel tones with extensive use of natural fabrics and finely grained New Zealand native Tawa wood. In the marbled bathrooms, you'll find sunken tubs, separate glass-enclosed showers and thick toweling robes. Each room also has a full-sized business desk with a phone to make business travel more comfortable.

The hotel has five bars and restaurants, including the all-day dining restaurant The Brasserie, the Lobby Lounge and the Lobby Bar. The award-winning Longchamps, named after the Parisian racecourse and celebrating New Zealand's horse-racing tradition, offers fine continental cuisine. Graced with Wedgewood china, fine crystal, silver and paintings of Auckland scenes, Longchamps is a formal showcase for gourmet dining. Sushi and Japanese a la carte dishes are offered at Sushi Bar Ariake and by room service.

Boasting extensive business and meeting facilities, The Regent is known as one of Auckland's best business hotels. Private dinners, cocktail parties, meetings and conferences are all catered for in the Regent Ballroom, which also divides equally into three self-contained rooms. The fully-equipped business center provides an "office away from the office".

When the time comes for relaxation, the rooftop pool is an excellent place to soak, swim, or simply lie under New Zealand's pollution-free skies. Sailing, fishing, water-skiing, international standard golf courses, tennis, galleries, museums, theaters and restaurants are all nearby and can easily be arranged for by the concierge.

Address: Albert St., Private Bay, Auckland, 1
Phone: (09) 309-8888, 800-545-4000, Fax: (64-9) 796-445, Telex: NZ 60079, Cable: REGAUCK
No. of Rooms: 313 **Suites:** 18
Credit Cards: All major
Services and Amenities: Concierge, Limousine service, Valet parking, Laundry/dry cleaning, Safe deposit fac., Porters, TV, Radio, Minibar, IDD/STD phone, Indiv. A/C ctl., Desk, Coffee/tea making fac., Hairdryer, Turndown service
Room Service: 24 hours
Restaurant: Longchamp, The Brasserie, Sushi Bar
Bar: Lobby Bar
Business Facilities: Secretarial, Telex/fax, Copying, Printing, Reference materials
Sports Facilities: Pool, Sundeck, Arrangements for waterskiing, sailing and golf
Attractions: Waitemata Harbour, Queen Street

SHERATON AUCKLAND

Located in Auckland's uptown commercial center and only 20 minutes from the airport, the Sheraton Auckland is actually two hotels in one—The Sheraton Hotel and The Sheraton Towers.

The main part of the complex is the Hotel. The circular marble lobby, with cascading waterfall, is usually busy. Nestled cozily off the main lobby is the Rendezvous Lounge, where you can enjoy a drink and the sounds of a grand piano.

The rooms in both the Hotel and the Towers are large and tastefully decorated. The Towers section is comprised of 30 deluxe rooms and 9 suites, and Tower guests enjoy additional amenities, such as attentive butler service.

Partington's, the hotel's award-winning restaurant, offers both New Zealand and continental cuisine. The popular Steam Biscuit Factory is available for more casual dining for breakfasts, lunches, and dinner buffets. Someplace Else is a relaxed drinking and eating pub with live music nightly. It is also an after-work hangout for many local executives. For a quieter spot, Greys offers cocktails in a less bustling atmosphere.

For those who wish to stay fit during their stay, the Sheraton has a complete health club with all the necessary equipment, and a swimming pool which is heated year-round.

Auckland is New Zealand's largest city and commercial center and offers many things to see and do. The hotel is minutes from shopping and financial districts and an easy walk to beautiful parks and gardens. Minutes away are beaches and harbors. The city is also a perfect base from which to explore New Zealand's snow capped mountains, lush valleys, crystal lakes and golden beaches.

Address: 83 Symonds St., P.O. Box 2771, Auckland 1
Phone: 0-9-379-5132, Fax: 64-9-377-9367, Telex: SHERAK NZ 60231
No. of Rooms: 407 **Suites:** 9
Room Rate: $$
Credit Cards: AmEx, DC, MC, JCB, Vs, AP
Services and Amenities: Parking, Laundry/dry cleaning, Currency exchange, Travel arrangements, Medical services, Babysitting, Duty-free shopping, TV, In-house movies, Minibar/refrigerator, ISD phone, Indiv. climate ctl., Coffee/tea making fac.
Room Service: 24 hours
Restaurant: Partington's, Steam Biscuit Factory
Bar: Rendezvous, Someplace Else
Business Facilities: Audio-visual, Secretarial, Fax/telex, Postal, Private office
Conference Rooms: 12, Capacity: 900
Sports Facilities: Pool, Health club, Sauna, Massage
Attractions: Victoria Park Market, botanical gardens, Underwater World, Auckland Harbour

MANDARIN ORIENTAL ~ MANILA

Opened in 1976 and completely refurbished in 1990, the magnificent 18-story Mandarin Oriental Manila stands in the heart of the Makati district, Manila's business and commercial center.

In the typical style of the Mandarin Oriental Hotel Group, which also runs the world-renowned Mandarin Hotel Hong Kong and Oriental Hotel Bangkok, the Mandarin Oriental Manila is truly one of Asia's grand modern hotels. The dramatic, sweeping lines of the circular lobby feature Italian marble and modern Oriental sculptures.

Guest rooms are elegantly appointed in cool shades of green and beige, with furniture of fine bleached wood, and feature spacious marble bathroom with built-in hair dryer, bedside controls for radio, T.V. and mood lighting, fully stocked mini-bar, security system and three international direct dial telephones. The Mandarin Suite, on the 18th floor, features two bedrooms and two marble baths, a circular living room, and a separate dining area overlooking a private pool.

Brasserie At L'Hirondelle specializes in French cuisine and fine wines in an elegant wood-panelled setting. Renowned classic guitarist Jose Valdez entertains in The Tivoli Grill, which serves up international cuisine and a la carte specialties. Tin Hau serves authentic Cantonese cuisine, including a versatile dim sum menu for lunch. Open from the crack of dawn to nearly midnight, The Brasserie offers a wide variety of food, including an excellent breakfast and international lunch buffet.

The Mandarin Oriental boasts one of the best Business Centers in Manila, and is an ideal place for a meeting or conference. The Ballroom, decorated in wood paneling and gold, can seat 650 for a banquet.

The hotel's swimming pool and full health spa offer the ultimate in relaxation, especially after a busy day of shopping in the nearby Makati Commercial Center. Tennis, squash and golf can be arranged at Metro Manila's exclusive sports and country clubs. You may wish to pursue a gambling adventure in Manila's casino. Just a short 10-minute walk away lies department stores, boutiques, restaurants, and theaters.

Address: 1299 Makati Ave., P.O. Box 1038, Manila, 3117
Phone: (2) 816-3601, Fax: (2) 817-2472, Telex: 63756 MANDA PN, Cable: MANDAHOTEL, MANILA
No. of Rooms: 468 **Suites:** 20
Room Rate: $$$
Credit Cards: AmEx, DC, MC, JCB, Visa
Services and Amenities: Concierge, Airport transfer, Car hire, Laundry/dry cleaning, Currency exchange, Travel desk, Barber/beauty shop, Gift shop, Medical/dental, Babysitting, Satellite TV, Minibar, IDD phones, Indiv. climate ctl., In-room safe, Fruit basket, Hair-dryer, Comp. newspaper
Room Service: 24 hours
Restaurant: Tivoli Grill, Tin Hau, The Brasserie
Bar: Captain's Bar
Business Facilities: Audio-visual, Secretarial, Fax/telex/cable, Private offices, Postal
Conference Rooms: 7, Capacity: 1,000
Sports Facilities: Pool, Health club, Sauna, Massage, Tennis, Golf, Aerobic classes, Scuba diving
Attractions: Shopping, casino, historic walled city, jeepney rides

THE MANILA HOTEL

An address of prestige. That is the reputation The Manila Hotel has enjoyed since its opening in 1912. Elegance, tradition, and over 75 years of history combine to make this one of the outstanding hotels in Asia. Located on Manila's shoreline, on the main boulevard, just 20 minutes from the airport, The Manila Hotel is close to shops, restaurants, and nightclubs. Upon entering the hotel, you'll find yourself in an elegant and stately lobby, with pillars, arches, and vaulted ceilings graced by elegant brass chandeliers.

All rooms and suites offer panoramic views of Manila Bay, the Walled City of Intramuros, or Rizal Park. Each spacious accommodation has a distinctive decor, which might include a four-poster bed, wicker chairs and night-tables reminiscent of Filipino-Spanish days, as well as luxurious amenities. There are also 64 marvelous suites. The MacArthur Club on the executive floor provides additional business amenities and services.

Seven restaurants, two bars, and a discotheque, provide sumptuous dining and entertainment. For example, the Champagne Room offers elegant French food and romantic dancing to an 11-string ensemble. At Maynila you can enjoy continental and Filipino cuisine in art nouveau decor and nightly Filipino music and dancing. The Cowrie Grill, with unique shell-covered walls, serves succulent steaks and seafood dishes. For light meals and snacks, you can visit Cafe Ilang-Ilang. The Tap Room Bar is the perfect place for drinks and refreshments, with its colorful Tiffany-style bay window.

The Manila Hotel's 13 function rooms can serve almost any size group. The Fiesta Pavilion can seat 1,300 for a banquet, or hold 2,000 for a reception. The Executive Services Center can cater to any executive need.

Outstanding recreational opportunities are offered through the hotel's Bay Club: a pool with swim-up bar, tennis, squash, sauna, gym, steam bath, massage, whirlpool, state-of-the art exercise equipment, and putting green. Just across the street is Club Intramuros, a golf club whose picturesque 18-hole course weaves around the historic Walled City built 400 years ago by Spanish Conquistadores.

Address: Rizal Park, P.O. Box 307, Manila, 3117
Phone: 47-00-11, Fax: 02-471-124, Telex: 63496 MHOTEL MANILHOTEL
No. of Rooms: 570 **Suites:** 64
Room Rate: $$
Credit Cards: All major
Services and Amenities: Travel arrangements, TV, VCR, In-house movies, Radio, Minibar, IDD phone, Indiv. climate ctl.
Room Service: 24 hours
Restaurant: Champagne Room, Cowrie, Cafe Ilang-Ilang, Maynila
Bar: Tap Room Bar, Pool Bar
Business Facilities: Audio-visual, Secretarial, Simult. translation, Printing
Conference Rooms: 10, Capacity: 1,800
Sports Facilities: Pool, Full health spa, Game room, Squash, Tennis, 6-hole putting green
Location: Rizal Park
Attractions: Walled city of Manila, shopping, museums, galleries

THE DYNASTY

Situated on the bustling Orchard Road, The Dynasty Singapore graces the city skyline with its spectacular 33-story octagonal tower, reminiscent of a Chinese pagoda. In the three-story lobby, the focal point is two enormous walls of Thai teak wood carvings. Consisting of 24 panels, each 42 feet high, the awe-inspiring walls depict, in relief, 400 to 4,000 years of Chinese history and well-known legends.

The theme of The Dynasty, a mix of Western functionality and Oriental opulence, is also carried throughout the 400 guest rooms. Warm woods, satin curtains, laquered paintings, marble, and oriental artworks appoint each room. Amenities include stocked mini-bar, color TV, direct dial telephones, and room safes.

Guests at The Dynasty can savor a variety of foods. For local food that even the locals talk about, the Golden Dew Coffee House is open 24 hours a day. The "beef kway teow" and "hae mee" soup are a must. The Stroller's Sidewalk Cafe is the open-air cafe where many guests watch the world go by. The "watering hole" is the handsomely designed Bill Bailey's Bar. The premier French restaurant, Truffles at The Dynasty, provides delightful French fare and an excellent selection of wines. Supervised by a 2-star Michelin chef, Truffles most celebrated entree is Scottish Lamb Saddle Renaissance, and for dessert, Hot Orange Souffle with Grand Marnier sauce. Chinese food lovers will appreciate the Tang Court Cantonese Gourmet Restaurant.

A fully-equipped Business Centre caters to all needs of the business traveler. The Dynasty Ballroom, fronted by two dramatic carved rosewood doors, opens out to a foyer and seats 600 comfortably.

Workout and/or relaxation are easily obtained at the cardio-fitness center, complete with fitness consultants, fully-equipped gymnasium, sauna, and steambath. The Willow Garden Pool is a calm place to sip jasmine tea, swim, sunbathe, or enjoy a poolside snack. Patterned after an ancient Chinese palace garden, the pool area is surrounded by waterfalls, Chinese pavilions and a rock garden. For recreation outside of the hotel, visit over 20 shopping centers within walking distance. The Botanic Gardens, National Museum, and Singapore handicraft center are all nearby.

Address: 320 Orchard Rd., 0923
Phone: 734-9900, Fax: 733-5251, Telex: DYNTEL RS 36633, Cable: DYNASTY SINGAPORE
No. of Rooms: 400 **Suites:** 21
Room Rate: $$
Credit Cards: AmEx, DC, JCB, MCh, Visa
Services and Amenities: Car rental, Airport limousine, Parking, Laundry, Valet service, Currency exchange, Tour desk, Barber/beauty shop, Medical services, Babysitting, TV, In-house movies, Radio, Minibar/refrigerator, DD phone, Indiv. climate ctl., In-room safe, Coffee/tea making fac., Hairdryer, Desk
Room Service: 24 hours
Restaurant: Tang Court, Truffles, Golden Dew
Bar: Bill Bailey's, Lobby
Business Facilities: Secretarial, Fax/telex/cable, Postal
Conference Rooms: 7, Capacity: 800
Sports Facilities: Pool, Fitness center, Sauna, Steambath

GOODWOOD PARK HOTEL

The Goodwood Park, a national treasure with a long and illustrious history, was first built as the exclusive Teutonia Club in 1900 and became a hotel after World War I. Situated on a beautiful 11-acre garden, the three-story Goodwood Park stands on a small hill just off Orchard Road in Singapore's prime residential and shopping district. For travelers seeking a haven from high-rises, this is the place.

The Goodwood Park's 235 rooms are all spacious, with comfortable sitting and working areas. Extravagantly furnished, the rooms combine Old World elegance with modern luxury amenities. Soft pastel shades create a relaxing atmosphere. The most classic rooms are in the original building, but the new garden rooms have the advantage of opening onto the two swimming pools. The Brunei Suite, a favorite of the Sultan of Brunei, is located in the tower and enjoys its own private lift. With beautiful furnishings, archways, columns, a rooftop garden, and private sauna, it is often called one of the most beautiful suites east of Suez.

Because the Goodwood Park is a small hotel, its service is superb. It is also reputed for its fine restaurants, whose cuisines range from Japanese, to Szechuan, to Scottish specialties and afternoon tea. The Gordon Grill is a popular place for guests and local business executives. Min Jiang Sichuan Restaurant and Garden Seafood Restaurant is known for its excellent Sichuan cuisine and seafood specialties. Should all rooms at the legendary Goodwood Park be booked before you arrive in Singapore, it is still worthwhile to dine at this famous landmark.

For luxurious meeting events, the lovely Tudor Room can hold up to 400 people. There are four other meeting rooms for smaller gatherings.

The two swimming pools, set amid the flowering gardens, offer relaxation and exercise. Orchard Road, just a short distance from the hotel, boasts prestigious international boutiques and shopping malls.

Address: 22 Scotts Rd., 0922
Phone: 737-7411, 800-421-0536,
Fax: 732-8558, Telex: RS24377
GOODTEL, Cable: GOODWOOD
No. of Rooms: 235 **Suites:** 112
Room Rate: $$$$
Credit Cards: AmEx, DC, CB, JCB,
EnR, V
Services and Amenities: Car hire,
Laundry, Tour services, Barber/beauty shop, Gift shop, Babysitting, TV, In-house movies, Radio,
Minibar, IDD phone, Indiv. climate
ctl.
Room Service: 24 hours
Restaurant: Chang Jiang, Gordon
Grill, Shima
Bar: Highland Bar, Lobby Bar
Business Facilities: Audio-visual,
Secretarial, Fax/telex/cable, Translation, Business center
Conference Rooms: 5, Capacity:
300
Sports Facilities: Pools
Location: Shopping district
Attractions: Shopping, entertainment

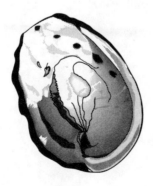

THE MANDARIN SINGAPORE

Offering "service in the tradition of emperors," the twin-towered Mandarin Singapore soars 40 stories high above Orchard Road, Singapore's fashionable shopping, tourist and entertainment district. Guests are greeted by turbaned doormen as they enter the main lobby, an expansive room graced with ceilings of gold leaf, walls of white and black marble, and touches of plush red. A crystal waterfall cascades from the ceiling and a gigantic marble frieze by a famous Chinese sculptor occupies an entire wall.

All the guestrooms at the Mandarin Singapore offer delightful views of the city or harbor. Those on the upper floors overlook parts of Malaysia and Indonesia, as well. Rooms are restful and charming, with soft colors and furnishing made from regional materials, such as cane and ramin wood. Of the hotel's 59 suites, five are presidential suites, each luxuriously furnished in a unique style. The Mandarin Suite, for example, features carved wood paneling, with the red carpeting and golden touches set off by rich hues of teak. The Japanese Suite, in contrast, emphasizes simplicity and tranquility, featuring pale gold and beige, with rosewood furnishings. The Persian Suite demands attention, with its four-poster canopied bed in midnight blue, trimmed with gold, and table lamps studded with semi-precious stones.

For a dining experience as grandiose as the Presidential Suites, reach for the Top of the M. Take in views of Singapore, Malaysia and Indonesia in this revolving restaurant, while dining on fine continental cuisine. The Stables, an English-style grill room on the hotel's fifth level, serves up all the old favorites, such as traditional steak and kidney pie and oxtail stew, paired with full bodied sherries and wines. Japanese delicacies are featured in Tsuru-no-ya, an intimate room seating only 35. And Beijing cuisine is the specialty at the Pine Court, where Peking Duck and Baked Tench are served amidst silk paintings and intricately carved woodwork.

A 24-hour business center, free shuttles to and from the financial district and the Botanic Gardens, a health club, and tennis and squash courts, are among some of the additional amenities the Mandarin Singapore has to offer.

Address: 333 Orchard Rd., 0923, P.O. Box 135, 9123
Phone: (65) 737-4411, 800-228-6800, Fax: (65) 732-2361, Telex: RS 21528 MANOTEL, Cable: MANRINOTEL
No. of Rooms: 1,200 **Suites:** 59
Room Rate: $$$
Credit Cards: AmEx, DC, JCB, MCh, Visa
Services and Amenities: Shuttles, Airport limousine, Valet parking, Safe deposit fac., Currency exchange, Travel desk, Barber/beauty shop, Shopping arcade, Medical clinic, Babysitting, TV, In-house movies, Minibar, IDD phones, Indiv. climate ctl., Hairdryer, Comp. newspaper
Room Service: 24 hours
Restaurant: Belvedere, Chatterbox, New Tsuru-No-Ya
Bar: Clipper, Kasbah
Business Facilities: Audio-visual, Secretarial, Fax/telex/cable, Copying, Printing, Postal, Message desk
Conference Rooms: 13, Capacity: 2,500
Sports Facilities: Pool, Health center, Sauna, Steam, Massage, Gym, Jogging, Squash, Tennis, Putting green, Sundeck, Cabanas
Attractions: Orchard Road, Botanic Gardens, Shenton Way

MARINA MANDARIN

Since its opening in 1987, the Marina Mandarin Singapore has been a favorite, especially among business travelers. The hotel is located in Marina Square, Southeast Asia's newest and largest shopping and entertainment complex. Built around an airy 21-story atrium, the hotel enjoys natural lighting in its reception area and hallways overlook ingthe atrium.

Accommodations combine the elegance of the East with the modern amenities of the West. Every room offers a unobstructed view of the harbor or the city skyline from its private balcony. The fully-marbled bathrooms feature twin wash basins, long tubs, telephones, and hairdryers. The top two floors have been especially designed for business travelers. The Marina View Suites offer either one or two bedrooms and parlor.

The hotel houses three excellent restaurants, two bars and an unique discotheque. The Brasserie Tatler serves popular Singaporean, Japanese and Western dishes. At the House of Blossoms, refined Chinese cuisine is served in private dining rooms, which are separated by carved screens. The Cricketer, an English-style pub, serves imported ales and light snacks. Set amid one of the world's largest open-air art galleries, the Atrium Lounge offers a relaxed yet classy atmosphere for enjoying drinks and snacks.

The hotel's Business Center provides a full range of secretarial and communication facilities. The Ballroom, the largest of the conference rooms, can hold 1,000 for cocktails or 800 theater-style. Simultaneous translations and state-of-the-art audio visual facilities are available.

Recreational opportunities include an outdoor pool, two squash courts, four tennis courts, and a fitness center, complete with gymnasium, sauna, and jacuzzi. The handsome and rich Reading Room contains a games room, billiards room, small theater, and many other interesting things to see. The shopping-inclined will delight in the four department stores and 250-shop mall found within the hotel and the Marina Square complex.

Address: P.O. Box 1217, 6 Raffles Blvd., Marina Square, 0103
Phone: (65) 338-3388, Fax: (65) 339-4977, Telex: RS22299 MARINA, Cable: MARINAMAND
No. of Rooms: 575 **Suites:** 33
Room Rate: $$$
Credit Cards: All major
Services and Amenities: Concierge, Limousine service, Parking, Laundry, Valet, Safe deposit fac., Currency exchange, Barber/beauty shop, Medical clinic, TV, Minibar, IDD phones, Indiv. climate ctl., Hairdryer
Room Service: 24 hours
Restaurant: Ristorante Bologna, House of Blossoms
Bar: Cricketer, Atrium, Reading Room
Business Facilities: Audio-visual, Fax/telex/cable, Secretarial, Simult. translation, Copying, Courier
Conference Rooms: 12, Capacity: 1,000
Sports Facilities: Pool, Health club, Sauna, Massage, Gym, Jogging, Squash, Tennis, Aerobics
Location: Marina Square
Attractions: City Hall, Cricket Club, Esplanade, Merlion Street, Orchard Road

OMNI MARCO POLO HOTEL

Located in the embassy district on four acres of landscaped grounds, the Omni Marco Polo Hotel is within walking distance of the shopping, entertainment, and business centers of Orchard Road, yet away from the bustle of the tourist belt. Because of its location and service, the Marco Polo Hotel has earned a reputation as being one of the top hotels in the world, especially among business travelers. Upon entering the 12-story hotel, you will find yourself in an elegant lobby, decorated in marble, European-style draperies, and Austrian hand-etched lanterns hanging from the ceiling.

All guest accommodations are furnished with king- or queen-size beds, a large executive desk, and comfortable armchairs. Guests can control lighting, music, air-conditioning and television from bedside. The Continental Wing accommodations resemble rooms of a fine European residence and exude an understated elegance. The terrace rooms open onto a private patio from which you can walk directly to the pool. Deluxe suites offer luxurious space for entertaining guests.

Le Duc is the premier restaurant of the hotel. Continental haute cuisine, complemented by a wide selection of vintage wines, is served in an elegant setting. For French provincial cooking, visit the charming, boulevard-style La Brasserie. Just off the main lobby, the Marco Polo Lounge is a popular place to enjoy drinks, conversation and nightly musical entertainment.

Several function rooms are available for conferences and banquets. The San Marco Room, reminescent of Venetian splendor, can graciously host 150 for a banquet. The hotel's Business Center provides all the necessary support for the individual business traveler or group.

The hotel is close to the Botanic Gardens and the famed shopping and entertainment area of Orchard and Scotts Roads. After a conference or a busy day in Singapore, you might enjoy a workout at the hotel's Clark Hatch Physical Fitness Center or take a dip in the outdoor pool. Later still, you might descend to the lower level and visit The Club, a disco with art deco ambiance.

Address: Tanglin Rd., 1024
Phone: 4747141, Fax: 4710521, Telex: 21476 OMPS RS, Cable: OMNIMPS
No. of Rooms: 545 **Suites:** 58
Room Rate: $$
Credit Cards: All major
Services and Amenities: Limousine/car rental, Valet parking, Laundry/dry cleaning, Safe deposit fac., Currency exchange, Valet service, Barber/beauty shop, Shopping arcade, Medical office, Babysitting, Florist, TV, In-house movies, Radio, Minibar, IDD phone, A/C, Hairdryer
Room Service: 24 hours
Restaurant: Le Duc, La Brasserie, Parrots
Bar: Marco Polo Lounge, The Club
Business Facilities: Audio-visual, Secretarial, Fax/telex/cable, Translation, Copying, Postal, Computers, Reference library
Conference Rooms: 10, Capacity: 300
Sports Facilities: Pool, Health club, Sauna, Massage
Location: Tanglin District
Attractions: Botanic Gardens, Orchard/Scotts Road shopping, museum, Sentosa Island, zoo

THE ORIENTAL SINGAPORE

The Oriental Singapore, a 21-story triangular hotel built around an 18-story atrium, is located in Marina Square, Southeast Asia's largest and newest shopping and entertainment complex. The hotel is in a prime location overlooking beautiful Marina Bay.

The Oriental's guest rooms are beautifully decorated, with soft tones of peach and green, and some original artworks. All have color television, writing desk, individual direct dial telephones, private bar offering a full range of liquor in quart bottles, refrigerator, and a bedside panel with built-in clock and lighting. There are 62 spacious suites with a variety of layouts, each individually designed to reflect Asian, animal, and maritime themes. All bathrooms are luxuriously finished in Italian marble and feature separate shower enclosure, king-size bath, and hairdryer. Service is emphasized at this hotel, and each floor has its own room attendants.

The main dining room is Fourchettes, serving top notch Continental cuisine, complemented by excellent wines. Szechuan and Hunan specialties are offered at the Cherry Garden. One can enjoy light meals at Cafe Palm. According to *The Straits Times*, The Oriental's L'Aperitif Lounge serves the best afternoon tea in Singapore. Light entertainment and dancing, along with drinks, can be found at the Captain's Bar.

The fan-shaped Oriental Ballroom can accommodate 800 for cocktails and 700 theater-style. Seven elegantly decorated banquet suites are available for smaller groups. The hotel has a complete Business Center with seven private offices where meetings or interviews can be held.

The Health Center features a pool with underwater sound system, sauna, exercise area, hot and cold spa, and massage. A health buffet breakfast is served every morning at the Pool Terrace. In addition to the two tennis courts, many guests enjoy jogging on the track along the nearby waterfront promenade.

Address: 5 Raffles Blvd., Marina Square, 0103
Phone: (65) 339-0066, 800-526-6566, Fax: (65) 339-9537, Telex: RS29117 ORSIN, Cable: ORSINHOTEL
No. of Rooms: 518 **Suites:** 61
Room Rate: $$$
Credit Cards: All major
Services and Amenities: Concierge, Limousine/car hire, Valet parking, Laundry/dry cleaning, Valet service, Currency exchange, Shopping arcade, Medical services, Babysitting, TV, In-house movies, Radio, Minibar/refrigerator, IDD phones, Indiv. A/C ctl., In-room safe, Hairdryer
Room Service: 24 hours
Restaurant: Fourchettes, Cherry Garden, Cafe Palm
Bar: Captain's, L'Aperitif
Business Facilities: Secretarial, Fax/telex/cable, Translation, Offices, Computers, Postal
Conference Rooms: 7, Capacity: 1,000
Sports Facilities: Pool, Health center, Sauna, Spa pools, Gym, Jogging track, Squash, Tennis, Arrangements for Golf, Windsurfing, Fishing
Attractions: Shenton Way, Satay Club, Victoria Theatre, Chinatown, Esplanade, Change Alley

RAFFLES HOTEL

The Raffles Hotel is a traveler's paradise in the heart of Singapore's business district. Its unparalleled service, classical architecture and lush tropical gardens have made it a favorite home away from home for kings, queens, film stars and writers. Somerset Maugham stayed often. It is said he spent his mornings working under a frangipani tree in the Hotel's famous Palm Court, turning bits of gossip and scandal overheard at dinner parties into his famous stories. He wrote, "Raffles stands for all the fables of the exotic East."

Established in 1887, Raffles embodies all the grace and grandeur of its elegant past. A $160 million restoration was completed in 1991, resurrecting the ambiance of the Hotel's glory days from the turn of the century to the 1930's. Meticulous attention has been paid to historical and architectural detail. Many of the original furnishings and artifacts still remain.

Upon entering their spacious suite, guests step into a bygone era of absolute comfort and old world opulence. Fourteen-foot moulded ceilings arch gracefully above elegant period furnishings. Exquisite oriental carpets dress the teak, marble and tile floors. Raffles offers a wide variety of fine and casual dining. Traditional tiffin curries can be savored in the renowned Tiffin Room, which also offers an informal buffet. The Tudor-style Elizabethan grill offers international fare highlighted by English specialties. Visit the Long Bar, where the famous Singapore Sling was created. In the Writers Bar, a wall of bookcases is filled with the signed, hardbound volumes of first editions from the visiting authors who are part of Raffles' literary heritage.

Designated a National Monument, Raffles Hotel has long been considered one of the world's grand hotels. The hotel's museum chronicles its romantic past as a world center during the Golden Age of Travel. Its 19th century style theater playhouse features audio-visual and cultural presentations.

Address: 1 Beach Road, 0718
Phone: 337-1886, Fax: 339-7650,
Telex: RS 20396 RINTL
No. of Suites: 104
Room Rate: $$$$
Credit Cards: AmEx, DC, JCB, MC, Visa
Services and Amenities: Concierge, Airport limousine, Theater hall, Hotel museum, Barber/beauty shop, Shopping arcade, Ceiling fans, Indiv. A/C ctl.
Room Service: 24 hours
Restaurant: Raffle's Grill, Empress Room, Tiffin
Bar: Writers Bar, Long Bar
Business Facilities: Secretarial, Fax/telex, Copying, Postal, Business center
Conference Rooms: 12, Capacity: 1,200
Sports Facilities: Pool, Health club, Sauna, Massage
Location: Business district
Attractions: Raffles Hotel Museum, Orchard Road shopping

SHANGRI-LA HOTEL SINGAPORE

Shangri-La Singapore is repeatedly ranked among the world's best hotels. Situated on 12 quiet acres of landscaped greenery, yet only a 5-minute walk from bustling Orchard Road, the Shangri-La Singapore features landscape as a major attraction. Lush greenery, garden areas, and the refreshing use of streams, waterfalls, reflecting pools, and fountains create a unique ambiance.

The Shangri-La is comprised of three wings. The 24-story Main Building has over 500 beautifully appointed rooms, all with balconies. The presidential Singapore Suite and five two-bedroom theme suites are also located in this wing.

The 9-story Garden Wing is one of the most popular hotel annexes in the world. The rooms are built around a spectacular open air atrium, which contains over one hundred varieties of tropical plants and flowers. Decorated in Oriental style, each room opens onto a private balcony, from which deep pink bougainvillea cascade.

The 17-story Valley Wing has 24 suites and 112 deluxe guest rooms. This exclusive wing has its own driveway, entrance and registration area. Adjoining the lobby is the semi-circular Summit Room, a VIP conference room for 60.

The hotel's food and beverage outlets are located in the Main Building. Shang Palace offers fine Chinese cuisine in a setting reminiscent of an emperor's palace. For gourmet Western specialties, visit the Restaurant Latour. Nadaman is an excellent Japanese restaurant, specializing in kaiseki. For informal dining, the Waterfall Cafe and 24-hour Coffee Garden are casual and offer tempting dishes. Drinking spots include the Peacock Bar and the Lobby Court.

The hotel is well equipped to handle small and large gatherings. The Island Ballroom, which can accommodate 1,400 theater-style, is the largest of the function rooms. A complete Business Center and Banquet Convention office provides full support for any business or meeting planning.

For relaxation, you can try out the tennis courts, squash courts, putting green, and health club. The health club offers state-of-the-art exercise equipment, sauna, pool, and health bar. A complimentary morning bus shuttle takes joggers and walkers to and from the nearby botanic gardens.

Address: 22 Orange Grove Rd., 1025
Phone: 737 3644, Fax: 733 7220, Telex: RS 21505, Cable: SHANGRILA
No. of Rooms: 750 **Suites:** 60
Room Rate: $$
Credit Cards: All major
Services and Amenities: Airport limousine, Parking, TV, In-house movies, Radio, Minibar/refrigerator, Indiv. climate ctl.
Room Service: 24 hours
Restaurant: Restaurant Latour, Shang Palace, Nadaman
Bar: Peacock Bar, Lobby Lounge
Business Facilities: Secretarial, Fax/telex/cable, Translation, Copying, Courier, Reference library, 24hr business center
Conference Rooms: 13, Capacity: 1,400
Sports Facilities: Pool, Health center, Squash, Tennis, 3-hole putting green
Attractions: Botanic Gardens, National Museum

YORK HOTEL

Resplendent in its multi-million dollar renovation, the York Hotel's decor is classic European style with a touch from the French Louis XV era. This accent can be noted in the recessed ceiling lights, period furnishings, and crystal chandeliers. The hotel's two entrances, via Scotts Road and Mount Elizabeth, open to an expansive lobby where elegant maple wood panels line the walls and pillars, and Italian marble spills out from under your feet.

All 400 guest rooms and suites offer modern amenities, luxurious fittings and spacious roomy beds, including direct dial phones and stocked minibars. The Tower Suites offer the utmost privacy for the business traveler, and feature a working area complete with desk, lounge and bar counter.

For exquisite Thai Teochew cuisine, you will want to dine at the Zen Restaurant. The White Rose Cafe is more casual and offers excellent local and western fares. Those who enjoy a perfect cup of coffee or tea will delight in the Coffee Bar, housing the finest coffee blends, teas, and local snacks. For entertainment, the Carriage Bar is a modern pub with live bands and state-of-the-art karaoke facilities.

Six differently-styled function rooms can accommodate any type of gathering. The rooms, elegantly appointed with English carpets, American wallpapers, curtains, imported chandeliers and furniture, are excellent settings for successful meetings. The business center can take care of all business needs.

For relaxation, the swimming pool and Nautilus Health Center, with professional instructors, are available.

Conveniently located in the heart of the city, York Hotel is only a short distance from the central business district and a 5-minute walk to Orchard Road, the main entertainment and shopping belt of the city.

Address: 21 Mount Elizabeth, 0922
Phone: 7370511, Fax: 7321217, Telex: RS 21683 YOTEL
No. of Rooms: 400
Room Rate: $$
Credit Cards: All major
Services and Amenities: Parking, Laundry, Safe deposit fac. Shopping arcade, Drugstore, Babysitting, TV, In-house movies, Minibar, IDD phone, A/C, Coffee/tea making fac., Hairdryer
Room Service: 24 hours
Restaurant: Zen Restaurant, White Rose, Coffee Bar
Bar: Carriage Bar
Business Facilities: Business center
Conference Rooms: 6, Capacity: 800
Sports Facilities: Pool, Health center, Jacuzzi
Attractions: Orchard Road, shopping

HOTEL LOTTE/LOTTE WORLD

Hotel Lotte is Seoul's largest and most sophisticated hotel, housing more than 1,484 rooms and 128 suites. Furnishings throughout Hotel Lotte reproduce an era of classical magnificence and old world comfort. Marble floors, luxuriously upholstered couches and armchairs, fresh flowers, gold fixtures, porcelain figures, crystal chandeliers, and ceiling artworks emulate the great palaces of Europe. Although the hotel is large, great care has been taken to ensure that all areas of the hotel provide personal attention and an international level of service.

Accommodations feature deluxe amenities, including extras, such as hairdryer, bath robe, video service, and evening chocolate. Rooms are decorated in a classical period style. The Royal Suite and Presidential Suite, lavishly appointed in Rococo style, are favorites for royalty and heads of state.

Hotel Lotte houses more than 31 restaurants, lounges and nightclubs. Schoenbrunn, the hotel's signature restaurant, is described as "high", not only for it's 35-floor view, but also for its acclaimed Continental "haute cuisine". Lovers of Italian cuisine congregate at Venezia for hearty fare in a merry atmosphere. Other eating options include the hotel's buffet restaurants and cafes. The cuisines of Asia are also represented by two Korean, two Japanese, and one Chinese restaurant.

The Executive Salons provide business facilities and bilingual assistants. Sixteen impressive meeting rooms, from extravagant Rococo to elegant, make for unforgettable meetings. Even conferences of 3,000 requiring simultaneous translation in eight languages can be handled by Hotel Lotte's experienced staff.

After a hard day, ease away stress and aches by stepping into the health club and indulging in a sauna, massage, or dip in the indoor pool. The extensive sports center features a golf clinic, squash courts, a track, a bowling alley, and fitness equipment.

Situated in the heart of the principal financial, shopping and entertainment district, Hotel Lotte is also near historical landmarks and tourist attractions, such as Toksu Palace, Namdaemun Gate, Namsan and the National Museum. Adjoining the hotel, the 10-story Lotte Department Store features an extensive Duty Free Shop.

Address: 1, Sogong-Dong, Chung-Ku CPOBx 3500, Seoul, 100-070
Phone: (82-02) 771-10, 800-225-6883, Fax: (82-02)752-3758, Telex: K23533/4 LOTTHO
No. of Rooms: 1,484 **Suites:** 120
Room Rate: $$$$
Credit Cards: AmEx, JCB, DC, MC, Visa
Services and Amenities: Concierge, Comp. airport pickup Shopping arcade, TV, VCP, Indiv. climate ctl.
Restaurant: The Schoenbrunn, 22 others
Bar: Windsor, Bobby London
Business Facilities: Audio-visual, Secretarial, Fax, Simult. translation, Copying, Business library
Conference Rooms: 15, Capacity: 3,000
Sports Facilities: Pool, Full health spa, Sauna, Massage, Gym, Jogging track, Indoor golf driving range
Attractions: Toksu Palace, Secret Garden, Namsan Mountain, Han River

WESTIN CHOSUN

Seoul's Westin Chosun is an elegant retreat in the midst of a rapidly growing metropolis; a 20-story landmark known for its luxurious ambiance and irreproachable service. The philosophy of the hotel is that guests should be "treated like Kings." No doubt this royal treatment is what attracted many dignitaries to stay here while visiting Seoul.

In the hotel's beautiful garden is "The Temple of Heaven." Now a historic monument, this much revered temple was built in 1897 in the style of a pagoda, and stands on what was once Korea's "most sacred ground." The lobby is sophisticated and intimate; striking Oriental murals adorn the walls and elevator doors above cool marble floors.

Hotel services have been superbly designed for the business traveller; executive packages offer additional amenities, including an Executive Club Concierge, complimentary buffet breakfast and cocktail hour, free access to the Fitness Center, premium quality toiletries and amenities, luxurious terry robe and bathroom slippers, and turndown service with complimentary Ginseng Jelly. Executive Club members receive a complimentary departure gift, as well. Spacious guestrooms and suites are handsomely appointed in pastel shades and feature private voice mail systems. A non-smoking floor is available.

Dining at The Westin Chosin is always a delight. The Ninth Gate Restaurant, with its tranquil atmosphere and view of the Temple of Heaven, serves exquisite international gourmet cuisine. O'Kim's Irish Pub & Sports Bar offers Guiness draught, the finest selection of beer in town and live music from an Irish band.

Take a refreshing dip at the Poolside Terrace, where snacks, cocktails and an evening barbecue are available. For an interesting day excursion, the Sejong Cultural Center, Toksugung Palace and Modern Art Museum are close by.

Address: C.P.O. Box 3706, Seoul 100
Phone: (82-02) 7710500, Fax: (82-02) 7568848, Telex: CHOSUN K24256
No. of Rooms: 480 **Suites:** 17
Room Rate: $$$
Credit Cards: AmEx, DC, MC, JCB, CB, Vs
Services and Amenities: Concierge, Limousine/car hire, Parking, Laundry/Valet, Safe deposit fac., Currency exchange, Travel arrangements, Shopping arcade, Babysitting, Satellite TV, Minibar/refrigerator, IDD phone, Indiv. climate ctl., Desk, Voice mail
Room Service: 24 hours
Restaurant: Ninth Gate, Cafe Royale, Sushi-cho
Bar: O'Kim's Pub & Sports Bar
Business Facilities: Audio-visual, Secretarial, Fax/telex, Simult. translation, Copying, Postal, Internat'l courier
Conference Rooms: 5, Capacity: 950
Sports Facilities: Pool, Fitness center, Sauna
Attractions: Sejong Cultural Center, Toksugug Palace, Temple of Heaven

GALLE FACE HOTEL

Billed as "The Only Seaside Resort In the Heart of Colombo," Sri Lanka's Galle Face Hotel was established in 1864 and may be the oldest Grand Hotel in Asia. Extensive renovations have been carried out to upgrade the hotel, yet the architecture and decor retain the hotel's original splendor. The North Wing looks out onto the famous Galle Face Green, which was at one time used by the British for horseracing. Just beyond the palm studded grounds and saltwater swimming pool, guests sun themselves on the hotel's private beach. An ocean breeze sweeps through the light-filled lobby, where old world charm is enhanced by a fantastic collection of antique furnishings, an old-fashioned lift, and delightful marble bird-baths in which frangipani blossoms float.

There is no piped in music at the Galle Face Hotel, no discotheque or stand up bar; only the sound of the Indian Ocean lapping on the shore and the happy chirping of the sparrows that nest in the upper rafters. For more than 125 years, the hotel's incomparable service (the employee to room ratio is over three to one) and delicious tranquility have attracted an impressive list of royalty and celebrities.

The Royal Suites are known worldwide for their luxury and exceptional spaciousness, lovely marble bathrooms and panoramic views of the ocean. The King Emperor Suite is one of the largest and finest deluxe suites to be found anywhere. Ocean-view, jumbo-sized apartments are superbly outfitted.

Restaurants at The Galle Face Hotel feature a fine selection of European and Oriental delicacies. The Royal Room, once the hotel's ballroom, is now a dining room. The Terrace Restaurant, overlooking the pool, serves cool drinks and light meals.

The shopping village offers a wide selection of Sri Lanka's fabulous gemstones, curios, handicrafts and clothing. Beyond the hotel, Sri Lanka, with its rich history and mystique, beckons the traveler to explore.

Address: P.O. Box 63, 2 Kollupitiya Rd., Colombo 3
Phone: 54-1010
No. of Rooms: 70 **Suites:** 21
Room Rate: $
Services and Amenities: Butler service, Limousine service, Laundry, Shopping arcade, Phone, A/C
Room Service: 24 hours
Restaurant: Galle Face Restaurant
Bar: Veranda
Business Facilities: Secretarial, Fax/telex, Copying

HOTEL CEYLON INTER-CONTINENTAL

Some people say that the location of the Hotel Ceylon Inter-Continental is the best piece of real estate in Colombo. Not only does this hotel overlook the ocean, it is also merely steps away from government offices, businesses, banks, airline offices and shopping centers.

Its 250 rooms and suites have all the amenities, including color TV with in-house movies and 24-hour Reuters News Service. The spacious and elegant Presidential Suite on the 8th floor has a panoramic view of the Indian Ocean and the city.

The Hotel Ceylon can host up to 500 persons for banquets and up to 800 persons for conferences. Its Business Center offers complete secretarial service with telex, fax, and photocopying facilities.

There are many recreational facilities at the hotel, including an outdoor swimming pool, and a full health spa with sauna and massage. The Sports Center has three glass-fronted, boarded floor, air conditioned squash courts and three synpave tennis courts. After a game of tennis or a swim, one might have a refreshing drink at the 100 Pipers Pub, a meal at the open-air Thananga Terrace, or a pizza at the open-air Pizzeria. Sultry breezes off the Indian Ocean can also be enjoyed at the Pearl Seafood Restaurant, a dinner spot with music. At rooftop level there is the Palms Roof Top Restaurant and Bar, offering buffet luncheons, evening dining and entertainment, and great views of the ocean and city. The Continental Club Casino has gambling along with dining. The 24-hour Emerald Tea and Coffee Shop offers an international menu highlighting Sri Lankan specialties.

Attention to friendly service has earned the Hotel Ceylon Inter-Continental the sobriquet "warmest heart in Colombo."

Address: 48 Janadhipathi Mawatha, Box 408, Colombo, 1
Phone: 21221, 26880, Fax: 547326, Telex: 21188, Cable: INHOTELCOR
No. of Rooms: 250 **Suites:** 26
Room Rate: $
Services and Amenities: Laundry, Valet service, Travel counter, Beauty salon, Shopping arcade, Drugstore, Casino, TV, In-house movies, Radio, Minibar/refrigerator, IDD phone, Indiv. climate ctl., Hairdryer
Room Service: 24 hours
Restaurant: Palms, Pearl Seafood, Pizzeria, Emerald
Bar: Aquamarine, 100 Pipers', Palms
Business Facilities: Secretarial, Fax/telex/cable, Translation, Copying, Meeting room, Library
Conference Rooms: 3, Capacity: 800
Sports Facilities: Pool, Full health spa, Sauna, Massage, 3 Tennis courts, 3 Squash courts
Location: Fort
Attractions: Shopping malls, bazaars, museums, Galle Face Green, Old Parliament Building

TAJ SAMUDRA HOTEL

Situated on Galle Face, Colombo's promenade along the Indian Ocean, is the beautiful Taj Sumadra Hotel. While located outside the heart of bustling Colombo, it is only 5 minutes away from the commercial district. The hotel is situated on 11 landscaped gardens.

Its 222 rooms are all air conditioned and have TV, in-house movies, piped music, and mini-bars. The front rooms have magnificent views of the beach and ocean, while the back rooms have views of the gardens and city. For maximum space and luxury, try the two-bedroom deluxe suites which offer a large living room, dining room, three bathrooms, service pantry and two balconies. The suites offer extra touches that make a visit so enjoyable: flowers, fruit basket, soap baskets, newspapers and magazines, and personalized stationery.

A variety of cuisine is available at the Taj Sumadra. Navratna offers Indian dishes, The Golden Dragon specializes in Chinese fare, and Cote D'Azur serves continental meals. Ports of Call is a charming 24-hour restaurant offering cuisines from different Asian and European countries, countries that took part in the spice trade of long ago. Aquarius, an open-air restaurant, serves succulent barbecued specialties. Temperatures in Colombo range from 26-31 degrees C. (73-88 degrees F.), making open-air dining delightful.

The Taj Sumadra can accommodate up to 350 for a conference. Secretarial service is available, along with a range of audio-visual equipment, including simultaneous translation facilities for French, German, and Japanese.

Other opportunities for relaxation are found at the swimming pool, at the health club which offers sauna, steam jacuzzi and massage, and at the tennis courts, squash courts and jogging track.

Visit Sri Lanka's beautiful zoological gardens, the nearby museum and art gallery, or enjoy shopping at Liberty Plaza.

Address: 25 Galle Face Centre Rd., Colombo, 3
Phone: 0941 546622, Fax: 0941 546348, Telex: 21729 TAJLAN CE, Cable: PALACE
No. of Rooms: 400 **Suites:** 28
Room Rate: $
Credit Cards: AmEx, CB, MC, Visa
Services and Amenities: Car rental, Laundry, Valet service, Currency exchange, Bank, Travel office, Barber/beauty shop, Shopping arcade, Doctor, TV, VCP, In-house movies, Radio, Minibar, IDD phone, Indiv. A/C ctl., Balconies
Room Service: 24 hours
Restaurant: Golden Restaurant, Rendezvous, Navaratna
Bar: Lobby
Business Facilities: Audio-visual, Secretarial, Fax/telex/cable, Translation, Copying, Postal
Conference Rooms: 4, Capacity: 350
Sports Facilities: Pool, Full health spa, Sauna, Jogging track, Squash, Tennis, 3-hole Golf, Casino
Location: Galle Face
Attractions: Zoological gardens, museum, Liberty Plaza shopping

HOTEL ROYAL TAIPEI

The centrally located Hotel Royal Taipei was designed by Paris-based specialists to capture the elegance of a stately European residence. Guests praise the hotel for its individualized service and warm, cheerful atmosphere. In the lobby, Italian white marble and sparkling Austrian crystal chandeliers rise three floors in a soft play of light. Guests can relax in true European style on the Mezzanine Floor, with its graceful white column archways and inviting wicker chairs.

Guest rooms are decorated with a bright but delicate floral motif, and have been designed to offer the best in traditional comfort and modern convenience. The interior of the Royal Suites is a French style in soft shades of green, grey and blue. Fine chinaware and contemporary artwork complement the comfortable modern and Oriental furnishings. All rooms have double doors for added privacy and quiet, and include turndown maid service twice a day.

Dining in Les Celebrites is an experience not to be missed. Delectables are served in the finest French tradition. A recent dinner featured Artichoke Salad with Pan-Fried Fattened Duck Liver, Grilled Quail Breast and Hazelnut Oil Dressing; Poached Sole Fillet, Red Wine Sauce with Clams and Bacon and Sauteed Spinach; and for dessert, a mouthwatering Hot Grand Marnier and Orange Tart, baked on the order, served with Chocolate Ice Cream.

The large rooftop pool offers a refreshing reprieve from busy city life. Guests can work out in the fully equipped gym at the Health Club, enjoy the sauna, or treat themselves to a relaxing massage. The hotel's lovely Greenhouse, located next to the pool, houses a lush botanical world of seasonal plants and flowers.

Address: 37-1 Chung Shan N. Rd., Sec. 2, Taipei, 10149
Phone: (02) 542-3266, Fax: (02) 543-4897, Telex: 23915 ROYALHTL, Cable: ROYALHTL
No. of Rooms: 203 **Suites:** 20
Room Rate: $$$
Credit Cards: All major
Services and Amenities: Airport transp., Limousine service, Valet parking, Barber/beauty shop, Shopping arcade, Tailor, Shoeshine, Satellite TV, In-house movies, Radio, Minibar/refrigerator, IDD phone, Indiv. climate ctl., Bathrobes, Comp. toiletries
Room Service: 24 hours
Restaurant: Les Celebrites, Ming Court, Nakayama
Bar: El Dore Bar, Lounge
Business Facilities: Secretarial, Fax/telex, Translation, Copying
Conference Rooms: 7, Capacity: 336
Sports Facilities: Pool, Health club, Sauna, Greenhouse
Location: Chung Shan district
Attractions: Palace Museum, shopping

LAI LAI SHERATON HOTEL TAIPEI

The Lai Lai Sheraton is centrally located in one of Taipei's busiest areas. Shopping, business, entertainment, cultural, and transportation centers are either a close walk or short taxi ride away.

Rising 18 stories, The Lai Lai Sheraton houses 705 guest rooms and suites. All accommodations include minibars (restocked daily with complimentary soft drinks), safe deposit boxes, in-room English movies, and daily turndown service.

Fourteen restaurants and bars each offers its own unique cuisine. The Antoine Room features classical French cuisine in opulent 19th-century surroundings, and the Pizza Pub serves up Italian pastas and pizzas baked in an authentic firewood oven. The cuisines of Asia are also well represented. The Chinese restaurants, decorated in the elaborate style of the Chinese dynasties, provide a backdrop for the sumptuous food presented by waitresses dressed in regional or traditional costumes. A wide range of Japanese dishes are prepared in traditional style in the hotel's Momoyama and Teppan-Yaki restaurants. For a mix of two continents, try the cozy Four Seasons Cafe, offering Western and Chinese favorites, and Hunan Garden, for savory Chinese cuisine, Western style. Night life centers around Le Bar and Lai Lai Disco Nightclub.

Banquet and convention facilities can handle up to 2,000 persons. The complete business center also offers professional secretarial services available in several languages.

The Lai Lai Sheraton has one of the most extensive recreational facilities in Taipei. The Lai Lai Executive Club features a fully equipped gymnasium, squash courts, an 80-meter rooftop jogging track, tennis and golf practice areas, a rooftop swimming pool, sauna, and massage.

For "in-house" shopping, The Lai Lai Sheraton has a shopping area of its own—two floors of 57 shops in a quietly cosmopolitan arcade, selling everything from designer handbags to oriental antiques. Other famous shopping areas are Haggler's Alley and the renowned Sogo Department Store. Cultural and historical attractions include the National Palace Museum and Martyrs Shrine.

Address: 12 Chung Hsiao E. Rd., Sec. 1, Taipei
Phone: (02) 321-5511, Fax: (02) 394-4240, Telex: 23939
No. of Rooms: 705 **Suites:** 72
Room Rate: $$$
Credit Cards: All major
Services and Amenities: Airport transport, Parking, Laundry/dry cleaning, Safe deposit fac., Currency exchange, Tour counter, Barber/beauty shop, Shopping arcade, Medical clinic, Babysitting, Satellite TV, In-house movies, Radio, Minibar/refrigerator, IDD phones, Indiv. climate ctl., In-room safe, Message light, Turndown service
Room Service: 24 hours
Restaurant: Antoine, Pizza, Jade Garden, Teppan Yaki
Bar: British Pub, Peacock, Lobby
Business Facilities: Secretarial, Telex/cable, Translation, Dow/AP news wires, Reference materials
Conference Rooms: 6, Capacity: 2,000
Sports Facilities: Pool, Full health spa, Sauna, Massage, Gym, Jogging track, Squash
Location: Commercial district
Attractions: National Palace Museum, Haggler's Alley, Snake Alley

RITZ TAIPEI HOTEL

At the Ritz Taipei, luxury and hospitality are tradition. Located in the center of a commercial district, The Ritz Taipei is just minutes from the domestic airport and major freeways, and 40 minutes from CKS international airport. A hotel limousine will pick you up at the airport. Upon arrival, there is no front desk check-in. Instead, you are shown straight to your room and welcomed by flowers, cake and a bottle of spirit. The atmosphere is intimate, and the decor throughout the hotel is reminiscent of the sophisticated French Art Deco era.

All rooms and suites have every amenity, including extras, such as, refrigerator, minibar, complimentary English movies, large writing desk, and floor safe. The bathrooms are superbly fitted with fine toiletries, toweling bathrobes, makeup mirrors, and hairdryers. Suites are more like luxury apartments—all beautifully decorated in the striking Art Deco motif. Every guest receives personalized stationary and name cards, as well as a complimentary fruit basket upon arrival.

Dining at any of the three Ritz Taipei restaurants is definitely an experience. La Brasserie is the only French Tiffany-designed bistro in town. A perfect place for a light meal or superb traditional fare, La Brasserie is *the* place to see and be seen. The Chinese Restaurant serves classic Hunan and Hangchow cuisine prepared traditionally by master chefs. Don't miss their celebrated dish, traditional pressed duck. Step into the romance of Paris in the 30's at Paris 1930. A selection of French delicacies and fine wines await you. Live music nightly complements such specialties as angler fish with sweet and sour pepper sauce. In Aldebaran, sip after-dinner drinks while listening to the keyboard maestro. Every in-house guest is extended an invitation to Ritzy Hour, a welcome cocktail party held Mondays, Wednesdays and Fridays.

For an invigorating workout or tension easing, guests can use the fully equipped health center. The Health Centre has a gym, jogging track, massage, open air whirlpool, sauna, sundeck, and weight lifting.

The Ritz Taipei is a relaxing hideaway for travelers when in the bustling city of Taipei.

Address: 155 Min Chuan E. Rd., Taipei, 10460
Phone: (02) 597-1234, Fax: (02) 596-9223, Telex: 27345 THERITZ
No. of Rooms: 204 **Suites:** 100
Room Rate: $$$
Credit Cards: AmEx, DC, JCB, MC, Visa
Services and Amenities: Concierge, Airport limousine, Valet parking, Laundry/dry cleaning, Currency exchange, Luggage storage, Barber/beauty shop, Gift shop, 24 hr. doctor, Babysitting, Comp. shoeshine, TV, In-house movies, Radio, Minibar, Indiv. climate ctl., In-room safe, Alarm clock, Desk, Hairdryer, Bathrobe, Stationery
Room Service: Room service
Restaurant: Paris 1930, La Brasserie, Chinese
Bar: Aldebaran
Business Facilities: Secretarial, Fax/telex/cable, Translation, Copying, Postal, Beeper service
Conference Rooms: Capacity: 300
Sports Facilities: Health center, Sauna, Massage, Gym, Jogging track

DUSIT THANI HOTEL

The Dusit Thani Hotel is centrally located, just a few minutes' walk from Bangkok's downtown business, financial and entertainment centers. It occupies 10 landscaped acres in the center of the city, and is adjacent to Asia's largest landscaped park.

Its 525 rooms feature all the amenities one would expect in a deluxe hotel, and many have balconies overlooking the park. All of the rooms are beautifully decorated with Thai paintings, silks and ceramics. The motif of the Royal Heritage Thai Suites employ decorative arts and crafts from various royal kingdoms that have played an important part in the history of the country. Each suite has its own balcony overlooking the city and boasts two bedrooms, living room, dining area, and pantry. The suite most frequented by Thailand's royal family when they attend a function at the hotel is the Royal Suite, which is luxuriously decorated in shades of blue tapestried silk.

Tiara, the rooftop dining room with breathtaking views of Bangkok, offers French cuisine and an international floor show in the evening. Delicious steaks and lobster can be savored at Hamilton's. The elegant Dusit-Bussaracum serves Thai specialties for lunch and dinner. Other restaurants include Mayflower, a Chinese restaurant, and Shogun, a Japanese restaurant. Library 1918 is both a reading room and cocktail lounge. Other popular drinking and meeting spots include the Lobby Lounge, with live entertainment, and Landmark Lounge, reserved for guests staying in the Landmark rooms.

The Dusit Thani's Ballroom can hold 2,000 for a reception. A range of smaller conference and meeting rooms are available, with support services offered through the hotel's business center.

A swimming pool, full health spa, tennis courts, and squash courts are found on the premises of the hotel.

From the Dusit Thani one can walk to such famous shops as Jim Thompson's for Thai silk, or Frank's for jewelry. It is also easy to plan excursions to the Grand Palace, The River of Kings, the National Museum, the house of Jim Thompson, and the house of Princess Chumbhot, a collector of fine Thai antiques.

Address: 946 Rama IV Rd., Bangkok, 10500
Phone: (66 2) 236-0450, Fax: (02) 236-6400, Telex: 81170/81027 TH
No. of Rooms: 525 **Suites:** 33
Rates: $$
Credit Cards: All major
Services and Amenities: TV, VCR, Radio, Minibar, Indiv. climate ctl.
Restaurant: Pavilion Cafe, Mayflower, Shogun, Tiara
Bar: Lobby Bar, Bubbles Disco
Business Facilities: Secretarial, Translation, Business services
Conference Rooms: 5, Capacity: 2,000
Sports Facilities: Pool, Full health spa, Squash, Tennis
Location: Downtown
Attractions: Shopping, Grand Palace, "River of Kings," National Museum

HOTEL SIAM INTER-CONTINENTAL

The Siam Inter-Continental is a beautiful low-rise hotel situated within the 26 landscaped acres that are part of the Srapatum Royal Estate. Yet it is close to the commercial, shopping and cultural centers of Bangkok. Guests arrive at the towering pagoda-shaped main building and are greeted by the elegant lobby. Gardens and waterfalls combine with marble and Thai decorations to make the lobby a continuation of the hotel's exterior beauty.

Guests are escorted to luxurious quarters in the two garden wings. Many rooms have their own private terraces. Teak-panelled bathrooms feature radio and telephone extensions and built-in hairdryers. The suites each have a panelled private study furnished in luxurious silks and leather and a dining room or area spacious enough for private luncheons or small cocktail receptions.

Avenue One, serving "nouvelle Thai" cuisine, is the hotel's main restaurant. The Talay Tong Seafood Inn offers fresh seafood, usually caught that very same day.

Functions may be held in the hotel's five function rooms which can accommodate 80-600 for a meeting. The grounds of this hotel offer spectacular opportunities for outdoor receptions and buffets for up to 5,000. Thai Village, a grouping of Thai-style houses built on the lake and surrounded by lush greenery, is the setting for Thai Night once a week in the dry season, where all guests at the hotel may enjoy a sumptuous buffet of local delicacies, and experience an evening of Thai music, dancing, and martial art performances. On the other nights, Thai Village is available to private groups for their own theme parties with up to 350 guests. The Siam Inter-Continental has a complete Business Center.

Portions of its extensive grounds have been used to create excellent sports facilities, which include the only golf driving range and putting green in a downtown Bangkok hotel, two night-lighted tennis courts, two jogging trails, a swimming pool, an outdoor fitness center and petanque lanes.

Address: 967 Srapatum Palace Pr., Rama 1 Rd., Bangkok
Phone: 253 0355, 253 0357, Fax: 253 2275, Telex: 81155 SIAMINT TH, Cable: INHOTELCOR BANGKOK
No. of Rooms: 353 **Suites:** 47
Rates: $$
Credit Cards: AmEx, DC, MC, JCB, BA
Services and Amenities: Laundry, Valet service, Travel arrangements, Barber/beauty shop, Shopping arcade, Drugstore, TV, VCR, In-house movies, Radio, Minibar, DD phone, Indiv. climate ctl., Hairdryer
Room Service: 24 hours
Restaurant: Avenue One, Talay Thong Seafood, Sivalai
Bar: Terrace Bar
Business Facilities: Secretarial, Fax/telex/cable, Translation, Newswire, Postal
Conference Rooms: 5, Capacity: 600
Sports Facilities: Pool, Fitness center, Petanque, Jogging trails, Tennis, Driving range, 6-hole putting green
Location: Siam Center
Attractions: Grand Palace, Crocodile Farm, Floating Market, Ancient City

THE ORIENTAL BANGKOK

The Oriental Hotel has been voted "Best Hotel in the World" for ten consecutive years by Institutional Investor Magazine, and consistently garners top awards in other polls. Superbly situated on the east bank of the enchanting Chao Phya River, The Oriental is just minutes away from Bangkok's business district. In the distinctive lobby, giant teak Thai temple bells have been transformed into fascinating light fixtures that hang from the high ceilings. White marble floors stretch across the room. A string quartet serenades guests while they sip their tea and gaze out through the lobby's floor to ceiling windows at lush tropical gardens and at the Chao Phya River beyond. It's not surprising that royalty and notables from all over the world have chosen the Oriental for their home in Bangkok.

Guest rooms and suites offer river views and are handsomely appointed with deluxe amenities. Theme suites offer an exceptional traveling experience. The Oriental Suite is similar to summer palaces built at the turn of the century; a grand entrance hall with marble floors and oriental carpet opens onto a living room with silk wall coverings, Georgian hand-cut crystal chandeliers, and spectacular view of the river. The master bedroom features four poster bed and handpainted ceiling design. The Normandie Restaurant offers fine French cuisine. Located on the Hotel's rooftop, The Normandie boasts a breathtaking view and the highest rated Master Chefs from France. Tea or cocktails in the Author's Lounge, located in the original wing of the hotel, rekindles the romance of the 19th century, when famous authors like John Steinbeck and Joseph Conrad often stayed at The Oriental.

Discover the secrets of Thai cooking at The Oriental's famous Thai Cooking School; relax in the Spa or Sports Center, or take a riverboat to explore magnificent temple ruins and ancient palaces.

Address: 48 Oriental Ave., Bangkok, 10500
Phone: 662-236-0400, 800-448-8355, Fax: 662-236-1939, Telex: 82997 ORIENTL TH, Cable: ORIENHOTEL
No. of Rooms: 360 **Suites:** 34
Room Rate: $$$
Credit Cards: All major
Services and Amenities: Limousine/car rental, Laundry, Valet service, Safe deposit fac., Currency exchange, Travel arrangements, Barber/beauty shop, Clinic, Thai cooking classes, TV, In-house movies, Radio, Minibar/refrigerator, IDD phones, Indiv. A/C ctl., Fruit, Comp. newspaper, Hairdryer, Bathrobes, Slippers
Room Service: 24 hours
Restaurant: Ciao, Terrace, Verandah, Normandie
Bar: Bamboo
Business Facilities: Audio-visual, Secretarial, Fax/telex/cable, Translation, Copying, AP wire, Postal, Reference materials
Conference Rooms: 6, Capacity: 1,500
Sports Facilities: Pool, Sauna, Gym, Jogging track, Squash, Tennis, Golf driving range
Attractions: River cruises to Bang-Pa-In, Sala Rim Naam

THE REGENT BANGKOK

The Regent Hotel, Bangkok, is situated in the heart of Bangkok's commercial and business area overlooking the Royal Bangkok Sports Club. Its three interconnecting structures follow a traditional Thai design: a 9-story central building flanked by two lower buildings.

The Regent's two lower buildings house most of the guest rooms and suites. Each accommodation has a luxurious sitting area, a large writing desk, and a desktop phone which plugs into the bedside table at night. The Rajadamri Suite, occupying the entire ninth floor of the main building, consists of a private dining room, large sitting room, master bedroom with dressing area, bath, jacuzzi, and massage, plus six connecting bedrooms.

The central building houses The Lobby, which is not only a reception area, but also an elegant all-day restaurant, featuring a string quartet at tea-time. Other restaurants are Le Cristal, which serves fine European cuisine in a sophisticated Thai setting; La Brasserie, where the decor is wood panelling and brass and the food is French provincial; and The Spice Market, which offers Thai cuisine in an Oriental bazaar setting. Before or after dinner, sink into the leather chairs of the Rommanee Lounge, and enjoy a drink and a little piano music.

The Business Center offers executive offices, private meeting room, library, multilingual secretarial services, and the latest in electronic communications. All this plus function rooms for 350 make The Regent a good choice for a conference or small convention.

The Regent boasts the largest hotel pool in the city. Its Rimsra Terrace serves charcoal barbecue and pizza. Beside the pool area is the Fitness Center with squash courts, jacuzzi, massage rooms, health bar, and gym.

Address: 155 Rajadamri Road, Bangkok, 10330
Phone: (66-2) 251-6127, 800-545-4000, Fax: (66-2) 253-9195, Telex: 20004 REGBKK TH, Cable: REGHO
No. of Rooms: 400 **Suites:** 39
Room Rate: $$$
Credit Cards: All major
Services and Amenities: Limousine/car rental, Parking, Laundry/dry cleaning, Safe deposit fac., Barber/beauty shop, Shopping arcade, Doctor, Babysitting, Comp shoeshine, Satellite TV, In-house movies, Radio, Minibar, ISD phone, Indiv. climate ctl., Desk, Comp. newspaper, Hairdryer
Room Service: 24 hours
Restaurant: Regent Grill, La Brasserie, Spice Market
Bar: Rommanee Lounge
Business Facilities: Secretarial, Fax/telex/cable, Translation, Copying, Private office, Reference library
Conference Rooms: 8, Capacity: 1,000
Sports Facilities: Pool, Full health spa, Sauna, Jacuzzi, Massage, Gym, Squash, Golf, Para-medical staff
Location: Rajadamri
Attractions: Pratunam shopping area, Peninsula Plaza, Siam Square, Lumpiri Park

ROYAL GARDEN RESORT HUA HIN

Two and one half hours south of Bangkok by bus, lies the tranquil fishing village of Hua Hin, where the royal family of Thailand has kept a vacation palace since the 1920s. Today, all travelers can enjoy regal accommodations at the Royal Garden Resort Hua Hin, while savoring the beauty of Thailand's gulf coast.

Rooms and suites are decorated in wicker furnishings and Thai touches and feature all the modern amenities. Suites are comprised of a dining area, lounge, large bedroom and an equally spacious dressing area and bathroom. Two of the seventh-floor penthouse suites have their own private rooftop gardens, while the others have balconies overlooking the pool.

Several restaurants and bars offer gastronomic delights and cool libations. The Thai Restaurant features Thai cuisine along with Thai performances. The Seafood Market specializes in fresh seafood and also provides live music. The Garden Coffee Shop is a popular place for a variety of light meals, where guests can choose to sit indoors or outdoors in a garden setting. The Jungle Disco is Hua Hin's first, and perhaps still the only, swinging night spot.

The hotel has conference and banquet facilities for 200. With enough advance notice, the staff can arrange to have an arriving group greeted by an elephant wearing the company logo.

The large swimming-pool area, encircled on three sides by the resort buildings is a relaxing place to swim or sun. On the fourth side is the beach, where waterskiing, para-sailing, windsurfing, and a variety of watersports equipment and lessons are available. Land sports at the resort include tennis on night-lighted courts, and 18 holes of golf at the nearby Royal Golf Course. A children's playground and children's pool make the young set feel welcome at The Royal Garden Resort. The hotel also has several large seawater aquariums where one can see colorful marine life.

Cultural shows, performances, and holiday celebrations at the hotel make one's visit unforgettable. The tour desk will also help arrange excursions about town, and farther afield to sugar and pineapple plantations, and the national parks.

Address: 107/1 Phetkasen Beach Rd., Hua Hin, 77110
Phone: (032) 511881-4, Fax: (032) 512422, Telex: 78309 ROGAHUATH
No. of Rooms: 222 **Suites:** 5
Rates: $
Credit Cards: All major
Services and Amenities: Concierge, Laundry/dry cleaning, Safe deposit fac., Currency exchange, Travel arrangements, Barber/beauty shop, Shopping arcade, Babysitting, TV, Radio, Minibar, Phone, Indiv. climate ctl.
Restaurant: Garden, Market Seafood, Bar-B-Q Terrace
Bar: Nautilus Cocktail Lounge
Business Facilities: Audio-visual, Secretarial, Translation
Conference Rooms: 2, Capacity: 200
Sports Facilities: Pool, Fitness center, Petanque, Games room, Badminton, Croquet, Tennis, Watersports, Children's playground, 18-hole golf nearby
Location: Hua Hin
Attractions: Kaeng Krajarn National Park, fishing villages, Wang Daeng Cave, night market

AMANPURI

Tucked away among the palms of a century old coconut plantation, Amanpuri's 40 individual pavilion suites offer guests the ultimate privacy, and service so impeccable, it has been called "invisible." Located on the tropical island of Phuket, overlooking the pristine Andaman Sea, this exclusive 5-star hotel is the perfect place for an intimate getaway with a loved one or to indulge in peaceful solitude.

On arrival, Amanpuri's gracious staff greets you in an open-air Grand Sala with 40-foot ceilings. There, a manager is assigned to ensure that all your requests are fulfilled. The staff to guest ratio is better than two to one; Amanpuri's staff of 220 will do everything from packing and unpacking your bags for you, to carrying you food on bamboo poles. It is not unusual, upon returning to your room, to discover that delicate orchids have been sprinkled on your bed.

The identical suites, designed with the grace of a Thai Temple, are connected by a network of winding paths and stone stairways. Curved, spired roofs are barely visible among the trees, yet each pavilion retains the natural openness of a beachside cottage. Suites are finely appointed with teak floors, soft taupe silks and cottons, hand-carved furniture, sunken tub and black marble shower. Handsome teak paneled doors slide open onto a private sundeck and open air sala.

The resort's two restaurants offer a choice of gourmet Thai or Italian food, guaranteed to tantalize any palette. Getting around in Amanpuri does require some stairclimbing; it is 82 steps down from the pool to the ocean. But it's worth it. There is nothing like a swim in Amanpuri's iridescent black onyx swimming pool, or relaxing all day by the azure waters of the Andaman Sea. For the adventurous, extensive water sports and island cruises are available.

Address: P.O. Box 196, Pansea Beach, Phuket 83000
Phone: (076) 311 394, Fax: (076) 311 100, Telex: 69529 AMANPURI TH
No. of Suites: 40
Room Rate: $$$$
Credit Cards: AmEx, DC, MC, Visa
Services and Amenities: Personal manager, Car rental, Laundry/dry cleaning, Postal, Currency exchange, Drugstore, Gift shop, Medical services, Airport transfer, Comp. newspaper, Stereo, Minibar/refrigerator, Hairdryer, Indiv. A/C ctl., In-room safe, Daily fruit basket, Thai sala, Private sundeck
Restaurant: Terrace (Thai), The Restaurant (Italian)
Bar: The Bar
Sports Facilities: Pool, Library, Sauna, Gym, Squash, Tennis, Island cruises, Sailing, Windsurfing, Scuba diving, Deep-sea fishing
Location: Pansea Beach
Attractions: Beaches, jungles, temples, markets, cruises to nearby islands

PHUKET YACHT CLUB HOTEL & BEACH RESORT

The Phuket Yacht Club Hotel opened in 1986. It is located on the southern tip of Phuket, an island off the west coast of Thailand's southern peninsula.

From the white sands of Nai Harn Beach, the staterooms and suites rise up a gentle slope, commanding panoramic views of breathtaking beauty. All accommodations have separate bedroom and sitting areas decorated with natural materials and local design motifs. Each has a covered patio, and a private sundeck offering views of the beach, the Andaman Sea, and the islands. Lush tropical greenery adorns the patios and fills the landscape.

The dining and recreational facilities are located on two levels at the foot of the hill. On the upper level is the Quarterdeck, an informal open-air restaurant serving three meals daily. On the lower level is the Chart Room Grill and Lounge, serving European and Thai gourmet food. At the foot of the cliff is the swimming pool, set in a peaceful tropical garden, complete with cascading waterfall. Cool drinks and light refreshments are available there from The Poop. On the beachfront, Western and Oriental snacks are served in The Promenade Coffee Shop.

Relax on the pristine beach, or, if you like, choose from a full spectrum of water sports available, from sailing and windsurfing to scuba diving. Five-minutes drive form the Phuket Yacht Club is the resort's private sports complex, with tennis courts, fitness center, and clubhouse.

The Phuket Yacht Club can accommodate only small conferences. However, if you are attending a larger conference in southeast Asia, you might well consider flying to this resort and relaxing for a few days after your business is completed.

Address: Nai Harn Beach, Phuket, 83130
Phone: (076) 214020-6, Fax: (076) 214 028, Telex: 69532 YACHT TH
No. of Rooms: 100 **Suites:** 8
Credit Cards: AmEx, DC, MC, Visa
Services and Amenities: Car hire, Laundry, Valet, Safe deposit fac., Tour desk, Barber/beauty shop, Babysitting, TV, In-house movies, Minibar, IDD phone, Indiv. climate ctl.
Room Service: 24 hours
Restaurant: Quarterdeck, Chart Room, Promenade
Bar: Regatta Club
Business Facilities: Audio-visual, Secretarial, Fax/telex/cable
Conference Rooms: 1, Capacity: 60
Sports Facilities: Pool, Fitness center, Tennis, Watersports
Location: Rawai
Attractions: Nai Harn Beach, Phromthep Cape

LA PLAYA HOTEL

The "grand lady of Carmel-by-the-sea," as local residents have known this Mediterranean-style villa since artist Chris Jorgensen built it for his bride in 1904, is now grander than ever. A resort since the 1920s, La Playa was acquired in 1983 by the Cope family (owners of San Francisco's incomparable Huntington), who have done extensive restoration and renovation to make it Carmel's only full-service resort.

The subtly exquisite decor accents pale pastel walls and upholstery with custom hand-loomed area rugs, paintings by contemporary artists, and the Cope family's extensive collection of California antiques and heirlooms. Rooms afford views of the garden, the ocean, or residential Carmel. Handcrafted furnishings incorporate La Playa's mermaid motif in hues of soft rose and blue. The baths have marble floors and inlaid decorative tile. La Playa's five guest cottages offer the luxuries of a private vacation home. Complete with kitchens, wet bars, fireplaces, terraces, and patios, La Playa's cottages are ideal for a private getaway or family outing.

The Spyglass restaurant's gorgeous terrace is a perfect spot to watch the sunset. The wood-paneled interior of the restaurant provides a cozy dining atmosphere amid Corinthian columns. An extensive international wine list and a fine collection of old ports and sherries set the stage for tempting cuisine.

For the meeting-minded, a conference coordinator is on the premises and complete business facilities are available.

If you can pull yourself away from La Playa's lush formal gardens and heated swimming pool, there are myriad recreational options in the area, including Pebble Beach, Spyglass, and Carmel Valley Country Club golf courses. The boutique shops and galleries of Carmel Village are just four blocks from the hotel.

Address: Camino Real & Eighth, P.O. Box 900, Carmel, California 93921
Phone: 408-624-6476, 800-582-8900, Fax: 408-624-7966
No. of Rooms: 75 **Suites:** 2
Room Rate: $
Credit Cards: AmEx, MC, Visa
Services and Amenities: Concierge, Valet service, Babysitting, TV, Radio, Toiletries, On request: Bathrobe, Sewing kit, Iron, Ironing board
Restrictions: No pets
Room Service: Room service
Restaurant: Spyglass Restaurant
Bar: Spyglass Lounge
Business Facilities: Audio-visual, Secretarial, Message center, Translation, Copying
Conference Rooms: 3, Capacity: 125
Sports Facilities: Outdoor swimming pool
Location: Carmel Village
Attractions: 2 blocks to beach, shopping, 17 Mile Drive, Point Lobos

INN L'AUBERGE DEL MAR

Recently affiliated with the prestigious Hotel Bel-Air, L'Auberge Del Mar is located on the site of the original Hotel Del Mar, which was a playground to the stars in Hollywood's heyday.

As one enters the marble and wood lobby, an expanse of French doors reveals the blue Pacific. The grand double-sided stone fireplace is a replica of that which welcomed visitors in days gone by.

All guest rooms have private balconies, many with spectacular ocean views. The country French decor includes poster beds, television in the armoire, wet bar, and a large marble bath. Many of the rooms feature cathedral ceilings and fireplaces.

The Bistro Garden features contemporary California regional cuisine, stylized after the hotel Bel-Air, whose food has become a west coast tradition, comprising the freshest of seafood, the finest of beef and an abundance of fresh herbs and vegetables.

Spa Del Mar, a full-service health and beauty spa, blends the healing qualities of the ocean with modern spa therapy. Guests may enjoy hydrotherapy massage, herbal wraps, Fango packs, and facials, plus water-aerobics in the pool, or a jog along the beach. Two outdoor swimming pools and lighted championship tennis courts enhance opportunities for exercise.

L'Auberge Del Mar has complete conference and business facilities. Meeting rooms are named for Hollywood stars of yesteryear and one might run into some of today's well-known personalities at the Jimmy Durante Pub, at afternoon tea near the lobby fireplace, or strolling through the nearby shops and cafés of the picturesque village of Del Mar.

For pampered European elegance in that wonderful southern California climate, this is the place.

Address: 1530 Camino del Mar, Del Mar, California 92014
Phone: 619-259-1515, 800-553-1336, Fax: 619-755-4940
No. of Rooms: 123 **Suites:** 8
Room Rate: $$
Credit Cards: AmEx, DC, MC, Disc, Visa
Services and Amenities: Concierge, Car hire, Parking, Valet service, Currency exchange, Game area, Gift shop, Library, Babysitting, Comp. shoeshine, Cable TV, Radio, Comp. toiletries, Robes
Restrictions: No pets
Room Service: Room service
Restaurant: Bistro Garden
Bar: Jimmy Durante Pub
Business Facilities: Audio-visual, Secretarial, Telex, Translation, Copying, Message center, Full business serv.
Conference Rooms: 9, Capacity: 250
Sports Facilities: Pool, Full health spa, Tennis, Polo, Riding, Sailing, Bicycling, Hiking
Location: N. County San Deigo
Attractions: San Diego Zoo, Balboa Park, Sea World, Seaport Village

CHECKERS HOTEL

In the sprawling, eclectic City of Los Angeles, what a treat to discover a small elegant hotel in the downtown area. Checkers Hotel, with 188 rooms including 15 suites, woos the guest with graciousness and service which extends to its fully-tailored business facilities. Opened in 1927 and carefully updated as recently as 1989, the Spanish-Moorish design initiates its hospitality in the lobby, where two antique mother-of-pearl elephants serve as chaperones to the entrance.

Charm and intimacy mark the guest rooms, where soft hues form the background for hand-carved headboards, rose-colored duvet covers marble tables and elegant accessories, such as minibars, in all rooms. Marble bathrooms include phones, robes, complimentary toiletries and TV/radio with speakers in bath. Two Penthouse suites, carpeted in muted gold hues, boast living room fireplaces flanked by inviting seating. Dining room walls are upholstered, and other regal appointments combine exquisite taste with pure comfort.

Wedgewood place settings, gleaming silver and linens grace the columned Checkers Restaurant, artfully designed to provide intimacy for the dinner guest. Among the celebrated entrees are Lobster Cioppino with Pesto and Garlic Toast, Smoked Salmon with Grilled Scallion Bread, and Ragout with a Wild Rice Waffle. A modified menu is available in the Health Spa, and afternoon tea is available in the lounge and library. Leisure time may be spent in the lap pool, jacuzzi and sauna in the spa retreat. Corporate visitors will appreciate the assistance and attention of the staff in all details.

Attractions galore dominate the Los Angeles scene, such as numerous superb museums, landmark buildings, escorted tours, colorful Olvera Street, Chinatown, Little Tokyo—and just a bit further, Disneyland and Universal Studios.

Address: 535 South Grand Ave., Los Angeles, California 90071
Phone: 213-624-0000, 800-628-4900, Fax: 213-626-9906, Telex: 403-525 CHECKER
No. of Rooms: 188 **Suites:** 15
Room Rate: $$
Credit Cards: All major
Services and Amenities: 24hr concierge, Car hire, Valet parking, Laundry/dry cleaning, Valet service, Currency exchange, Babysitting, Shoeshine, TV, Radio, Minibar, Multiline phone, Comp. toiletries, Robes, Comp. newspaper
Room Service: 24 hours
Restaurant: Checkers Restaurant
Bar: Checkers Bar
Business Facilities: Audio-visual, Secretarial, Telex, Teleconferencing, Copying, In-room FAX avail.
Conference Rooms: 4, Capacity:
Sports Facilities: Outdoor lap pool, Health spa, Jacuzzi, Massage, Weight room, Sauna
Location: Downtown Los Angeles
Attractions: Museums, Music Center, Olvera St., 20 mi. to Disneyland

HOTEL BEL-AIR

Where else can you be surrounded by fountains and courtyards, beside waterfalls tumbling into a lake that hosts a family of white swans, that's just a short drive from Rodeo Drive?

Nestled in an eleven-and-a-half acre estate garden, where redwoods, pampas grass, orchids, lilies and roses blend to create a fabulous color array, Bel-Air is a most private, secluded and unhurried Shangri-La. Accommodations are in mission-style buildings and bungalows. The designers who worked on the project are James Northcutt, Louis Cataffo, Therese Wills, Kalef Alaton and Betty Garber. Each spacious guest room or suite is individually decorated, reflecting the different designers' styles. The atmosphere is opulent, luxurious and quintessentially comfortable. Wood-burning fireplaces, bay windows with window seats, and hand-stencilled ceilings are featured throughout. The lush baths and separate vanity areas gleam with marble and brass fixtures.

The Hotel Bel-Air Restaurant is renowned for its California-inspired cuisine. Original art enhances walls upholstered in peachy beige; strikingly beautiful carpeting in a moss green and beige floral pattern unifies the whole. Tables are set with the finest crystal, china and silver.

Our recent dinner experience at the Bel-Air began with California Shellfish, Crispy Sweetbreads and Foie Gras Salad served warm with curly lettuce, walnuts and mint. As an entree, Salmon Grilled over Charcoal with Garlic Cream, or Squab with Sweet Corn and Red Pepper Relish, is exquisite, as is the Pine Nut Tart with homemade ice cream for dessert. Weather permitting (and it usually is), al fresco dining is available by the pool or on the bougainvillaea draped terrace overlooking the hotel gardens.

The wood-panelled bar has a baby grand piano, fireplace, and fresh flowers. Howard Hughes used the Bel-Air's bar as an informal "office," and the aura of intimacy remains.

Address: 701 Stone Canyon Rd., Los Angeles, California 90077
Phone: 213-472-1211, Telex: 674151
No. of Rooms: 92 **Suites:** 33
Room Rate: $$$
Credit Cards: All major
Services and Amenities: Concierge, Car hire, Parking, Laundry, Valet service, Currency exchange, House doctor, Babysitting, Comp. shoeshine, Cable TV, Radio, Phone, Robe, Comp. toiletries
Room Service: 24 hours
Restaurant: Hotel Bel-Air Restaurant
Bar: Hotel Bel-Air Bar
Business Facilities: Services on request
Sports Facilities: Pool, Golf arranged
Attractions: Rodeo Drive, close to Century City, Beverly Hills, Westwood

WESTWOOD MARQUIS

This ultra-elegant new all-suite hotel is located in residential Westwood Village, within walking distance of fashionable boutiques, restaurants, theatres and the U.C.L.A. campus. Handsome magnolias frame your approach to the Westwood Marquis, and the hotel gardens offer winding pathways, grassy knolls, flowering shrubs and shade trees for tranquil contemplation in the heart of the city. Here, privacy is of primary importance.

Each suite is individual in design and decor. All share the European style grand hotel ambience, accented by fine furniture, paintings, art objects and live plants. Bedrooms have king, queen or twin beds and color television. The living room has a sofa, easy chairs and desk. The dining room is separate. The 17 suites on the Penthouse Floor have a private butler. Splendid views include palatial Bel-Air estates, the Santa Monica Mountains, the city and the ocean.

The Dynasty Room, the hotel's private dining salon, serves Continental/Nouvelle cuisine, most recently the "Menu Minceur" has been designed for health-conscious clientele. The room is named not for a television series but rather for its display of T'ang Dynasty porcelains from the "Magnificence of China" exhibition. The Garden Terrace restaurant is best known for its Sunday brunch, which Los Angeles restaurant critics have called, ". . . the finest brunch I have ever been to in the world," and, ". . . the buffet brunch against which all buffet brunches have to be judged." A harpist helps set the mood for relaxed afternoon tea in the lounge, as grand piano performances do for evening cocktails.

Men's and women's health spa facilities offer saunas, steam baths and jacuzzis. An exercise room features Universal equipment and a Life Cycle. Massages, facials and cosmetic artistry are available by appointment.

Throughout, the Westwood Marquis creates a garden resort feel in the midst of the city.

Address: 930 Hilgard Avenue, Los Angeles, California 90024
Phone: 213-208-8765, 800-421-2317, Fax: 213-824-0355, Telex: 181835 MARQUIS
No. of Suites: 258
Room Rate: $$
Credit Cards: All major
Services and Amenities: Concierge, Comp. limousine, Car rental, Valet parking, Valet service, Currency exchange, Barber/beauty shop, Florist, Doctor on call, Babysitting, Comp. shoeshine, Cable TV, Radio, Refrigerator, Phones, Hairdryer, Robe, Toiletries
Room Service: 24 hours
Restaurant: Garden Terrace, Dynasty Room
Bar: Bar
Business Facilities: Audio-visual, Secretarial, Fax/telex, Translation, Copying, Message center
Conference Rooms: 6, Capacity: 150
Sports Facilities: Pools, Sauna, Whirlpool, Massage, Exercise room, Men's & women's health spa
Location: Westwood Village
Attractions: Westwood, near Rodeo Drive, Beverly Hills, Santa Monica

HOTEL PACIFIC

The Monterey Peninsula's newest luxury hotel is a graceful adobe structure in the heart of the historic district, adjacent to California's First Theater and directly across from the Monterey Conference Center. The main hall of the Hotel Pacific features original artworks, distinctive artifacts, antiques, handcrafted tile floors and a warm fireplace. Hand-woven Indian rugs accent the southwestern traditional motif.

The Hotel Pacific is among the finest of the new breed of all-suite hotels. Each guest unit is a 560-square foot executive suite, complete with wood-burning fireplace, custom furniture in rich earth tones, goosedown feather beds, remote control color TV, fresh-ground coffee and brewer, and imported teas. Custom cabinetry houses a refrigerator and honor bar. A tiled desk area separates the living area from the sleeping room. Unusually spacious bathrooms feature separate showers and tubs, scales, TV, and telephone. Each room has a private patio or terrace with a view of the ocean or the hotel's lavish garden courtyards with spas and hand-carved fountains.

Special services for guests include complimentary continental breakfast, afternoon tea, wine and cheese, nightly maid service and turn-down with chocolates. Chauffeured Rolls-Royce limousine service is available by advance reservation to take guests to and from the Monterey Airport. The hotel's meeting rooms will accommodate an intimate board meeting or a conference for up to 60 participants.

Walk outside this tranquil hideaway and find yourself in the heart of downtown Monterey. Visit Monterey Aquarium, Carmel galleries and shopping, Carmel Mission Basilica, Fisherman's Wharf and 17-Mile Drive. Nearby sporting facilities include 18 world-famous golf courses, a jogging and bike trail, riding, sailing, scuba diving, fishing, and whale-watching.

Address: 300 Pacific St., Monterey, California 93940
Phone: 408-373-5700, 800-554-5542, Fax: 408-649-3743
No. of Suites: 106
Services and Amenities: Concierge, Airport limousine, Parking, Laundry/dry cleaning, Valet service, Game area, Babysitting, Nightly maid service, Cable TV, TV in bath, Minibar, Phone in bath, Comp. newspaper, Coffee/tea making fac., Robes, Priv. patio/terrace
Restrictions: No pets
Room Service: Room service
Business Facilities: Audio-visual, Secretarial, Fax, Translation, Copying, Message center
Conference Rooms: 3, Capacity: 100
Sports Facilities: Whirlpool, Jogging & bike trail, Golf, Sailing, Riding, nearby Fishing, Scuba diving
Location: Historic downtown
Attractions: Monterey Aquarium, Carmel Mission Basilica, Carmel shopping

CAMPTON PLACE

The exterior is Spanish revival, the James Northcutt interiors contemporary, and the location the best: one-half block from Union Square, and only 4 blocks from San Francisco's financial district. Opened in 1983, Campton Place is the proud result of an $18 million total renovation of two turn-of-the-century buildings.

The peach-and-taupe color scheme used throughout complements exquisite furnishings and distinctive objets d'art. The 126 rooms and suites are residential in character and quite luxurious. Armoires conceal remote control color TV. Beds are made up with the softest sheets, down comforters and down pillows. Bathrooms are of travertine marble with brass fixtures. Other amenities include a wall telephone in the bathroom, a full complement of I. Magnin toiletries and a bathrobe. The service is professional, friendly and prompt.

Campton Place Restaurant has emerged during the past few years as one of California's leading restaurants. The dining room decor shines with Wedgwood china, fine linen, crystal, and oriental porcelains but the food itself upstages all else. Chef Jan Birnbaum is a culinary master and a natural in the kitchen. Don't miss breakfast, whether a fluffy omelette of Smithfield ham and Farmhouse Cheddar with Red Onion Conserve, or Spiced Compote Of Nectarines, Boysenberries, Bananas and Apples. Lunch and dinner specialties include Warm Asparagus with Morels, Stuffed Soft Shell Crab with Corn Pancetta and Crayfish Ragout, Grilled Rib-Eye Steak with red onion rings and Maytag Bleu Cheese and Banana Cream Pie for dessert. Everything on the restaurant menu (which changes daily) is also available via room service for en suite dining privacy.

Address: 340 Stockton St., San Francisco, California 94108
Phone: 415-781-5555, 800-647-4007, Fax: 415-955-8536, Telex: 6771185 CPTN
No. of Rooms: 126 **Suites:** 10
Room Rate: $$
Credit Cards: AmEx, DC, DC, MC, Visa
Services and Amenities: 24hr concierge, Parking, Laundry, Packing/unpacking, Currency exchange, House doctor, Babysitting, Comp. shoeshine, Phone in bath, Robes, Comp. newspaper
Room Service: Room service
Restaurant: Campton Place Restaurant
Bar: Campton
Business Facilities: Secretarial, Telex, Copying, Message center
Conference Rooms: 2, Capacity: 20
Location: Union Square
Attractions: Maiden Lane shopping, Union Square shopping, near cable car

THE DONATELLO

"Italian design, craftsmanship, cuisine and staff are perfectly integrated at the Donatello," says A. Cal Rossi, the creative force behind this remarkable hotel in the heart of San Francisco's fashionable shopping and theatre district. The Italian sculptor Donatello was a major figure in 15th-Century Renaissance art, and the hotel bearing his name reflects classic European spirit.

The interiors, designed by Andrew Delfino, blend travertine, Italian marble, Venetian glass and European antiques. The spacious guest rooms are luxuriously decorated in soft pastels and designer prints, with Ming and Biedermeier furnishings. In the marble-clad baths you will find fine soaps and full-length terry cloth robes. Our favorite suite has a bedroom done in cream color with dark details, with a fine corner view. The living room has walls covered in Fortuny fabrics, couches in pale rose, and an impressive marble entryway.

Ristorante Donatello has been an international success since the day it opened. Its two dining rooms are done in Fortuny fabrics with Veronese marble floors. The atmosphere, while elegant and formal, maintains an intimate ambiance and charm.

A springtime dinner opened with a Creamy Risotto with Truffles and Wild Mushrooms, followed by Fresh Monkfish sauteed with two pepper sauces, accompanied by Favorita di Santa Vittoria d'Alba. The next course was Medallions of Veal sauteed with fresh sage and butter. Dessert was the Dark Chocolate Fondant in a light orange-scented custard, delicious with Moscato Rosa. The feast would have impressed even the Medici. Besides daily special dinners such as this, there is an extensive a la carte menu.

Sophisticated travelers from the U.S. and abroad have fallen in love with *la dolce far niente* at the Donatello. You will too.

Address: 501 Post St., San Francisco, California 94102
Phone: 415-441-7100, Telex: 172875
No. of Rooms: 95 **Suites:** 5
Room Rate: $$
Credit Cards: AmEx, DC, JCB, MC, Visa
Services and Amenities: Concierge, Car hire, Parking, Laundry, Valet service, House doctor, Babysitting, Comp. shoeshine, TV, Radio, Phone in bath, Robes, Fine soaps, Comp. newspaper
Restrictions: No pets
Room Service: Room service
Restaurant: Ristorante Donatello
Bar: Ristorante Donatello
Business Facilities: Audio-visual, Secretarial, Telex, Translation, Copying
Conference Rooms: 2, Capacity: 65
Sports Facilities: Full health spa, Sauna, Whirlpool, Outside health clubs
Location: Union Square
Attractions: Boutique shopping, major theater district

HUNTINGTON HOTEL - NOB HILL

The height of elegance in San Francisco is to be found atop Nob Hill in the classic and understated Huntington. Built as a residence hotel in 1924 by the architectural firm of Weeks and Day, the Huntington is now the pride of the Cope family, innkeepers extraordinaire.

You will sense the atmosphere of quiet luxury and security as the doorman admits you to the intimate lobby, and you will understand why visiting nobility and celebrities of opera, symphony, and stage choose The Huntington.

The stylish, comfortable rooms, each different, have been designed by Anthony Hail, Lee Radziwill, and Elizabeth Bernhardt. All are spacious and elegantly furnished. Of the 30 suites, our personal favorite is the Ambassador Suite (#1207), with its ornate gilt ceiling and 17th- and 18th-century Italian furnishings. Robert Redford slept here; so did Baron Edmond de Rothschild. Luciano Pavarotti's choice, Suite #514, is done in delightful yellow and aqua English chintz with a Chinese motif.

The Big Four Restaurant and Bar, named for the Central Pacific railroad magnates, offers continental cuisine in a refined atmosphere of green leather banquettes and rich gleaming mahogany. We recommend the Boule de Niege for dessert. The cozy bar is a San Francisco favorite.

Address: 1075 California St., San Francisco, California 94108
Phone: 415-474-5400, 800-227-4683, Fax: 415-474-6227
No. of Rooms: 140 **Suites:** 38
Room Rate: $$
Credit Cards: AmEx, CB, DC, MC, Visa
Services and Amenities: Concierge, Limousine service, Parking, Laundry, Valet service, Gift shop, House doctor, Comp. shoeshine, Cable TV, Radio, Nightly turndown, Comp. toiletries, Sun lamp, Comp. newspaper
Room Service: Room service
Restaurant: The Big Four
Bar: The Big Four
Business Facilities: Audio-visual, Secretarial, Telex, Translation, Copying, Message center
Conference Rooms: 4, Capacity: 60
Location: Nob Hill
Attractions: On cable-car line, Chinatown, Fisherman's Wharf

MANDARIN ORIENTAL

The Mandarin Oriental San Francisco opened in 1987 as the first U.S. hotel of the Hong Kong-based Mandarin Oriental Hotel group, whose other locations include six Asian cities. The company claims that both its Hong Kong and Bangkok Mandarin Oriental Hotels are consistently voted among the top three hotels in the world. That bold assertion sets the new downtown San Francisco hotel an exacting standard to live up to, a task that general manager Wolfgang Hultner, formerly manager of Mandarin Oriental hotels in Manila and Hong Kong, has undertaken enthusiastically. The Mandarin Oriental occupies the top eleven floors of First Interstate Center, the San Francisco skyline's new 48-story landmark. Guest rooms are in two diagonal towers, connected at each level by a glass-enclosed skybridge affording incomparable views of the city 400 feet below. Each floor of the two towers has only seven rooms, creating a private, personal feel.

Accommodations feature electronic security doors, large closets, built-in luggage racks, hidden televisions and minibars. The contemporary oriental decor, delicately orchestrated in earth tones, features Canadian maple woodwork, beige wool carpeting and coffered ceilings with recessed lighting. The bathrooms, tiled in beige Roman Travertine, have separate showers and bathtubs with Jacuzzi whirlpools, as well as all imaginable amenities, including a full complement of English bathing products. Silks, the hotel's gourmet restaurant, has recently received critical acclaim. It is widely expected to rank among San Francisco's finest dining establishments. Menus change daily. Chef Michele Sampson supervises not only Silks' kitchen but also a separate kitchen exclusively for room service.

The hotel's business center provides state of the art facilities for visiting executives: personal computers, word processing service, telex, facsimile transmission and photocopying machines, international direct dial telephones and a business library.

Address: 222 Sansome St., San Francisco, California 94104-2792
Phone: 415-885-0999, Fax: 415-433-0289
No. of Rooms: 154 **Suites:** 6
Room Rate: $$$
Credit Cards: All major
Services and Amenities: Concierge, Car hire, Parking, Laundry, Valet service, Currency exchange, Babysitting, Comp. shoeshine, No pets, Cable TV, In-house movies, Radio, Comp. toiletries, Heat lamps, Robes, Comp. newspaper
Room Service: 24hr room service
Restaurant: Silks
Bar: Mandarin Lounge
Business Facilities: Audio-visual, Secretarial, Fax/telex, Full business center, Copying, Message center, Business library
Conference Rooms: 4
Location: Financial district
Attractions: Near cable car line, Embarcadero Center shopping

THE MARK HOPKINS INTERCONTINENTAL

Celebrating its 65th year in 1993, Mark Hopkins Intercontinental, located on prestigious Nob Hill, has had a history filled with visits from celebrities, royal figures, heads of state and other notable guests. Inside this 19-story hotel, the lobby is elegantly decorated in shades of pale jade green, gold and rose, and set off by crystal chandeliers and fresh flowers. Adjacent to the lobby, the Room of the Dons contains artistic murals and architectural treasures of Early California.

Fresh fruit and a complimentary bottle of champagne greet you when you first arrive at your room. The 393 guest rooms and suites are neoclassic in styling, with quilt chintz bedspreads, damask wall coverings, and a handsome cherry amoire encasing a television and minibar to complement the decor. Many rooms offer some of the finest views of San Francisco and the bay area. The luxurious marble baths feature bath telephones, hairdryers, and bathrobes. There are 19 suites, including the popular Jacuzzi suite with a large jacuzzi overlooking a magnificent Golden Gate view.

The Nob Hill Restaurant is the hotel's lobby-level restaurant, and is a favorite among locals as well. Specializing in French cuisine using fresh California produce, the restaurant offers specialties such as Sauteed Escalope of Goose Foie Gras and Roast Quail Salad in hazelnut oil, balsamic vinegar and duck glaze dressing. The wine list is extensive as well. On the 19th floor, the glass-walled cocktail lounge, Top of the Mark, features a spectacular 360-degree view of San Francisco, Golden Gate, Pacific Coast mountains, the Pacific Ocean, and surrounding cities. It is truly a spectacular view during the day and a glittering treasure chest at night.

The Mark Hopkins is equipped to handle conferences of up to 1,100 for receptions and 670 for banquets. All the hotel's function rooms are soundproof, fully-carpeted and tastefully furnished.

Recreational facilities at the hotel include a fitness center. The city offers a host of activities, including Golden Gate Park, with gardens and museums, Union Square shopping, Fisherman's Wharf and Chinatown.

Address: One Nob Hill, San Francisco, California 94108
Phone: (415) 392-3434, Fax: (415) 421-3302
No. of Rooms: 393 **Suites:** 29
Credit Cards: All major
Services and Amenities: Concierge, Car rental, Parking, One-day laundry, Valet service, Currency exchange, Q-DAT ticket service, Barber/beauty shop, House doctor, Babysitting, Comp. shoeshine, TV, Desks, Minibar, Phone, Indiv. climate ctl., Video messages, Turndown service, Robe, Comp. toiletries
Room Service: 24 hours
Restaurant: The Mark Hopkins
Bar: Top of the Mark
Business Facilities: Audio-visual, Fax/telex, Private offices, Coordinators
Conference Rooms: 15, Capacity: 750
Sports Facilities: Fitness center, Sauna, Jacuzzi, Massage, Exercise classes, Nautilus
Location: Nob Hill
Attractions: Cable car, Chinatown, Union Square, Fisherman's Wharf, Golden Gate Park

PARC FIFTY FIVE

Located in downtown San Francisco, the Parc Fifty Five is within walking distance to most of the grand sights and activities of this colorful city. Cable cars, China Town, shops in Union Square, the theater district and Moscone Convention Center are all within walking distance.

The 32-story hotel houses 1,003 guest rooms, including 23 suites. All rooms have bay windows. The deluxe Concierge Club accommodations feature additional amenities and services, including private access floors and a private lounge.

The 60-seat Corintia Ristorante serves elegant Italian dinners in an intimate setting. Specialties include pastas, risotti, fresh seafood and Italian wines. The menu also includes low cholesterol selections. Additional places to eat at the hotel: The Rikyu Restaurant serves Japanese cuisine; The Veranda Restaurant serves breakfast, lunch and dinner in a casual, garden-like setting; The Piazza Lounge is the place to meet for favorite drinks while enjoying live piano music in the hotel's spacious atrium; The Sanae Piano Lounge features a Karaoke bar, with entertainer Sanae Tanaka playing the piano and singing favorite songs in different languages.

The hotel features a complete business center and 20 meetings rooms totaling 18,000 square feet. This makes for successful meetings or receptions of anywhere from 30 people to 1,500 people.

At the end of a busy day, you can work off the day's tensions in the hotel's full service fitness center.

Address: 55 Cyril Magnin, San Francisco, California 94102
Phone: (415) 392-8000
No. of Rooms: 1,003 **Suites:** 23
Room Rate: $$$
Credit Cards: All major
Services and Amenities: Concierge, Valet parking, Laundry, Valet service, Gift/sundry shop
Room Service: Room service 6am-1am
Restaurant: Corintia Ristorante, Rikyu, Veranda
Bar: Piazza, Sanae Piano Lounge
Business Facilities: Business center
Conference Rooms: 20, Capacity: 1,500
Sports Facilities: Full fitness center
Attractions: Cable Cars, San Francisco Centre, Moscone Convention Center

RITZ CARLTON SAN FRANCISCO

The Ritz Carlton is a historic landmark building located on Nob Hill. Bordering the Financial District, Chinatown and Union Square, Ritz Carlton is convenient to all San Francisco attractions. The hotel is also a regular stop on the California Street cable car line.

One first notices the beauty of the neoclassic exterior. A block-long facade of Ionic columns, rich filigree patterns, and carved lionheads are showcased by outdoor lighting. The architectural beauty of the hotel is also extended inside, where the interior is decorated in Italian marble, silk wall coverings, antique furnishings, and an abundance of museum-quality art works.

Accommodations provide all the amenities, including extras such as fully stocked honor bars with refrigerators, in-room safes, and VCRs and video tapes on request. Residents of every floor also receive a morning newspaper and twice-daily maid service. Italian marble bathrooms offer terry robes, double sinks, and phone extensions. For the utmost in residential luxury, the rooms and suites on the Ritz-Carlton Club levels provide this and extra pampering as well.

The hotel's signature restaurant is "The Dining Room," where traditional French is served in an intimate, formal setting. The menu changes weekly and guests are encouraged to compose their "tasting" meals of 2 to 4 courses to suit their preferences. "The Restaurant" serves innovative Northern California cuisine and features a delightful Sunday Jazz Brunch, where jazz music soothes the mind, and caviar, fruits, cheeses and smoked salmon excite the palate. The Garden Courtyard offers terrace dining for open-air breakfast, lunch, dinner and Sunday Brunch.

The prominent Ritz-Carlton ballroom can host banquets for up to 825. Nine other meeting rooms are available, with all the necessary equipment for a successful meeting.

For relaxation after a busy day in San Francisco, the hotel provides a fitness center and spa with indoor lap pool, whirlpool, steam, sauna, and massage therapy rooms. Certified personal training instructors are also available.

Address: 600 Stockton St., San Francisco, California 94108
Phone: (415) 296-7465, Fax: (415) 296-8559
No. of Rooms: 336 **Suites:** 44
Room Rate: $$$
Credit Cards: All major
Services and Amenities: 24hr concierge, Valet service, Valet parking, Gift shops, Babysitting, City transportation, Remote ctl. TV, VCR on request, Radio, Stocked minibar, Refrigerator, Phone, In-room safe, Twice daily maid, Robes, Comp. newspaper
Room Service: 24 hours
Restaurant: The Dining Room, The Restaurant
Bar: Lobby Lounge, Ritz Bar
Business Facilities: Audio-visual, Secretarial, Translation, Teleconferencing
Conference Rooms: 9, Capacity: 825
Sports Facilities: Pool, Fitness center, Spa, Whirlpool, Steam, Sauna
Location: Nob Hill
Attractions: Cable car, Chinatown, Union Square shopping, Golden Gate Park

SHERATON PALACE HOTEL

Right in the middle of downtown, Sheraton Palace Hotel is a turn-of-the-century Belle Epoch Beaux Arts building. The interior is grandly decorated with polished marble walls and floors, and is highlighted by vaulted ceilings, marble columns and African and Honduran mahogany.

All rooms are luxuriously furnished in beige, gray and rose color schemes, in a traditional decor built around antique reproductions, including four poster beds. Each bathroom is finished in marble and the finest fixtures, with hair dryer and telephone. All suites have a living room with writing table, sofa, antiques, and reproduction fixtures.

Sheraton Palace Hotel features the world-famous Garden Court restaurant, where expansive elegance surrounds you while dine or enjoy cocktails. You are seated among rich marble columns and potted palms, all under crystal chandeliers, gold-leaf sconces, and a spectacular leaded glass-dome ceiling. One celebrated lunch entree to try is the Palace Court Salad with Green Goddess Dressing. For more intimate and casual dining, Maxfield's Restaurant offers Old San Francisco cuisine of grilled and light fare in a setting of dark wood paneling. Acclaimed as the "Best Sushi Bar in Town", Kyo-ya Restaurant offers an extensive menu of authentic Japanese delicacies.

Meeting and convention space has been expanded to 45,000 square feet, and includes a new, ultra-modern business center. Three historic ballrooms host receptions of up to 1,000 people or banquets of up to 800.

The new health spa on the fourth level sports an exercise room, whirlpool and sauna. The beautiful indoor lap pool is covered with a skylit domed ceiling.

Sheraton Palace Hotel is situated in an ideal downtown location, just a short walk to Moscone Center, Union Square and the Financial District. In addition, all the famous sights of San Francisco are nearby, from the Golden Gate Bridge to Coit Tower, the Palace of Fine Arts to Embarcadero Center.

Address: 2 New Montgomery St., San Francisco, California 94105
Phone: 415-392-8600, 1-800-325-3535, Fax: 415-453-0671
No. of Rooms: 550 **Suites:** 32
Room Rate: $$$
Credit Cards: All major
Services and Amenities: Concierge, Car hire, Parking, Laundry, Valet service, Currency exchange, Specialty shops, Babysitting, Cable TV, Iron & board, Radio, Refrigerator, Phones, Bath phone, In-room safe, Comp. newspaper, Robe, Hairdryer, Computer/fax hookup
Room Service: 24 hours
Restaurant: Garden Court, Maxfield's, Kyo-ya
Bar: Garden Court, Pied Piper Bar
Business Facilities: Audio-visual, Secretarial, Fax, Translation (avail.), Copying, Postal, Teleconferencing, Fax rental
Conference Rooms: 22, Capacity: 1,000
Sports Facilities: Pool, Health spa, Sauna, Whirlpool, Massage, Gym, Tennis club privileges
Location: Downtown
Attractions: Financial District, Union Square, Embarcadero Center, theaters

STOUFFER STANFORD COURT HOTEL

This legendary grand hotel of Nob Hill reflects the gracious hospitality of an earlier era. The entrance to the hotel is a fountained courtyard with a Tiffany-style glass dome. Once inside, you will notice the fresh-cut flowers, fine antiques and original art collected from around the world that welcome you.

Each of the 402 guestrooms and 34 suites is a charming blend of fine 19th century European reproductions, antiques and oriental classics. Bathrooms feature Carrara marble and are complete with many extra amenities, such as two guest robes, a heated towel rack and a bathroom television.

The hotel restaurant, Fournou's Oven, is one of San Francisco's most charming. Colorful handmade tiles adorn immense roasting ovens and garlands of herbs hang among exquisite antiques and art work. Specializing in contemporary American cuisine, the menu includes fresh seafood and succulent roasts of lamb, veal and beef cooked over oak embers in the massive ovens. It's 20,000-bottle award-winning wine cellar offers an impressive selections of wines from around the world. The Lobby Bar provides afternoon tea, wine and champagne by the glass. At the romantic International Bar, you can sip classic cocktails or espressos while looking at the panoramic view of the city skyline.

As a complimentary service during the weekdays, a vintage Rolls Royce Phantom IV or Mercedes Benz limousine can take you to the theater, shopping, restaurants or any location in downtown San Francisco.

Address: 905 California St., Nob Hill, San Francisco, California 94108
Phone: (415) 989-3500, Fax: (415) 391-0513
No. of Rooms: 402 **Suites:** 34
Room Rate: $$$
Credit Cards: All major
Services and Amenities: Concierge, Comp. limousine, Valet parking, 24hr laundry/valet, Currency exchange, Shopping arcade, Babysitting, Comp. shoeshine, Remote ctl. TV, TV in bathroom, Radio, Newspaper, Phones, Desk, Hairdryer, Nightly turndown, Bathrobes, Heated towel rack
Room Service: 24 hours
Restaurant: Fournou's Ovens
Bar: International Bar, Lobby
Business Facilities: Audio-visual, Secretarial, Fax, Translation, Copying, Notary
Conference Rooms: 13, Capacity: 800
Sports Facilities: Health club privileges nearby
Location: Nob Hill
Attractions: Cable Car, Union Square, Chinatown, Financial district

WESTIN SAINT FRANCIS

From its prestigious address on Union Square, The Westin St. Francis overlooks San Francisco's exclusive shopping area and the bustling Financial District. Since 1904, St. Francis has hosted international dignitaries, royal figures, celebrities and prominent city events, becoming very much a part of San Francisco's history and tradition.

The opulent Powell Street lobby is decorated with crystal chandeliers, an inlaid marble floor, gilded woodwork and elaborate rosettes which adorn the ceiling. The St. Francis is the only hotel in the world that washes its money. The unprecedented tradition began in 1938 when the manager noticed that dirty money was soiling the ladies' white gloves. 55 years later, the hotel still continues to turn out sparkling clean coins.

Each of the 1,200 guestrooms is decorated with elegant wood furnishings and tasteful floral fabrics, and contains all the amenities one would expect from an international first-class hotel.

Victor's, the award-winning restaurant on the 32nd floor of the Tower building, is named after St. Francis' first chef Victor Hirtzler. Victor's menu delights the palate with seasonal California Cuisine, prepared from the freshest and finest available seafood, produce, and meats. A caffelier offers patrons a selection of fresh, individually ground coffees blended to taste at your tableside. 20-foot floor-to-ceiling windows frame downtown San Francisco and the Bay Bridge while you eat. The Compass Rose is San Francisco's opulent "Grand Bar", serving lunch, afternoon tea, caviar, tasting menu, champagne and cocktails. Four additional bars and restaurants offer guests a wide variety of dining and relaxing.

Meeting facilities, which range from elegant meetings halls to sumptuous dining rooms, are first-class, and St. Francis has been awarded numerous awards for its meeting facilities. A full service convention staff and business center will insure every meeting is a success.

The city's world famous cable cars stop in front of the hotel and can take you for a thrilling ride to Fisherman's Wharf or Chinatown.

Address: 335 Powell St., San Francisco, California 94102
Phone: (415) 397-7000, Fax: (415) 774-0124, Telex: 278584, Cable: STFRANCIS
No. of Rooms: 1,200 **Suites:** 85
Room Rate: $$$
Services and Amenities: Concierge, Airport limousine, Valet parking, Laundry/Valet, Safe deposit fac., Currency exchange, Car rental, Barber/beauty shop, Gift shop, Babysitting, Japanese guest desk, TV, In-house movies, Minibar/refrigerator, Phone, In-room safe, Robes
Room Service: 24 hours
Restaurant: Victor's, St. Francis Grill
Bar: Compass Rose, Deweys
Business Facilities: Audio-visual, Secretarial, Fax/telex, Postal, Copying, Computers, Cellular phones, Voicemail
Conference Rooms: 26, Capacity: 1,500
Sports Facilities: Fitness center
Location: Union Square
Attractions: Shopping, Financial district, Cable Car, Fisherman's Wharf, Moscone Convention Ctr.

HOTEL DE ANZA

Originally built in 1931, the De Anza Hotel is now a registered historical landmark. Marble predominates throughout: in the lobby there are gold-tone walls with marble affect, stark and elegant, softened by silk draperies, plush seating arrangements and rare antiques. Marble is repeated in the floors and walls of the dining room and in the guest rooms, where it is used on countertops as well as in the baths.

Suites have king-sized beds, parlor areas, 3 telephones (one in the bath) and three televisions, also one in the bath.

The dining room is in Art Deco style with warm gold-tone walls. After a dinner featuring Linguini Con Frutti De Mare, and Chocolate Truffle Cake for dessert, diners may repair to the lounge to be entertained by a jazz trio, a swing band, or an opera singer.

With San Jose growing as it has, the hotel is ideally situated in the heart of town, three blocks from the Convention Center and Pavilion Shops, and minutes from the Center for the Performing Arts. Out-of-town guests are transported to and from the airport in the hotel's limousine.

Address: 233 W. Santa Clara St., San Jose, California 95113
Phone: 408-286-1000, 408-286-0500
No. of Rooms: 101 **Suites:** 1
Services and Amenities: Concierge, Comp. limousine, Valet parking, TV, VCR, Videotapes, Minibar, Voice mail, Fax port, Robes, Comp. coffee and paper, Hairdryer, Turndown service
Restaurant: Dining Room, "Raid the Pantry"
Bar: Club Room, El Capitan
Business Facilities: Audio-visual, Secretarial, Fax, Translation, Pagers, Personal computers, Cellular phones, Fax machine on req.
Conference Rooms: Capacity: 100
Sports Facilities: Exercise facilities
Attractions: San Jose Convention Center, Center for Performing Arts

HYATT REGENCY WAIKOLOA

They pulled out all the stops for this $400 million mega-resort that stands out above all, if for sheer size only. On the sunny Kohala Coast north of Kailua, in spectacular sunset territory, sits this extravagant, elaborate newcomer. You'll detect Water Swami Howard Field's touch as you're carried from level to level in the river pool's gentle current. Landscaped with lagoons, pools, waterfalls and Japanese gardens, the resort houses guests in three 66-story buildings. The main wings are connected with a mile-long walkway and house an art collection fit for a museum. A sleek tram and a fleet of Venetian-style boats will whisk you to your suite or nearby golf courses. Most of the guest rooms have ocean views, and water seems to be everywhere. All of it is for play.

This is a conference planner's dream come true, as there is a ballroom area measuring nearly a acre, capable of hosting 6,200 people. Restaurants and lounges? Try nineteen of them and they run the gamut from a Polynesian buffet to the Orchid Cafe, serving light California fare. There's so much to do here, you'll need an activities director so you don't miss anything. Try tennis on eight courts with two clay courts in a garden setting, including an exhibition court, a gigantic health spa, racquetball/squash courts, jogging trails and swimming pools. Nearby is horseback riding, deep sea fishing, sailing, windsurfing and helicoptering. Nothing was spared in providing a wildlife lesson, as you feast your eyes on parrots, swans, cranes, flamingoes, Japanese koi, and tame Atlantic bottlenose dolphins.

You'll have your choice of a Robert Trent Jones, Jr., course and a new $16 million Jay Moorish/Tom Weiskopf. Set on lava beds with the dormant volcano Mauna Loa looming in the background, the Kings' Course is a typical Scottish design. For every hole into the wind, you'll find one with the wind. Number five, a par 4, is a go-for-the-green drive, but you'll have to avoid two large lava boulders on the left and a deep bunker on the right. A gigantic pristine double green serves both the third and sixth holes in case you want to pretend you're at St. Andrews. You won't be disappointed with this new gem which also boasts an attractive, airy clubhouse.

Address: One Waikoloa Resort, Big Island of Hawaii, 96743
Phone: 808-885-1234 800-233-1234
No. of Rooms: 1,241
Rates: $$$
Services: Concierge, Valet, Beauty shop, Barber shop, Laundry, International currency exchange, Babysitting, House doctor, Library, Sundries shop, Room service
Restrictions: No pets
Restaurant: Several
Bar: Many
Business Fac.: Full conference facilities, Conf. rm. cap.: 6,200
Sports Fac.: Tennis, Pools, Health spa, Racquetball
Location: Kohala Coast
Attractions: Windsurfing, sailing, volcanoes, tidal rock pools

Course: King's Course
Distance: 6,010
Rating: 75, No. of holes: 18
Guest Policy: Resort guests may book in advance
Phone Club-House: 808-885-1234
Pro's Name: Joseph Rool
Reservations: Make reservations 2 days in advance
Season: Year round
Guest Carry Clubs: No

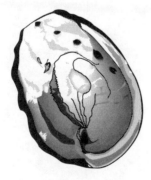

HOTEL HANA-MAUI

The lovely Hotel Hana-Maui "The world's most romantic hide-away," is in the exclusive, secluded Hana area of the island of Maui. 96 accommodations, including sea ranch cottages with ocean views, are scattered throughout 66 acres of landscaped gardens within a 4,700-acre working ranch. These accommodations feature a striking decor of white with natural wood beams and shuttered windows. Plantation ceiling fans whir overhead. Orchids and other tropical plans bloom indoors as well as out. The luxurious baths have sunken tubs, and outside each bath is an enclosed private garden.

The sporting life is in full swing at this resort. Facilities include two swimming pools, tennis courts, a croquet lawn, and a well-equipped riding stable. A full range of water and ranch sports are available at the hotel. Our Wellness Center features programs designed to enhance the quality of life.

The Hotel Hana-Maui Restaurant takes pride in the innovative Pacific-American cuisine of chef Amy Ferguson-Ota. A favorite meeting spot for guests and residents alike, the Paniola Lounge features local entertainment nightly.

The Hana area is rich in Hawaiian lore and replete with visitor opportunities. View the local botanical gardens, enjoy hiking trails in Waianapanapa State Park, Ohe'o Gulch and Hana Ranch. To stay at Hotel Hana-Maui is to experience "the Hawaii that used to be."

Address: P.O. Box 8, Hana, Maui 96713
Phone No.: 808-248-8211
Toll-free: 800-321-HANA
FAX: 808-248-7202
Reservation Services: 800-321-HANA
Rates: $$$$
Credit Cards: Visa, MC, AmEx
No. of Rooms: 96
Services and Amenities: Valet service, Library, Car hire, Laundry, Babysitting service, Game area, Phone in bath, Robes, Complimentary toiletries, Coffee grinder-brewers, Refrigerators
Restrictions: No pets
Concierge: 7:00 a.m.-9:00 p.m.
Restaurant: Hotel Hana-Maui Restaurant 7:30-10:00 a.m., 11:30 a.m.-2:00 p.m., 6:30-10:30 p.m.
Bar: Paniola Lounge, 11:00 a.m.-10:30 p.m.
Sports Facilities: Tennis courts, croquet, practice golf, horseback riding, snorkeling, bicycling, swimming, fishing, hula, massage, Wellness Center
Location: Hana Ranch
Attractions: Museum and cultural center, Waianapanapa State Park, botanical gardens, Seven Pools at Ohe'o, Hasegawa General Store

HALEKULANI

Halekulani means "House Befitting Heaven," a name given a century ago by Hawaiian fisherman to the original private beachfront estate. Today, this modern luxury resort, voted "Top Tropical Resort" in Conde Nast's 1992 Reader's Choice Awards, is known throughout the world as Hawaii's home away from home for international royalty, celebrities and discerning travelers.

Spacious guest rooms are decorated in an elegant white on white scheme, featuring 15 shades of white. Most rooms offer sweeping views of Waikiki beach. Ceramic tiled bathrooms include deep soaking tub and his and her bathrobes.

La Mer offers extraordinarily fine dining in an environment of premier elegance overlooking the Pacific Ocean. Chef Mavrothalassitis dazzles guests with his Salad of Sauteed Foie Gras and Baby Corn with red currant vinaigrette, Risotto of Pacific Crab and Avocado with fresh tomato nage; and the La Mer's signature Onaga (long-tailed snapper) baked in Thyme and Rosemary Rock Salt Crust with a sauce of fresh herbs.

Nothing is more luxurious than lounging around the Halekulani's lush swimming pool. Beneath the pool's clear waters, sparkles a huge multicolored cattelya orchid, created from over one million imported glass tiles. Poolside service is superb. A complimentary Junior Program for children is available during Easter, summer and winter vacations.

Don't miss the traditional sunset cocktails on the beach lawn, where Hawaiian music is provided by top entertainers beneath a towering, century-old Kiawe tree.

Address: 2199 Kalia Road, Honolulu, Hawaii 96815
Phone: (808) 923-2311, (800) 367-2343 (Fax): (808) 926-8004
No. of Rooms: 412 **Suites:** 44
Room Rate: $$$
Credit Cards: AmEx, VISA, Diners Club, MC, CB, JCB, Optima
Services and Amenities: Welcome bowl of assorted fresh fruits and chocolates, Mini-refrigerator with bar accessories, Remote color cable T.V., T.V. audio in bathroom, Bathrobes, Private label toiletries, Three telephones, In-room safe, Daily morning newspaper, Twice-daily turndown service with memento each night, Full-service concierge, Laundry,
Restrictions: A select number of rooms specifically designed for wheelchair occupants.
Room Service: 24 hours
Restaurant: House Without a Key, La Mer, Living Room
Bar: Lewers Lounge
Business Facilities: Complete business and secretarial services,
Conference Rooms: 4, Capacity: 650
Sports Facilities: Pool, Complimentary fitness room and program, Water sports
Location: Waikiki Beach
Attractions: Waikiki Beach, Shopping, Boat cruises

KAHALA HILTON

The Kahala Hilton is a tropical masterpiece on the island of Oahu. Only ten minutes from Wakiki Beach, this thoroughly modern hotel is set amidst the unspoiled natural beauty of Oahu's prestigious Waialae Kahala district.

Consistently voted as one of the top ten resorts in the world, the Kahala has perfected the art of indulging its guests in luxurious seclusion. Guest rooms are among the largest in Honolulu, offering spectacular views of the ocean, mountains or the resort's private lagoon. Upon arrival, travelers receive a fresh pineapple, complementary amenities, and the use of a Japanese robe and slippers. Fresh orchids are placed on guests' pillows in the evening.

Kahala's Maile Restaurant has garnered numerous top awards, including a five diamond rating (the highest rating possible) from AAA for four years running. Chef Dominique Jamain continues his divine culinary innovations, serving up such mouthwatering delicacies as Hawaiian Spiny Lobster Medallions with Tangy Pineapple Salsa and Coconut Trio Delight with Passion Fruit and Chocolate Sauce.

Guests may enjoy an enchanting encounter with the penguins, sea turtles and tropical fish that inhabit the resort's private blue lagoon. The Kahala's 800 foot stretch of private, uncrowded beach is the perfect place for solitary walks or relaxation. The adventurous should be sure to sample the windsurfing around the Kahala's private island, or embark on one the resort's fabulous scuba diving and deep sea fishing excursions.

Address: 5000 Kahala Avenue, Honolulu, Hawaii 96816
Phone: (808) 734-2211, (800)367-2525 (Fax): (808) 737-2478
No. of Rooms: 340 **Suites:** 29
Room Rate: $$$
Credit Cards: All major
Services and Amenities: Fresh pineapple upon arrival, Dressing robes and slippers, Refrigerator, Mini-Bar, Remote control cable TV, Bedside clock radios, Hair dryers, Makeup mirrors, Assorted toiletries, Direct dial telephones, Nightly turndown service with orchid on pillow, Barber & beauty salon, Shops, Concierge, Multi-lingual staff, Dolphin Lagoon, Gourmet picnic baskets available.
Room Service: 24 hours
Restaurant: Maile Restaurant, Hala Terrace, Plumeria Cafe, Gazebo Snack Bar
Bar: Maile Lounge, Hala Bar, Lobby Lounge
Business Facilities: Complete business and secretarial services,
Conference Rooms: 7 Capacity: 400
Sports Facilities: Pool, Paddle boating and kayaking around hotel's private island, Tennis, Water sports
Location: Waikiki Beach
Attractions: Private beach, Daily dolphin shows, Maunalua Bay Tennis club, Ala Moana Shopping Center, Sea Life Park, Yacht cruise of Pearl Harbor, Eight-hour Oahu Circle Island tour

THE ROYAL HAWAIIAN RESORT

Serenely nestled among Honolulu's towering highrises, the Royal Hawaiian Hotel faces the shores of Waikiki Bay in traditional elegance, a regal testament to a bygone era of gracious living and tropical romance. The Royal, affectionately known as the "Pink Palace of the Pacific," has consistently ranked among the world's Grand Hotels since it opened its doors in 1927.

The Hotel's Mediterranean architecture was the rage of its time. Long hallways with Spanish-style arches open onto the azure waters and white sands of Waikiki beach. Vaulted Moorish ceilings with crystal chandeliers, Spanish-style cupolas and exquisite tropical gardens recall the exotic grandeur of a Moroccan castle.

And if these pink walls could talk . . . Mary Pickford and Douglas Fairbanks stayed here, as did President Franklin and Jack Benny. The Royal survived even "Beatlemania," when eager teenage fans crowded the lobby to catch a glimpse of John, Paul, George and Ringo. More recently, the likes of Kevin Costner, Michael Caine and Rosanna Arquette have basked in the Royal's luxurious atmosphere.

After a relaxing day of sunbathing on the white sands of Waikiki (the Royal's attendant will smooth the sand for you and remind you to turn over ever 20 minutes), how about a grand feast under the stars at the Royal's Hawaiian Luau? And be sure to catch the dinner show at the world-famous Monarch Room, where Hawaii's Brothers Cazimero and the Royal Dance Company entertain with a traditional song and dance spectacular.

Address: 2259 Kalakaua Avenue, Honolulu, Hawaii 96815-2578
Phone: (808) 923-7311, (800)334-8484 (Fax): (808) 924-7098
No. of Rooms: 468 **Suites:** 58
Room Rate: $$$$
Credit Cards: All major credit cards
Services and Amenities: Multi-lingual concierge, Valet parking, Laundry, Air conditioning, Valet service, Electronic safe, In-room daily newspaper and magazines, Fresh banana bread, Fresh flower lei on arrival, Champagne on ice upon arrival, Fruit Basket and floral arrangement, Nightly turn-down with chocolate mints, Plush bath towels, Bathrobe and slippers, Color TV, In-house movies, Refrigerator, Modular phones for lap-top computer, 24-hour nurse and doctor, Specialty shop, Babysitting, Barber and beauty shop, Limousine.
Room Service: 24 hours
Restaurant: Surf Room, Monarch Room, The Royal Luau, Tea Dance
Bar: Mai Tai Bar
Business Facilities: 24-hour telex and fax services, Secretarial services,
Conference Rooms: 5, Capacity: 4,000
Sports Facilities: Private beach at Waikiki, Freshwater swimming pool, Preferential tee-off times at Makaha Resort and Golf Club.
Location: Honolulu, Waikiki Beach
Attractions: Shopping at Waikiki, The Royal Luau

MAUI PRINCE HOTEL

Nestled on a sandy beach in a secluded cove, the Maui Prince Hotel at Makena Resort offers the visitor Hawaii as it was meant to be—private and beautiful—with golf, tennis, swimming, sailing and sunning in Hawaii's best climate.

The six-story V-shaped building embraces a central atrium courtyard with cascading waterfalls, rock gardens, streams, footbridges, stone lamps and exotic foliage. The open-air lobby is enhanced with warm teak paneling, teak furnishings and colorful woven carpets that cover the tile floor. An original bronze sculpture and large original oil painting complete the lobby decor. Outside, a 300,000-gallon fresh-water pond surrounds the courtyard with over 1,000 colorful Japanese koi.

This 310-room hotel includes 20 suites with panoramic views of the ocean and nearby islands of Molokini and Kahoolawe. Guest rooms are appointed with oak furnishings and feature private lanais. All baths are spacious and include special bath amenities, and separate room commodes and telephones.

Teak woodworking and brass railings are set off by romantic candlelight and stunning views at the award-winning Prince Court restaurant serving innovative Hawaiian regional cuisine. Two other exquisite restaurants, the Japanese Hakone restaurant and the open air Cafe Kiowai provide superb dining opportunities for guests. Evening brings the soothing sounds of classical strings wafting upward from the courtyard as the classical musicians entertain for the dinner hour.

The 18-hole championship Makena Golf Course is the creation of Robert Trent Jones, Jr. Much of the natural setting has been worked into the design, resulting in a challenging course affording ocean vistas from virtually every fairway. Breathtaking views of the Pacific Ocean and Haleakala Crater can be appreciated from the Makena Clubhouse, where a pro shop, restaurant and locker rooms are located. The resort also has a 5-star, award-winning tennis facility with six plexi-paved courts, including two lit for night play. Beautifully landscaped pathways lead to the two outdoor swimming pools, a fully equipped ocean activities center and a serene quarter-mile white-sand beach. A sleek 46-foot sailing catamaran is available for snorkeling trips, sunset cruises and whale watching.

Address: 5400 Makena Alanui, Kihei, Hawaii 96753
Phone: 808-874-1111, 800-321-6284, Fax: 808-879-8763, Telex: 510-600-6992
No. of Rooms: 310 **Suites:** 20
Room Rate: $$$
Credit Cards: AmEx, CB, DC, Visa
Services and Amenities: 24hr concierge, Car rental, Parking, Laundry, Valet service, Currency exchange, TV lounge, Game area, Gift shop, House doctor, Babysitting, Cable TV, Radio, Indiv. climate ctl., Comp. toiletries, Comp. newspaper
Room Service: 24 hours
Restaurant: Prince Court
Bar: Molokini Lounge
Business Facilities: Audio-visual, Fax/telex, Japanese translation, German translation, Copying, Message center
Conference Rooms: 3, Capacity: 180
Sports Facilities: Pools, Weight training, Aerobics, Massage, Croquet, Tennis, 18-hole golf, Horseback riding, Water sports
Location: Makena Area
Attractions: Beach, historical tour of Makena's undeveloped beaches and ancient lava flows

MAUNA LANI BAY HOTEL

Nestled in a 16th century ebony lava flow, this six-story 351 room resort, is the newest of the great golf and tennis destinations along this breathtaking coast. The atrium lobby is the most incredible feature, with six stories of lush rain forest foliage, waterfalls and a fish-filled lagoon. Acres of King Kamehameha I's ancient spring-fed fishponds and gardens provide solitude, picnic grounds and even a private swimming hole. 15th century rock shelters were left untouched during construction.

Ocean and mountain views highlight large light rooms, decorated in tones of burgundy and ivory. The Le Soliel is the signature restaurant here. Opening onto a seaside garden, the casually elegant award-winner boasts one of Hawaii's most extensive and impressive wine cellars. The other eateries, too, deserve applause.

Flanked by the island's four great mountains, the showpiece resort's recreational facilities are excellent. The Tennis Garden, with a five-star rating, has ten 3-speed outdoor courts. A large free-form pool, and jogging and bike trails are guaranteed to tempt a confirmed couch potato. The white sandy beach is slide show perfect, plus you can scuba dive, sail, fish for marlin, snorkel, or try an outrigger canoe.

The magnificence of the Francis H. I'i Brown Course has moved players and naturalists to praise the vast lava sculpture whose green fairways snake through a treasure trove of ancient cave-homes, shrines and petroglyphs as well as the historic King's trail. The Homer Flint design, a 6,259 yard par 72, features four ocean holes, three lakes, 43 fairway bunkers, plenty of green traps, and a spectacular ocean shot from the 6th tee. A second 18 hole course is under construction and due to open in early 1991.

Address: One Mauna Lani Dr., Kohala Coast, Island of Hawaii, 96743
Phone: 808-885-6622 800-367-2323
No. of Rooms: 351
Rates: $$$
Services: Medical clinic, Beauty/Barber shop, Hawaiian Quilting, Hula Lessons, Lei making, Weaving, Historic Tour, Hawaiian Massage Demonstration, Floral Demo.
Restaurant: Le Soleil and Canoe House
Bar: The Bar
Business Fac.: Audio-visual, Conf. rm. cap.: 400
Sports Fac.: Tennis, Pool, Windsurfing, Health club
Attractions: Mauna Kea, North Kohala Tour, Kailua Kona

Course: Francis H. I' Brown
Distance: 6,259, Par: 72
Rating: 70.5, No. of holes: 18
Guest Policy: Call for availability
Phone Club-House: 808-885-6655
Pro's Name: Jerry Johnston
Fees: **
Reservations: Telephone for tee times
Season: Year round
Guest Carry Clubs: No

MAUNA KEA

A vision of Laurance Rockefeller, and now under the helm of Westin, this splendidly understated vacation destination welcomed its first guests in 1965, as the most luxurious hotel ever constructed in Hawaii. The renowned hotel sits on a hillside overlooking a white sandy beach and crystal waters. Landscaping and architecture are imaginative, with lofty palms towering over public areas where gentle breezes play. But what's most memorable here is the antique art displayed in public areas. A majestic seventh-century Buddha, Japanese tansu chests, and a remarkable collection of Hawaiian quilts are just a few of the treasures from Pacific Islands. Rooms are large, fanned by tradewinds, with attractive wooden shutters, wooden ceiling fans, private lanais, polished brick floors, and wicker furniture. Large floral lithographs in bright island colors by Hawaii's Lloyd Sexton inspire the decor. There are also 10 suites and 8 villas. Expect impeccable service, handsomely appointed tables and an innovative menu in the exotic, split-level Batik Room with its Ceylonese motif. There are five other restaurants, and five lounges scattered about the main building. Don't miss the weekly luau, with traditional roasted pig and local favorites such as guava and poi palau, and the music of Hawaii. There is excellent snorkeling, windsurfing and boogie boarding from the beach. And of course, a beautiful pool, thirteen tennis courts, and badminton courts. Also available are Lasers, and Scuba and deep sea fishing excursions aboard the resort's 58 foot catamaran. Try horseback riding, play volleyball, go hunting, or take a sightseeing helicopter trip and look down on the rivers of lava created by the Kiluea volcano. Or relax under a palm tree and ask yourself where else you can snow ski down a dormant volcano in the morning, and body surf in 75 degree clear water in the afternoon.

The Robert Trent Jones, Sr. 18 hole course is something to behold. Ready for play in 1964, the challenging course has won numerous awards. With lush grass growing on ancient lava that spills dramatically into the sea, the par 72 layout was recently toughened and softened, with four tees to challenge all playing levels. The spectacular par-three third hole carries 200 yards over the ocean from the blue tees. Hook it and you can kiss that little ball good-bye.

Address: P.O. Box 218, Kohula Coast Amuea, 96743
Phone: 808-882-7222 800-228-3000
No. of Rooms: 310
Rates: $$
Services: Clinic, Fitness center, Barber/Beauty shop, Beach Service Center, Safe Deposit Boxes, Room service
Restaurant: Cafe Terrace, Batik Room
Bar: Gazebo Bar
   Conf. rm. cap.: 180
Sports Fac.: Tennis, Pool, Volleybal, Snorkeling
Attractions: Helicopter tours, archaeological sites

Course: Mauna Kea
Distance: 6,365, Par: 72
Rating: 70.7, No. of holes: 18
Guest Policy: Call for availability
Phone Club-House: 808-882-7222
Pro's Name: JD Ebersberger
Fees: *
Reservations: Call for tee times
Season: Year round
Guest Carry Clubs: No

THE KAPALUA BAY HOTEL & VILLAS

On the northwest tip of Maui, above white sand beaches sheltered by lava peninsulas, Kapalua Bay Hotel & Villas is a 750-acre tropical paradise certain to delight even the most demanding international traveler. The neighboring islands of Lanai and Molokai are visible across the brilliant blue waters of the bay from this full service resort, which boasts thirty-six holes of golf designed by Arnold Palmer, and a tennis garden with ten plexi-pave courts arranged in separate pairs to eliminate distractions. Beside the hotel is a gallery of twenty-two unique international boutiques and shops.

The spacious guest rooms are done in relaxing pastels, with natural wood accents throughout. Each air-conditioned room has a private sitting area and lanai. Sometimes you can even watch whales cavorting from your terrace. The baths feature "his-and-her" amenities and oversized dressing areas.

The Plantation Veranda, one of several fine dining options, is elegantly decorated with Pegge Hopper murals on the walls. Ceiling fans do a slow dance overhead. Special touches, like complimentary Kir Royale and an orchid spray for every lady, complement the lovely environment. A harpist plays nightly. Your divine dinner might begin with pates or Melon in Strawberry Liquour, followed by a Plantation Salad. Seafood may be poached with saffron and tomatoes or sauteed with lobster and Beurre Blanc. From the Kiawe charcoal grill come Noisettes of Spring Lamb in Tomato Coulis and Chanterelles. A fresh tropical fruit sorbet ends the meal on a note of perfection.

Other dining choices include the Pool Terrace and the Bar with its sporty atmosphere. The wine list here is a connoisseur's dream. The Bay Lounge offers tea service from 3:00 to 5:00 and hors d'oeuvres thereafter. The lounge is ideal for sunset views or whale-watching, best appreciated with the aid of the house specialty drink, the Kapalua Butterfly.

Internationally renowned since it opened in 1978, the Kapalua Bay Hotel is the centerpiece of an award winning community and a remarkable hotel experience not to be missed.

Address: One Bay Dr., Lahaina, Hawaii 96761
Phone: 808-669-5656, 800-367-8000, Fax: 808-669-4694, Telex: ITT 669-6515
No. of Rooms: 194 **Suites:** 3
Room Rate: $$
Credit Cards: AmEx, DC, CB, MC, Visa
Services and Amenities: Concierge, Car hire, Parking, Laundry, Valet service, Currency exchange, Barber/beauty shop, Babysitting, Cable TV, Comp. toiletries, Robes
Restrictions: No pets
Room Service: Room service
Restaurant: Plantation Veranda, Bay Club, The Garden
Bar: Bay Lounge
Business Facilities: Audio-visual, Secretarial, Telex, Teleconferencing, Copying, Message center
Conference Rooms: 2, Capacity: 115
Sports Facilities: Aerobics, Sailing, 10 tennis courts, 54-hole championship golf

THE LODGE AT KOELE

The Lodge at Koele has the ambiance of a worldly plantation-owner's residence. It is designed in the manner of a grand estate or country lodge, with heavy timbers, beamed ceilings and natural stone fireplaces. A large porch with lounging chairs provides a relaxing spot from which to view spectacular sunsets or vast pineapple fields.

The Great Hall, the heart of the lodge, is appointed with comfortable, large-scale furnishings and unique art objects, paintings, sculptures and rare artifacts of the Pacific. Striking octagonal corner rooms feature musical recitals or film screenings.

The guestrooms continue the "plantation" theme with carved four-poster beds, quilted pillows, colorful paintings by local artists, and carpets custom-made in radiant Hawaiian colors. The bathrooms feature Brazilian marble counter tops and floors in blue and white tiles.

For casual dining, the Keole Terrace overlooks the Lodge's Great Hall and outdoor gardens. The Keole Dining Room is a formal dining area which features sophisticated cuisine, blending the best of Lana'i fresh fruits, meat and seafood with classic European and Oriental culinary techniques. A favorite dish here is the Lana'i venison loin with Moloka'i sweet potato puree. The Tea Room is a cozy area for drinks, hors d'oeuvres and music.

Address: P.O. Box 774, Lanai City 96763
Phone No. 808-565-7300
Toll-free: 808-329-4666
Fax: 808-565-4561
Rates: $$$$
Credit Cards: All major credit cards
No. of Rooms: 102 **Suites:** 14
Services and Amenities: Valet service, Beauty shop, Garage and parking, Car hire, Laundry, Gift shop, TV Lounge, International currency exchange, Complimentary shoeshine, Baby-sitting service, Card/game area, Library, Fireplaces (4 suites), Balconies, VCR, Radio, Wet bar (2 suites), Robes, Complimentary toiletries
Restrictions: Children under 8 free with parents, No pets allowed, 2 rooms equipped for handicapped
Room Service: 6 a.m. - 10 p.m.
Concierge: 6:30 a.m. - 10:30 p.m.
Restaurant: Koele Terrace, Koele Dining Room (dress code evening: men must wear jackets
Bar: Tea Room, 11 a.m. - 11 p.m.
Business Facilities: Secretarial service, Copiers, Audio-visual
Conference Rooms: 4, capacity: 25 (full-scale facility at Lana'i Conference Center)
Sports Facilities: Outdoor swimming pool, croquet, whirlpool, golf (18 holes), sailing, riding, tennis, scuba, fishing, horseback riding, hunting, jeep rides, lawn bowling, hiking, private picnicking
Location: 1 mile to Lana'i City
Attractions: Four-wheel drive excursions, mountain biking, tackle fishing, ocean rafting, snorkel

THE MANELE BAY HOTEL

The Manele Bay Hotel sits high above Hulopo'e Bay, Lana'i's finest white sand beach, overlooking the nearby island of Kaho'olawe. The brilliant red lava cliffs and rock formations provide a dramatic contrast to the blue-green waters of the sea below. Multi-level gardens are in five different themes—Hawaiian, Japanese, Chinese, Bromeliad and Cosmopolitan—with waterfalls, ponds and streams, exotic plants and flowers.

The lobby features stunning views and original works of Lana'i's native artists. Guests may browse through books and photography and handle artifacts on display.

Guestrooms are spacious and offer views of the ocean, sculptured gardens and waterfalls. Interior decor reflects Mediterranean and Asian influences—custom-designed tile and wall-coverings incorporate five different color schemes—English yellow, Caribbean blue, Mandarin red and other hues. The bathroom features a his and hers marble sink, wall mirror, marble counter top, separate shower stall and separate toilet room. A lighted make-up mirror, hair dryer and other accessories are available for guest use.

Ihilani (heavenly splendor) is a special dining room featuring fish and shellfish with a French flair. Here, guests will be greeted by staff and seated at tables with crystal and silver. A favorite dish is the Nage of Fresh Island Fish with julienne of cucumber & tomato. For dessert, don't miss the Strawberry Sunburst. Guests may also enjoy complimentary tea and pastries on the Kailani Terrace on Saturday afternoon.

For those with an adventuresome spirit, Lana'i is an explorer's mecca. There are many excellent hiking trails through lush forests, over rugged grasslands and beside pristine shorelines.

Address: P.O. Box 774, Lanai City 96763
Phone No. 808-565-7700
Toll-free: 808-329-4666
Fax: 808-565-2483
Rates: $$$$
Credit Cards: All major credit cards
No. of Rooms: 250 **Suites:** 28
Services and Amenities: Valet service, Beauty shop, Garage and parking, Car hire, Laundry, Gift shop, TV lounge, Complimentary shoeshine, Baby-sitting service, Card/game area, Library, Balconies, Complimentary newspaper, Cable TV, VCR, Radio, Ind'l A/C control, Robes, Complimentary toiletries
Restrictions: Children under 8 free w/parents, 4 rooms equipped for handicapped, No pets allowed
Room Service: 6 a.m. - 10 p.m.
Concierge: 7 a.m. - 10 p.m.
Restaurant: Hulopo'e Court, 7 a.m. - 11 a.m., 6 p.m. - 9:30 p.m.; Pool Grill, 11 a.m. - 5:30 p.m.; Ihilani (dress code: coat or jacket), Weds. - Sat. 6 p.m. - 9:30 p.m.
Bar: Poole Grille Bar, Hale Ahe Ahe, 5 p.m. - 11 p.m.
Business Facilities: Message center, Secretarial service, Copiers, Audio-visual,
Conference Rooms: 4, capacity: 20 (also Lanai Conference Center adjacent to hotel)
Sports Facilities: Outdoor swimming pool, croquet, jacuzzi, sauna, massage, aerobics, weight training, golf (18 holes) sailing, riding, tennis, nearby ocean activities: scuba, snorkeling, rafting, fishing
Location: Hulopo'e Bay
Attractions: Four-wheel driving jeep trails to sights, hiking, beach combing, Lana'i Nature Conservancy

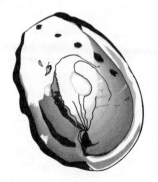

THE WESTIN KAUAI AT KAUAI LAGOONS

This 800-acre resort on the Garden Isle is only a mile and a half from Lihue, county seat. Billed as a "world unto itself," the resort takes the form of towers and wings surrounding a circular 26,000-square-foot pool with dramatic waterfalls spilling over marble walls, and five jacuzzis awaiting gleaming bodies. Rooms here are large, and number more than eight hundred, in addition to suites and 49 deluxe Royal Beach Club rooms. Decor is by Hirsch-Bedner, and features coral, pinks and off-white—all with views of beach, gardens, or the aquatic fantasyland unveiled below. Public areas are open, and evenings here around the lagoons resemble a lavish Hollywood production. Twelve tennis courts, racquet ball courts and a fully equipped European Spa and Wellness Center are guaranteed to help you work off the calories ingested in one of the 12 restaurants and lounges. Visit the Paddling Club for high-energy adult entertainment. If you happen to be car-less, you can opt for 19th century carriages drawn by Clydesdales, or cruise the 40-acre lagoon and wildlife refuge in an outrigger canoe or a mahogany launch. Beach activities range from sunning and surfing to thrill sailing on Keile IV, a 42-foot race catamaran, snorkeling, scuba diving, and boogie boarding. But you'll probably want to don a designer bikini from one of 30 world-class shops, and watch the activity at what some statisticians consider the world's largest resort pool.

Jack Nicklaus is the Director of Golf here, where you'll find two eighteen hole courses making their debut in an incredibly picturesque setting. Kiele Course, named "Best New Resort Coursee in America for 1989" by Golf Digest, is nestled above the Pacific. It is a stadium course created for tournament play. From the men's white tees, its 6164 yards, with lots of water. Hole #13 is a par 3 cliff-to-cliff toughie that's all carry across the pounding surf. Kiele touts many mesmeric vistas, and with time, it can only improve. The Lagoons Course was designed in the traditional links style, offers all levels of players the ultimate in shot-making opportunities. It was ranked among the "Top 10 Best New Courses in America in 1989" by Golf Magazine.

Address: Kalapaki Beach, Lihue, 96766
Phone: 808-245-5050 800-228-3000
No. of Rooms: 846
Rates: $$$
Services: Beauty/Barber Salon, Safety deposit boxes, Car hire, Valet and self-parking,, Room service
Restaurant: 9 restaurants
Bar: 3 lounges/clubs
Business Fac.: Secretarial, Conf. rm. cap.: 1,850
Sports Fac.: Tennis, Pool, Spa & Wellness center
Location: Kauai Lagoons
Attractions: Horses/carriages, wildlife island tour, catamaran

Course: Westin Kaui, Kiele Course
Distance: 7,070, Par: 72, No. of holes: 18
Guest Policy: Call for availability
Phone Club-House: 808-246-5061
Pro's Name: Frank Sullivan
Reservations: Guests—up to a month in advance
Season: Year round
Guest Carry Clubs: No

PRINCEVILLE RESORT

Princeville Resort acts as a gateway to the wonders of Kauai's spectacular North Shore. A verdant green promontory with seven miles of coastline, the resort overlooks Hanalei Bay and the Pacific Ocean. The resort features a wide variety of activities from watersports to tennis, horseback riding and even polo during summer months. Accommodations include the luxurious Princeville Hotel, managed by Sheraton, and a variety of condominium complexes and executive homes available for vacation rental. A shopping center and commuter airport complete the resort complex.

Sightseeing is a big attraction here, and what sights! Hiking to Kilauea Point, under the protection of the US Fish and Wildlife Service, visiting Hanalei Valley Lookout to see endangered koot and stilt, helicopter flightseeing, trail riding or raft trips along the Na Pali Coast, checking out the shopping, polo matches, or the occasional hukilau all contribute to the haole's vacation.

Makai, meaning "toward the sea" Golf Course consists of four nine hole courses; Ocean, Lake, Woods, and the newest, which will eventually be a full 18 hole course, Prince Course. Home of the 1978 World Cup, the Kauai Open, and the LPGA Women's Kemper Open, these Robert Trent Jones, Jr. wonders have attained high marks in their 17-year existence, and as such, it is the only course in Hawaii to have been listed within the Golf Digest's Top 100 for the past fifteen years. #3 on the Ocean Course, a par 3, is world-renowned as an achingly beautiful sight, as well as a formidable one. Only 125 yards, with dense grass on the left, a green protected on the left side and rear by threatening sand traps, a placid lake in front, and a thicketed canyon beyond, the player prays for respite from looking for a wayward ball. Lake Course boasts ocean views, jungle caverns and plenty of water coming into play, and Woods Course heads inland, graced with regal Norfolk pines and rock garden bunkers. The Prince, operated as a separate course from the other 27 holes, will offer the golfer natural waterfalls cascading down behind a lush green, deep verdant ravines, jungle, rocks galore, ancient mango trees, and vision of a machete to hack one's way back to the narrow fairway.

Address: P.O. Box 3040, Princeville, 96722
Phone: 808-826-3040 800-826-1166
No. of Rooms: 252
Rates: $$$
Services: Valet, Barber shop, Beauty shop, Garage and parking, Car hire, International currency exchange, Babysitting, Card/game area, Laundry, Room service
Restrictions: No pets
Restaurant: Cafe Hanalei,Hale Kapa
Bar: Ukiyo
Business Fac.: Secretarial, Telex, Conf. rm. cap.: 750
Sports Fac.: Pool, Tennis,Health spa, Croquet, Polo
Location: North coast of Kauai
Attractions: Waioli Mission House, Kilauea Light House

Course: Makai, Prince
Distance: 6,900, Par: 72
Rating: 72.6, No. of holes: 45
Guest Policy: Resort guests have preferred tee times
Phone Club-House: 808-826-3580
Pro's Name: R. Martinez
Fees: **
Reservations: Up to one year in advance
Season: Year round
Guest Carry Clubs: Yes

THE GRAND WAILEA RESORT

Just one year after opening in 1991, The Grand Wailea Resort and Spa was voted among the top five resorts in the world by Conde Naste Traveler's Reader's Choice Poll. Set on 40 acres of magnificently landscaped grounds, this world class hotel overlooks Maui's breathtaking coastline and blends Hawaii's rich natural and cultural heritage with the luxury of the turn-of-the century's Grand Hotels. Huge waterfalls at the hotel's entrance seem to catch the water from sacred Mount Haleakala. A large formal pool, bordered by 60-ft royal palms and magnificent sculptures, transforms at night into a brilliantly lit fountain. Original artwork by Hawaiian and legendary artists, including Pablo Picasso and Andy Warhol, are beautifully interwoven into the Resort's stunning interior decor and floral gardens.

Unusually spacious guest rooms are superbly appointed. Guest room wings are positioned on the gentle slopes above Wailea Beach, so each room features a view of Maui's pristine ocean. Extra-large bathtubs easily accommodate two people. Scenic lanais are perfect for leisurely breakfasts and sunbathing.

Connoisseurs of Japanese cuisine will enjoy Kincha, named by Esquire Magazine as one of the country's top new restaurants. Dining at Kincha is like eating art: velvet smooth sashimi is served on a shiso leaf in an ice igloo, tiny quail eggs are painted with faces and vegetables are carved into flowers of the season.

The Grand Wailea is the ultimate family resort. The opulent Spa Grande offers a unique array of relaxing international water therapies, as well as traditional Hawaiian body treatments. A 20,000-foot Action Pool offers the whole family a thrilling ten minute swim/ride through mountains and grottos, dropping guests a total of 325 feet and carrying them through a series of pools waterfalls, slides and rapids. Camp Grande is a special haven for children, featuring a movie theater, game room and crafts center, 1950's style soda fountain and outdoor playground with whale shaped swimming pool.

Address: 3850 Wailea Alanui, Wailea, Maui, Hawaii 96753
Phone: (808) 875-1234, (800) 888-6100 (Fax): (808) 874-5143
No. of Rooms: Suites:
Room Rate: $$$$
Credit Cards: All major credit cards accepted
Services and Amenities: Three telephones in guestroom, Spa Grande, Camp Grande (children's camp), Seaside Wedding Chapel
Restaurant: Kincha, Bistro Molokini, Cafe Kula, Grand Dining Room Maui, Humuhumunukunukuapua's, Luau Gardens
Bar: Volcano Bar, Tsunami
Conference Rooms: 22, Capacity: 2,000
Sports Facilities: 2,000-foot long activity pool, Formal swimming pool, Scuba diving pool, Game room, Weight training room, Golf courses, Tennis courts, Racquetball court, Aerobics room, Fishing and water sports
Location: Wailea, Maui
Attractions: Whale watching in winter, Sunset cruises

STOUFFER WAILEA BEACH RESORT

Spectacular scenery surrounds Maui's Stouffer Wailea Beach Resort: five white sand beaches, tropical gardens, shimmering waterfalls, and the 10,000 ft. high Mt. Haleakala, the world's largest dormant volcano. This 347-room resort is nestled in the gentle foothills of Mt. Haleakala, a natural 15.5-acre wonderland. Unerring service and superb accommodations earned Wailea Beach Resort the AAA Five-Diamond Award for eight consecutive years. A boundless dedication to pleasing guests is the creed of the resort's staff, reflecting sincere pride in Maui culture and ambience.

All rooms in the country club-like retreat are generous in size, and handsomely decorated in rattan, wicker and koa, the select Hawaiian hardwood. Included as well are private lanais with sweeping views, fully-stocked refreshment centers, and TV with in-room movies. Business and social gatherings are ideally held on the lobby level, with five fully-detailed meeting units for conventions, meetings or social gatherings. Theme parties for up to 600 people are immensely popular and easily arranged.

The award-winning Raffles' Restaurant recreates the decor of its famed Singapore namesake, complete with intimate seating, elegant foliage and Lenox china. Dinner fare includes wonderfully prepared Hawaiian seafood as well as continental cuisine. Raffles' too is the setting for Wailea's sumptuous Sunday brunch. Casual day-long dining is a tempting treat on the Palm Court Terrace, also the scene for champagne breakfast buffets and evening continental buffets. Other favorites are the Sunset Terrace, featuring nightly island entertainment, the Maui Onion, famed for its onion rings, and the Lost Horizon, for dancing, cocktails and nightly showtime. Ideal for the sports-minded, the resort provides superb golfing on its two championship courses, and the Tennis Club has 11 hard and 3 grass courts for your pleasure. Water sports abound: snorkeling, sports fishing, sailing, surfing, and swimming in the gentle Pacific and the resort's luxurious pool.

Your Maui idyll includes night torchlighting, luaus, lei-making, Island lore, sunset cruises, garden and reef tours, and whale watching adventures.

Address: 3550 Wailea Alanui Dr., Wailea, Maui, Hawaii 96753
Phone: 808-879-4900, 800-9-WAILEA, Fax: 808-874-5370
No. of Rooms: 347 **Suites:** 12
Room Rate: $$
Credit Cards: All major
Services and Amenities: Concierge, Car hire, Free parking, Laundry, Valet, Currency exchange, Library, Game area, Barber/beauty shop, Shopping arcade, Babysitting, Comp. shuttle, Cable TV, Radio, Comp. paper & coffee
Room Service: 24 hours
Restaurant: Raffles', Palm Court, Maui Onion
Bar: Sunset Terrace
Business Facilities: Audio-visual, Secretarial, Fax/telex, Message center, Full conference fac.
Conference Rooms: 5, Capacity: 400
Sports Facilities: Pool, World Gym privileges, 14 tennis courts, Croquet, Riding, 2 golf courses, Sailboarding, Snorkeling, Scuba diving, Surfing, Sailing
Location: 1/4 mi. Piilani Hwy
Attractions: Private beach, lush gardens on Mt. Haleakala, bi-weekly luaus, culture classes

THE HEATHMAN HOTEL

This National Historic Landmark in downtown Portland is next door to the Center for the Performing Arts and just a few steps from the Oregon Art Institute in the downtown business and shopping districts.

The Heathman was completely renovated in 1984 under the supervision of San Francisco's master interior designer, Andrew Delfino. Original works by leading American artists are displayed throughout the hotel. The lobby, featuring rare eucalyptus panelling, a grand piano, and cozy fireplace, is the setting for afternoon tea, a burgeoning Portland custom.

Each spacious guest room is decorated with teak wood and art deco furnishings. Carrara white and Verona red marble, Roman travertine, and Burmese teak have been artfully blended to create an unabashedly luxurious decor. A complimentary 225-plus film library is available to all guests. Baths are fitted with marble and provided with robes and abundant complimentary toiletries.

The Heathman has become a Portland dining favorite, thanks in part to its proximity to cultural events. The restaurant prides itself on serving the finest and freshest northwest regional seafood, vegetables, and meat. Menus change seasonally; in the spring, dinner began with Northwest Game Pâté with Red Rémoulade, then the Heathman Salad of Romaine Butter Lettuce, Garlic Croutons, Bacon, and Mint tossed together in a delectable dressing. The entrée was rack of Oregon Lamb, and dessert a Chocolate Raspberry Torte served along with the Heathman's house blend coffee.

The elegant Marble Bar, named for its exquisite marble furnishings, is a popular après-theatre meeting place, serving bistro-style small plates until 2:00 a.m.

The care and thought that have gone into refurbishing this hotel, combined with courteous professional service, will surely please.

Address: Southwest Broadway at Salmon St., Portland, Oregon 97205
Phone: 503-241-4100, 800-551-0011, Fax: 503-790-7110
No. of Rooms: 112 **Suites:** 40
Room Rate: $$
Credit Cards: All major
Services and Amenities: 24hr concierge, Car hire, Parking, Laundry, Valet service, Currency exchange, Library, Gift shop, Babysitting, TV, Video library, Radio, Comp. toiletries, Robes, Comp. newspaper
Restrictions: No pets
Room Service: 24 hours
Restaurant: Heathman Restaurant & Bar
Bar: Marble Bar, Lobby, Mezzanine
Business Facilities: Check with concierge
Conference Rooms: 7, Capacity: 80
Sports Facilities: In-room exercise equipment avail., Access to athletic club
Location: Downtown
Attractions: Shopping, business district, Performing Arts Center, Oregon Art Institute

SORRENTO HOTEL

Past the sparkling Italian fountain, one is admitted by the door-man from the entrance *porte cochere* into a lobby richly panelled with handcrafted Honduras mahogany. An intimate ambiance, aglow with warm subtle colors and textures, characterizes this newly-remodeled 1908 hotel.

The beautifully furnished guest rooms contain many antiques. Beds are made up with all-cotton sheets and goose down pillows. Special touches, such as twice-daily maid service and evening turndown with a chocolate, will make you feel pampered.

Almost half the hotel's guest accommodations are suites, including two penthouses. The largest is 3,000 square feet with a baby grand piano, fireplace, library, and terrace overlooking the city and Puget Sound. It is surely one of the finest hotel rooms in Seattle.

Begin your morning with a complimentary morning newspaper. Enjoy privileges at the Seattle Club, a prestigious downtown athletic club. Later, join other guests who gather daily in the Fireside Lounge for afternoon tea in the English manner.

The Hunt Club restaurant, with its rose and salmon color scheme and romantic atmosphere, serves the bounty of the Northwest, and particularly its fine seafood, with true continental flair. Assorted smoked fish and shellfish, warm quail salad, fresh Northwest salmon with yellow bell pepper and basil sauce, and a fresh fruit Napoleon are among delights that await you.

Seattle is a fascinating city set in the great natural beauty of the Pacific Northwest. The Sorrento Hotel is close to the Puget Sound waterfront, where ferries and harbor tours are available, and just an hour's drive from the pristine Cascade Ranges.

Address: 900 Madison St., Seattle, Washington 98104
Phone: 206-622-6400, 800-426-1265, Fax: 206-622-6400, Telex: 244206 SORRUR
No. of Rooms: 76 **Suites:** 32
Room Rate: $$
Credit Cards: AmEx, DC, MC, Visa
Services and Amenities: 24hr concierge, Car hire, Parking, Laundry, Valet service Florist, Babysitting, Comp. shoeshine, Cable TV, Cassette player, Phone, Comp. toiletries, Robes, Comp. newspaper
Room Service: Room service
Restaurant: Hunt Club
Bar: Hunt Club Louuge
Business Facilities: Audio-visual, Secretarial, Fax/telex, Teleconferencing, Copying, Message center
Conference Rooms: 3, Capacity: 100
Location: Downtown
Attractions: Close to Puget Sound waterfront, harbor tours, ferries, 1 hr. to Cascade Ranges

Elegant Small Hotels — A Connoiseur's Guide. This selective guide for discriminating travelers describes over 200 of America's finest hotels characterized by exquisite rooms, fine dining, and perfect service par excellence. Introduction by Peter Duchin. "Elegant Small Hotels makes a seductive volume for window shopping." — **Chicago Sun Times.**

Complete Guide to Bed & Breakfasts, Inns & Guesthouses in the United States and Canada—A best-selling classic now in its tenth fully revised edition. Over 6,000 inns listed and access to over 20,000 guesthouses. Includes specialty lists for interest ranging from bird watching to antiquing. "All necessary information about facilities, prices, pets, children amenities, credit cards and the like. Like France's Michelin . . ." **New York Times**

Golf Resorts — The Complete Guide. The first ever comprehensive guide to over 1,000 golf resorts coast to coast. Includes complete details of each resort facility and golf course particulars. Introduction by Fuzzy Zoeller.

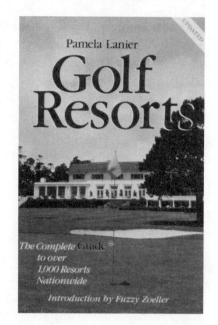

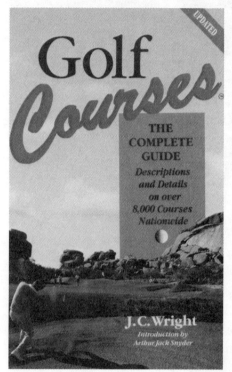

Golf Courses — The Complete Guide. It's about time for a definitive directory and travel guide for the nation's 20 million avid golf players, 7 million of whom make golf vacations an annual event. This comprehensive guide includes over 8,000 golf courses in the United States that are open to the public. Complete details, greens fees, and information on the clubhouse facilities is augmented by a description of each of the golf courses' best features. A beautiful gift and companion to *Golf Resorts—The Complete Guide*. Introduction by Arthur Jack Snyder.

Golf Resorts International. A wish book and travel guide for the wandering golfer. This guide, written in much the same spirit as the bestselling *Elegant Small Hotels*, reviews the creme de la creme of golf resorts all over the world. Beautifully illustrated, it includes all pertinent details regarding hotel facilities and amenities. Wonderful narrative on each hotel's special charm, superb cuisine and most importantly, those fabulous golf courses. Written from a golfer's viewpoint, it looks at the challenges and pitfalls of each course.

For the non-golfer, there is ample information about other activities available in the area, such as on-site health spas, nearby extraordinary shopping, and more.

AVAILABLE IN BOOK STORES EVERYWHERE

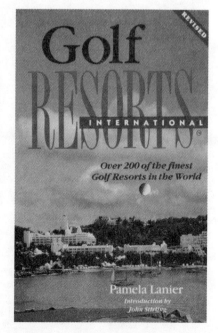

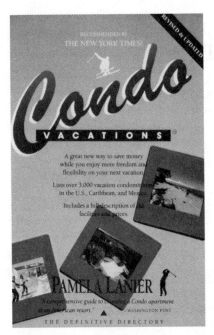

Condo Vacations — The Complete Guide. The popularity of Condo Vacations has grown exponentially. In this first ever national guide, details are provided on over 3,000 Condo resorts in an easy to read format with valuable descriptive write-ups. The perfect vacation option for families and a great money saver!

All-Suite Hotel Guide — The Definitive Directory. The only guide to the all suite hotel industry features over 1,200 hotels nationwide and abroad. There is a special bonus list of temporary office facilities. A perfect choice for business travelers and much appreciated by families who enjoy the additional privacy provided by two rooms.

"They appeal to every segment—individual, corporate travellers, long time stays, and meetings**." — Corporate and Incentive Travel.**

"One of the hottest trends in the industry."**—Time**

The Back Almanac — The Best New Thinking on an Age-Old Problem *by Lanier Publishing.* Just in the nick of time for the 4 out of 5 Americans suffering with back pain, a practical guide to back pain prevention and care. Delightfully illustrated. Internationally acknowledged experts offer the latest thinking on causes, treatment, and pain-free life, including Danger Signals, Sex and Back Pain, and What If Nothing Works? Resource guide lists back schools, pain centers and specialty items.
    Revised
"The editors have amassed a wealth of easy-to-find easy-to-read information . . ." **—HEALTHLINE**

Travel Books from

LANIER GUIDES

ORDER FORM

QTY	TITLE	EACH	TOTAL
	Golf Resorts - The Complete Guide	$14.95	
	Condo Vacations - The Complete Guide	$14.95	
	All-Suite Hotel Guide	$14.95	
	Golf Resorts International	$19.95	
	Golf Courses - The Complete Guide	$14.95	
	Elegant Small Hotels	$19.95	
	Elegant Hotels - Pacific Rim	$19.95	
	Complete Guide to Bed & Breakfasts, Inns & Guesthouses in the United States & Canada	$16.95	
	The Back Almanac	$14.95	
	Sub-Total		
	U.S.A. Shipping		$ 2.75 / 1 copy
	Foreign Shipping		$ 5.75 / 1 copy (each additional book 50¢)
	TOTAL ENCLOSED		$

Send your order to:

LANIER PUBLISHING INTERNATIONAL, LTD.
P.O. Box 20429
Oakland, California 94620

Allow 3 to 4 weeks for delivery

NAME _____

ADDRESS _____

CITY _____STATE_____ ZIP _____